Allan J. Janssen, Leo Koffeman (Eds.)

# Protestant Church Polity in Changing Contexts I

# Church Polity and Ecumenism

## Global Perspectives

edited by

Leo J. Koffeman, Allan J. Janssen
and Johannes Smit

Volume 2

LIT

# Protestant Church Polity in Changing Contexts I

## Ecclesiological and Historical Contributions

Proceedings of the International Conference,
Utrecht, The Netherlands, 7 – 10 November, 2011

edited by

Allan J. Janssen and Leo Koffeman

LIT

Cover image: Nico Thöne

This book is printed on acid-free paper.

**Bibliographic information published by the Deutsche Nationalbibliothek**
The Deutsche Nationalbibliothek lists this publication in the Deutsche Nationalbibliografie; detailed bibliographic data are available in the Internet at http://dnb.d-nb.de.

ISBN 978-3-643-90310-5

**A catalogue record for this book is available from the British Library**


Klosbachstr. 107
CH-8032 Zürich
Tel. +41 (0) 44-251 75 05
Fax +41 (0) 44-251 75 06
E-Mail: zuerich@lit-verlag.ch
http://www.lit-verlag.ch

LIT VERLAG Dr. W. Hopf
Berlin 2014
Fresnostr. 2
D-48159 Münster
Tel. +49 (0) 2 51-62 03 20
Fax +49 (0) 2 51-23 19 72
E-Mail: lit@lit-verlag.de
http://www.lit-verlag.de

**Distribution:**
In Germany: LIT Verlag Fresnostr. 2, D-48159 Münster
Tel. +49 (0) 2 51-620 32 22, Fax +49 (0) 2 51-922 60 99, E-mail: vertrieb@lit-verlag.de
In Austria: Medienlogistik Pichler-ÖBZ, e-mail: mlo@medien-logistik.at
In the UK: Global Book Marketing, e-mail: mo@centralbooks.com
In North America: International Specialized Book Services, e-mail: orders@isbs.com
e-books are available at www.litwebshop.de

# TABLE OF CONTENTS

# PREFACE

The essays offered in this volume, along with a companion volume, *Protestant Church Polity in Changing Contexts. Case Studies,* were first presented at an international conference of church order experts, held in Utrecht, the Netherlands, in early November, 2011. That conference drew scholars on church order from around the world. Most came from churches in the Reformed family to consider two matters, one material and the other formal.

The material question asked: to what extent is it (still) possible to speak of what has traditionally been understood as 'principles of Reformed polity'? Are there prescriptions in church order that may be considered essential to the nature of the church? As churches in the Reformed family express an increasingly global face, this question has become very pressing. That is the case not only in what until recently have been considered 'missionary' churches, but in established Western churches as well. The global nature of church membership in Western churches means that ethnic groups within those churches pose significant questions on the nature of church governance. Does, for example, the practice of communal decision-making reflect a Western bias? Is authority as expressed solely through the assemblies of the church essential to being Reformed? Many of the churches represented at the conference emerged from a Dutch Reformed heritage, and hence represented church orders that have the church order of Dordt as its originating source. Participants differed on the authoritative weight of the Dordt order.

Some essays from non-Western participants put the question pointedly in terms of their own contexts. Other essays, that of Nelus Niemandt, for example, ask the question from an ecclesiological perspective, in his case asking about the adequacy of the old order for what has been called a 'missional' ecclesiology.

Hence the second, formal consideration: the theological nature of church order as a sub-discipline. Taught to future ministers in seminaries and universities, church order is often treated as necessary but secondary. Leo Koffeman, my co-editor, in his introductory essay, notes that church order has been called the 'dark side of theology'. In many countries, there is a scarcity of literature on church order of an academic nature. The conference was called, in part, to rectify that lack even as it focused on the material question. The eager response to the call for papers evidences the readiness of scholars, often isolated, to rise to the challenge. The essays reflect the dialogue as experts in systematic theology, church history, and practical theology as well as from missiology and cross-cultural theology shared in the dialogue. And, it might be added, 'practitioners' in church order, those responsible at local and national levels for the execution of church order, also offered valuable input. Their various perspectives contribute to what is hoped to be the beginning of a rich global conversation.

There exists a crying need for a *theological* approach to church order at all levels of church life. This is the case in ecumenical discussions at both national and international levels. The Reformed-Roman Catholic dialogue, for example, again and again touches on the nature of ecclesiastical office. The need is also the case at very local levels, as is evident in case studies presented in the companion volume.

Leo Koffeman introduces this volume by posing the questions that frame a discussion not only for the conference, but for a broader consultation. He proposes a method that is ecclesiological, ecumenical, contextual and that engages with civil law. His recent book *In Order to Serve* — published in this same series — presents a more extensive introduction to this field of study.

A number of more theological essays ensue. Volker Küster contributes from a cross-cultural perspective as he describes the contextual and intercultural nature of theology, thereby setting church order in a context broader than the mono-cultural context that has characterized many of the churches. Mary-Anne Plaatjies van Huffel distills principles of a Reformed Church order, specifically in her South African Context. Joseph Small explores how Presbyterian polity in the United States has become 'captive' to regnant notions of democracy. As noted above, Nelus Niemandt discusses the implications of a missional ecclesiology. Harm Dane, from a Dutch context, evinces the pressures of a secularized society on church order. Rein Brouwer, from the same context, asks after the nature of ecclesiastical office, particularly with the appearance of 'interim' pastors. And Johannes Smit reflects on the theological pros and cons of giving human rights a place in a church order.

Several essays trace the origin and reception of the church order of Dordt. Fred van Lieburg offers an historical background. Pieter Coertzen, Henry De Moor, and Lazarus Purwanto detail how the Dordt church order has influenced churches in South Africa, North America, and Indonesia respectively.

Finally, Norman Doe, from an Anglican perspective, and Myriam Wijlens, from a Roman Catholic one, contribute two extended essays, thereby engaging in Koffeman's contention that theological discussion of church order be ecumenical.

Neither the conference nor the book would have been possible without the contribution of a number of persons and institutions. Leo Koffeman, professor of church polity and ecumenism at the Protestant Theological University, called together an international group of scholars to arrange the conference and to work together in collecting the essays presented in this volume: PoHo Huang, Mary-Anne Plaatjies van Huffel, Lazarus Purwanto, Johannes Smit, Robert Vosloo, and Allan Janssen. The Protestant Church in the Netherlands, its department for Mission and World Service 'Kerk in Actie', the Council for World Mission, and the Protestant Theological University were not only the organizing institutions but were strong financial supporters. Their support enabled a number of participants who otherwise did not have the means to travel to the Netherlands to participate, thereby not only enriching the conference, but enabling the conversation to become truly global.

The editors also owe a debt of gratitude to LIT-Verlag for their publication of the proceedings of this conference. Indeed, these volumes are to be among the first in a new series, 'Church Polity and Ecumenism. Global Perspectives'. This initiative is in part to fulfill the formal purpose of the international conference.

As an international conference, a common language was required: English. We are deeply grateful for participants for whom English is not their native language who thus worked doubly hard on their presentations, not only for oral presentation but for publication. We extend our thanks to them for their gracious engagement with the editors over style, word choice and syntax. Moreover, we extend a heart-felt thanksgiving to the Rev. Joshua Bode who reviewed the English and to the Rev. Gerard van Zanden for assistance in technical lay-out.

It is our hope as editors that these volumes will stand not only as the beginning of a dialogue on church order—and not only among Reformed, but ecumenically—but will act as encouragement to those engaged in church order both theoretically and practically.

Allan J. Janssen
*Epiphany, 2014*

# THE DARK SIDE OF THE GOOD NEWS?

## A Theological Approach to Church Polity

Leo J. Koffeman

Church polity is not among the most cherished subdisciplines in theology. The annual meetings of the American Academy of Religion may be the largest meeting of theologians worldwide, but, for instance, at the 2011 meeting only one out of hundreds of presentations dealt with issues of church polity, and so within the wider framework of 'ecclesiological investigations', focussing on the relationship between ecclesiology and church law in different denominations.

On internet, Roman Catholic liturgist Mark R. Francis presents a review of Ladislas Orsy's book *Receiving the Council*, and notes: "I once heard someone describe canon law as 'the dark side of the Good News'. This book, however, gives lie to such an assertion" (Francis 2010). The dark side of the Good News — it is an interesting but not really flattering characterization of church polity. I suppose that this rings a bell with most theologians working in this area. Those who are involved in theological education in the area of church polity will easily be able to recall moments that comparable doubt about the value of this discipline was expressed by students. Is it theological at all? Is it really academic? And even: is it salutary? Does it further church life? Or is it rather 'the dark side of the Gospel', indeed?

To find out, it makes sense to have an exchange of experiences and views regarding the contextualisation of Protestant church polity, with a view of strengthening this theological discipline both in terms of contents and of methodology.

### *Protestant Church polity — is it a matter of theology at all?*

A short survey of the way church polity research and teaching is being organized in worldwide Protestantism is not exactly encouraging. It is likely the case that no theological discipline is so often subject to misunderstandings — and consequently disapproval — as church polity. Its theological nature is controversial. Is it really a matter of theology?

In Germany the answer seems to be: no! There, church polity is studied and taught at the faculty of law rather than at the faculty of theology, mainly due to the fact that church law is part of public law.

In the Reformed—and more specifically the Dutch Reformed—tradition, the answer traditionally is 'yes'. But here church polity has usually been seen as closely related to church history. Not even this is a widely accepted point of view in Protestantism. Often, church polity is seen as a matter of the church rather than the faculty. Even well-known theological faculties like Princeton have no chair of church polity: retired or at least very experienced ministers of the church come and see their future colleagues for a few hours in order to introduce them into the church order of their particular denomination. So, in fact, it is not only the theological nature, but even the academic standing of church polity that is not at all self-evident.

Moreover, we can recognize some cultural reasons for scepticism about this discipline. Church polity has to deal with wide-spread suspicion about institutions; at least this is true for a Western context. For many reasons people do not place much value on the institutional aspects of church life. Often people are more interested in spirituality, events and—at best—short term commitments than in maintaining existing structures. And it is not only the so-called 'ordinary congregants' that are scarcely aware of the role of major assemblies like the classical assemblies and the general synod. I am afraid that, for instance in the Protestant Church in the Netherlands, even among elders and deacons—if not ministers—there is a great deal of scepticism with regard to such supralocal structures. For some decades now, historical churches in the Netherlands have been losing members to free congregations in the evangelical and Pentecostal tradition; in this case 'free' primarily connotes that there are no established rules, enacted at a 'higher' level, that bind these local congregations. In 1971, the Canadian sociologist Reginald W. Bibby introduced the term 'circulation of the saints' (cf. Bibby 2003), in order to point to the phenomenon of postdenominationalism and decreasing ecclesial loyalty, especially in conservative evangelical churches that seem to grow significantly. Bibby's research was repeated every decade since, and it shows a pretty consistent picture: about 70 % of evangelical church growth is due to people moving from one evangelical church to another. Church polity, however, is often regarded as nourishing rather than weakening denominationalism, if not as sheer ecclesial conservatism and self-conceit.

So, we have to face some sweeping questions implied in such misunderstandings in order to further a shared awareness of urgency and a common endeavour to respond. We are in need of a truly international and interdisciplinary discussion on both content and methodology of church polity. It is a matter of content, first of all: is there something that can be seen as a core of 'principles of Protestant/Reformed church polity', a kind of Protestant ius divinum? But that also raises issues of methodology. How can church polity be related to church history? To other theological disciplines, like practical theology or missiology? In order to answer such questions, we have to be aware of, and to seriously analyze the changing contexts we are part of. What is required in order to further a responsible contextualization of church polity? It is this kind of questions that I hope to deal with more extensively in my *In Order to Serve* (Koffeman 2014, cf. Koffeman 2009). In this contribution I have to limit myself to some main issues.

*A lacking international discourse*
What about the status of theological research in the area of Protestant church polity? Let us try to 'harvest the fruits' — to use an expression of Cardinal Walter Kasper (cf. Kasper 2009).

In The Netherlands the number of relevant publications is very limited. Dutch church polity experts like Doede Nauta, Wim van 't Spijker, Jan Plomp, Henk Weijland, Leen van Drimmelen, and Piet van den Heuvel have published either practical commentaries to the current church orders of their churches or historical studies. Only very few articles have been written in English or German.

We see a similar picture in South Africa. In 2004 Pieter Coertzen published his book *Decently and in Order* (Coertzen 2004), for its main part a translation of a similar book in Afrikaans, published in 1990. Its bibliography contains close to 200 titles, but only very few of them are in English. Most of them are rather historical in nature. Coertzen himself gives a thorough theological reflection on the order for, and the order in, the church — as the subtitle says. It includes interesting ecclesiological parts, but it does not take ecclesiology as such as its main point of departure, and rather focuses on issues of method and sources.

Also from a broader perspective, the harvest of publications that are accessible for an international — i.e. English speaking — public is meager, even in the English-speaking world. An important but mainly descriptive work is Edward Long's *Patterns of Polity* (2001). It distinguishes and describes the most important aspects and manifestations of the three main systems of governance of churches, usually referred to as the episcopal system, the presbyterial-synodical system, and the congregationalist system respectively. Long explicitly refrains from trying "to adjudicate which form of governance has the greatest biblical warrant or most adequately embodies the Christian heritage" (Long 2001, 151). So, he does not take a theological stand. However, his book is very helpful for understanding different church polity traditions.

A few other examples from the North American context can be mentioned here. As a quite common kind of books on church polity we see the commentaries on church orders of specific churches, like Henry DeMoor's *Christian Reformed Church Order Commentary* (DeMoor 2010). It is structured according to the set-up of the church order of the Christian Reformed Church in North America, adding questions and responses on issues the author had to deal with in decades of teaching and advising church bodies. Theological arguments, however, are present in a quite implicit manner. Basically, Allan Janssen's *Constitutional Theology* (Janssen 2000) follows a similar pattern. It is a commentary to *The Book of Church Order of the Reformed Church in America*. However, it also contains a short Introduction as well as a first Chapter dealing with the Preamble of the aforementioned church order; these parts do indeed point to some fundamental ecclesiological questions. Speaking more generally, commentaries on church orders usually refer only rather implicitly to theological pre-understandings — but they cannot fully do without.

More theological in nature is *Paradigms in Polity*, written by David Hall and Joseph Hall, and offering a collection of classical texts on Reformed church polity, including Calvin, as well as the continental European and the Anglo Saxon tradition. Foundational texts — confessions like the *Belgic Confession*, and constitutions like (an English translation of) the 1619 *Dordt Church Order*) — as well as classical authors in the area of church polity are made available for a wider audience. However, as the authors say themselves, "(i)t is, in the main, a book characterized by a historic flow" (Hall and Hall 1994, xi). In the way its Introduction focuses on Biblical foundations of church polity, it at the same time shows a strong apologetic inclination.

*Principles of Reformed church polity?*

In terms of content, we first have to consider the issue of the existence (or non-existence) of principles of Reformed church polity.

Of course, such principles can easily be identified from a phenomenological and/or historical perspective. We can distinguish certain common denominators in terms of church polity in most — if not all — churches within the Reformed tradition, even though there are major differences in detail. We could refer to the equality of three offices (minister, elder, deacon), to decision making in meetings (assemblies) at all levels, to the (relative) independence of local congregations — to name a few characteristics. It is no less evident that such common denominators can be traced back to the constitutive era of the Reformation. The *Dordt Church Order* (1619), a foundational church order for many churches in this tradition, contains the aforementioned characteristics of Reformed church polity. Nobody would argue the existence of such principles from an historical perspective.

The question we have to face, nevertheless, regards the theological character of such principles. What makes them to be understood as principles in the first place? Is not church polity 'only' church polity? Church polity is not self-evidently related to theology, certainly not in Protestantism. There rather is a tendency toward suspicion in this respect — which by the way is in itself based on theological views. Not a few Protestants would instinctively reject any attempt to give church polity a theological status, because they would see it as an inappropriate and even dangerous endeavor to safeguard specific power interests. It is what they see happening in debate on women's ordination: theological arguments are used (if not misused) in order to exclude certain categories of Christians from ordained office. A critical (and deeply theological!) view of ecclesial institutions is behind such analysis! We certainly have to be aware of the risk of using theological — or pseudo-theological? — arguments in order to maintain an ecclesial status-quo. It has happened and too often it still happens. But the alternative is not to refrain from theological thinking in church polity, but rather to intensify solid and critical theological and particularly ecclesiological thinking.

Traditionally, Protestant — and certainly Reformed — theologians would speak of 'biblical' or 'Scriptural' principles. And, indeed, a theological approach to church polity has to clarify its understanding of the relevance of Scriptural data. The Calvinist Reformation has a long tradition of applying the sola Scriptura to church polity issues as well as to other faith issues. However, the role of biblical theology in this respect requires some more consideration. Is an appeal to the Bible sufficient in theological thinking about church polity? Coertzen says: "To merely minister God's law from the Word, is not always simple" (Coertzen 2004, 145). He emphasizes that church polity is a continuous process, that it first of all is about maintaining the Lordship of Christ in the church, in a process of obedience and dependence.

The New Testament does not offer something like a prefabricated church order (cf. Bronkhorst 1947). There is a variety, depending on historical and contextual factors, as well as practical needs. Taking New Testament texts in order to apply them directly in a church order is even more unsatisfactory. The notorious words of 1st Corinthians 14:34 — that women should not be allowed to speak in the church — should not be taken as a biblical argument in order to deny women the ordination.

In the Reformed tradition 1st Corinthians 14:40 has played a major role: "do everything properly and in order" (CEV) or "Let all things be done decently and in order" (KJV/ASV). This seems to suggest a rather pragmatic approach of church life — and it is about worship rather than about church organization. In fact 'properly' or 'decently' (ευσχημόνωσ) suggests a certain adaptation to what is supposed to be the accepted norm in a specific context: the church should not be unnecessarily provocative nor get itself talked about. 'In order' (κατα τάξιν) refers to a common understanding in the Hellenistic context of the New Testament that there is a relationship between 'what is good', 'harmony', 'world order' and God (cf. 1st Cor. 14, 33 [ASV]: "God is not [a God] of confusion, but of peace"). One could say: whatever a Christian community does, including its legislation and its way of living in accordance with its regulations, should be done in a certain harmony both with the cultural context of this community and with an understanding of a normative framework that transcends that context. Nevertheless, it is clear that Paul's words do not say much about church polity as such.

A similar view has to be considered as to how church polity as a theological subject and confession are interrelated. Church polity undoubtedly is a matter of confession. The *Belgic Confession* sees 'the government of the church' as a matter of faith ( art. 30), and concludes: "There should be ministers or pastors to preach the Word of God and administer the sacraments. There should also be elders and deacons, along with the pastors, to make up the council of the church", seemingly as a direct consequence of 'the spiritual order that our Lord has taught us in his Word'.

However, we cannot argue theologically on a basis of church polity confessionalism, i.e. an uncritical continuation and justification of a specific tradition — e.g. either 'there should be bishops' of 'there never can be bishops' — with the one and only argument that this is the position of our confessional forebears. In practice this would mean that theological positions that were formulated at the moment that a certain church was born (often by splitting itself from an existing church) or challenged severely (e.g. in a time of conflict) are taken as axioms rather than as contextual historical views. Of course, historical reasoning plays a role in church polity, but it cannot be decisive as such — if theology wants to be academic!

Where pivotal theological questions occur, of course, some biblical and confessional considerations will have to play a role. A recent report of the Community of Protestant Churches in Europe, *Ministry — Ordination — Episkopé*, says with regard to the hermeneutic criteria and the sources from which the different understandings of ministry are drawn: "Scripture, tradition, reason and experience are sources from which the different forms of ministry, ordination and episkopé (along with their theological foundations) arise. Christian life has been confronted throughout history with the tension between the claim of Scripture and of present-day reality. For that reason the hermeneutic criteria are conformity with Scripture and with reality" (MOE, § 23, emphasis MOE).

Theology, as an academic discipline, is free. It is supposed to be accountable in academic discourse, both regarding its methods and its results. Theology is critical in nature, also with regard to existing structures, fixed opinions, and vested interests. This also goes for its relation to confession. Confessional arguments have to be taken seriously because of what they represent: the results of a sometimes long and intensive struggle for truth in a specific history and context. They signify what has crystallized out as being of major importance in terms of proclamation and faith, dialogue with culture and shaping the Christian community. But as such they cannot be decisive in theology. But contexts are changing, and they require new responses which as such should be confessional in nature. The *Barmen Theological Declaration* witnesses to this challenge, by saying: "We reject the false doctrine, as though the church were permitted to abandon the form of its message and order to its own pleasure or to changes in prevailing ideological and political convictions" ( art. 3). Also in its actions, as ruled by church polity, the church confesses.

### *Methodology*

If it is true that Scripture and tradition are not sufficient in order to provide for the contents of Protestant church polity, it is even more important to reconsider our methodology. A broad and multidisciplinary and therefore critical approach of Protestant church polity is the first requirement for an academic way of dealing with church polity. I suggest five aspects of such a critical approach: church polity should be related to (a) ecclesiology, (b) ecumenism, (c) missiology, (d) context, and (e) law.

#### a. *Ecclesiology*

We first of all need ecclesiological research—within a multidisciplinary set-up, indeed—to discover theological answers to the question what the nature and mission of the church is today, and how this should affect our church polity regulations. Key ecclesiological issues—like 'ordained ministry', the role of confession, inclusive forms of church life, and many others—have to be related to church polity practice in order to serve the church.

Churches are institutions, and like all institutions in society they have an in-build tendency to maintain the status quo. This is more or less self-evident: institutions usually are not eager to change. So, conservatism and bureaucracy are real threats to church life. They can only be tackled, not by resignation or by declaring church polity 'unnecessary', but by critical theological analysis and creative theological suggestions. That is what theological faculties are for, and that is also what churches should expect from those faculties connected with them.

So, in my view church polity is related to theology, either implicitly or explicitly. Every church order is based on theological choices made—e.g. regarding ministry and the role of laity—regarding human powers and the Holy Spirit, regarding local and supralocal manifestations of the church, or regarding the relation of the church to civil government and society. Sometimes these theological choices are quite obvious. More often such theological views are more or less implicit, and hidden in church order texts, and it takes some digging to expose them. In any case, this digging is necessary, and it is a critical action. Because a church order usually reflects a broadly accepted if not a kind of standard theology, these theological choices have to be treated from a critical theological perspective. This is where systematic theology is pivotal: are the theological views that lie behind specific church order texts (still) adequate in terms of current theological thinking? Or do they need to be reconsidered in relation to changed and changing contexts? Ecclesiology may be leading in this respect, but trinitarian theology, Christology, pneumatology or, for instance, soteriology will often have to be taken into account as well. And other theological disciplines, like biblical and practical theology, cannot be neglected.

In Protestant Germany and Austria a solid tradition of theological thinking about church polity has formed, due to excellent scholars like Karl Barth, Johannes Heckel, Emil Brunner, Erik Wolf, Hans Dombois, Albert Stein and many others. Although in quite different ways, they deal with the issue of church polity from an ecclesiological perspective. Roman Catholic theologians in the canon law tradition have for many decades taken it as a matter of course that canon law and ecclesiology are closely linked. The Belgian Roman Catholic canon lawyer Rik Torfs recognizes that theological interest in canon law has increased, and he also indicates some dangers in this development, like: "The increasing theologisation of canon law leads to a more idealistic but also to a more irenic approach. It seeks to avoid any possible field of conflict as far as possible" (Torfs 2004, 4). Few theologians have a clear picture of church polity as a dynamic process of relating theology and church polity.

The discipline of church polity needs to be informed by normative ecclesiological views on the nature and mission of the church, but at the same time it cannot do without a strong awareness of what happens in day-to-day church life. It is exactly the vulnerability of the empirical church that challenges church polity. No church order can guarantee the spiritual level and quality of church life, but at least churches are challenged to do whatever they can to make church life meet the highest standards in this respect (as they can be understood from an ecclesiological perspective), including the introduction and maintenance of adequate structures and procedures.

b. *Ecumenism*

In our tradition church polity is 'Reformed church polity'. I already referred above to so-called 'Reformed church polity principles'. Indeed, church polity often plays a role as the main defender of our own confessional inheritance. Procedures of church discipline are in place in order to maintain a strictly Reformed identity of the church. Church polity is supposed to focus on a specific confessional tradition, but therefore it might not be able to respond adequately to plurality, both in the church and in society. In other words, church polity and ecumenism seem to be natural enemies.

Again we need a truly theological approach to deal with this problem. The question is: is it necessary for church polity to be at odds with ecumenism? I do not think so. Not at all! On the contrary, in my view church polity has to be dealt with from an ecumenical perspective in the first place. In this respect I feel deeply indebted to the work of the German church law scholar H. Dombois (cf. Dombois 1961, Dombois 1974, and Dombois 1983). In his view, traditional apologetic — Dombois would rather say: transcendental — forms of church polity have lost credibility: they can no longer be convincing. All forms of legitimizing theology have to be abandoned. Therefore, now the time for ecumenical church polity has come.

His first point of departure in this respect is the conviction that church polity is ecumenical in nature. Ecumenical church polity is not just a matter of subjective idealism and personal commitment to ecumenical consensus. It is not a hobby. In a summary of his views he speaks about 'the objective ecumenicity of church polity as a historical fact' (cf. Dombois 1979, 230). This is true, he says, because of the undisputable fact that unity is not only something we seek, but also something we receive and believe. His second point of departure, equally important to him, is that we have to work from the conviction that the Holy Spirit has entered our human history, evoking historical manifestations. The church is among these manifestations, living in the power of the Spirit. The Holy Spirit creates visible forms, like the church. The relevance of this principle is that it determines the dynamics of church history. Church history, church polity and ecumenism have a process character. In church polity and in ecumenical life churches are involved in a movement that is rooted in the mission of the Lord and oriented towards the Kingdom of God to come.

The interesting contribution in Dombois' work is the connection he makes between ecumenism as a Spirit-led process and church polity as a similar process. He does not operate with the quite popular opposition between law and Spirit, as we, for instance, find it in the influential writings of Rudolph Sohm. Dombois takes the opposite stand, and in that manner he challenges the churches to see church polity as a full-blown theological matter as well. Ecumenism and church polity both have a dynamic nature, a process character. Both have to be understood from the perspective of the missio Dei, the mission of the Lord towards the Kingdom of God. And that is where they have to be related. Ecumenism as a process of unity has a church polity dimension, as it searches for sustainable forms of visible unity. And church polity as a process of law has an ecumenical dimension: it cannot put up with ecclesial divisions and confine itself to so-called 'internal matters'. The processes of growing unity and of legislation are intrinsically linked, since invisible unity does not exist. The consequences of such a view are far-reaching. Churches need each other, in church polity as in other matters. To make his point, Dombois even says: in terms of its visible and juridical structure every church is fundamentally deficient (cf. Dombois 1974, 87ff.).

If church polity it wants to be academic at all, it necessarily has to be ecumenical. In terms of methodology there is no Reformed way of doing church history or practical theology. Church historians and practical theologians — as well as biblical scholars and to a large extent even systematic theologians — use academic methods that are independent of a specific confessional tradition. If not, their work no longer deserves the name of academic theology. In church polity as well, the day of apologetics or confessional self-justification is over, both for academic reasons and for spiritual reasons. No theological argument can be valid for the sole reason that it is Reformed. At best it is Reformed because it is valid!

Church polity research has to be in touch with ecumenical ecclesiological thinking. Over the last decades the Faith and Order Commission of the World Council of Churches — and the Roman Catholic Church is a full member of the Faith and Order Commission — has taken ecclesiology as its main subject of studies. The same goes for many of the recent bilateral ecumenical dialogues like those between the Roman Catholic Church and the World Alliance of Reformed Churches (cf. TCUC 1991, CCCWKG 2007; cf. Meyer and Vischer 1984, Gros 2000, Gros et al. 2007). It is especially the Faith and Order document *The Nature and Mission of the Church* (NMC 2005) that has to be mentioned here. This result of a long study project presents an ecclesiological approach that shows major convergences in fundamental questions like the relation between the church and the Word of God, the role of tradition, the church as communion (koinonia), etc. Of course, it also lists a lot of differences and questions still to be resolved, but nevertheless it presents an ecumenical framework that can and should be made fruitful for church polity as well.

Ecumenical theology — and in fact ecclesiology as such — tends to be quite abstract. On the level of systematic theology it is easy to use many nuanced or even paradoxical formulations. For instance, it is a well-known ecumenical paradigm to speak of 'unity in reconciled diversity'. Nobody would seriously oppose this, as long as we can agree on a balance between unity, diversity and reconciliation. If church lawyers take part in an ecumenical debate on such views, they will bring forward the question what 'unity in reconciled diversity' would mean in practice. How can we organize it? What kind of legislation does it require? That in fact helps ecumenical dialogue to stay focused.

c. *A missionary approach*

There is an inevitable tension between a church's internal life and its mission. In many respects internal church issues tend to consume so much energy of those who are responsible in the first place that too little attention can be given to the role of the church in society and to its witness and service towards people outside the church. And, indeed, many of these internal church issues have obvious aspects of church polity. Is not church polity naturally focused on such internal church life? Is not it suffering from a high degree of introversion? It is an argument often heard against church polity: it is all about internal procedures and therefore it distracts attention from the really urgent issues, like the mission of the church. In other words: it is necessarily introverted, because it always and only has to do with internal organizational issues.

Nevertheless, in my view the only adequate response to this problem is: we need a different approach, i.e. a more theological and even a missionary approach to church polity. In this respect I do think that churches in traditionally 'Christian' countries like the Netherlands need to learn from churches in the South, like in Indonesia. We share the same inheritance in terms of Reformed church polity. But we should be aware of the fact that this presbyterial-synodical system is rooted in an era of a supposedly self-evident Christian society. In the sixteenth and seventeenth century the Netherlands was not seen as a mission field at all. The Reformed tradition developed in opposition to Roman Catholicism, but within a broader framework of the *corpus christianum*, a societal order in which church and state were seen as two institutional forms of the same Christian commonwealth. In many respects church polity in the Netherlands still draws upon this past, for instance in the way the so-called 'territorial principle' is maintained: in principle your home address is decisive as to the question to which congregation you belong. We are only starting to be aware of the challenges implied in a secular society, with a majority of the population not belonging to any church. I am aware that churches in Indonesia have a long history of coping with questions regarding the mission of the church. They have done so in a situation which is totally different from the Dutch context. It is only fair to ask if church polity has been experienced as helpful in terms of the mission of the church, or rather as a source of additional complications and frustrations.

We really need a missionary approach of church polity. In ecclesiology the mission of the church is one of the key issues. A lot of energy and creativity is spent in theological research and practical experiments with an aim of improving the missionary performance of the churches. As far as it is a fact that sometimes such efforts are confronted with church polity problems, these issues should be identified, explicitly described, and dealt with from a truly theological perspective. We do not need less church polity; we need more church polity research.

d. *A contextual approach*

Church polity—like most theological disciplines—is heavily influenced by history and context. But we are not always sufficiently aware of that fact. This brings me to a fourth aspect of an academic approach of church polity: it should be fully contextual.

My roots are in the Reformed Churches in the Netherland (RCN), founded by Abraham Kuyper. He is well known for having spoken about 'the curse of uniformity' in modern life. As a real romanticist he enjoyed what he called 'pluriformity'. Nevertheless, during the first half of the 20th century the RCN developed into a denomination with a high degree of uniformity. Whatever would deviate from what was supposed to be 'normal' (and therefore truly 'Reformed'!), was looked at with distrust and suspicion. An absolute understanding of truth implied that the same rules would apply in all circumstances and in all contexts. For decades it did not matter in which RCN congregation you would participate: there was hardly any difference. Church polity served such uniformity, and it often does. It tends towards uniformity, and therefore it reduces room for experiment and innovation. In a way that is self-evident, church polity works with general rules that should be applied in all circumstances in an equal way, is not it? Therefore it necessarily neglects the particularities of specific situations to a large extent.

However, Abraham Kuyper may have had another view! I am afraid that the second generation betrayed a basic intuition of Abraham Kuyper. In 1895 the general synod of Middelburg of the RCN dealt with the important issue of the mission of the church, especially with regard to mission work in what is now the Republic of Indonesia (cf. Reenders 2001). At that time Abraham Kuyper was not convinced that the young churches there should copy both the confessions and the church order of the RCN. In his view at least on the long run the churches here should express themselves in terms of confession and church order in a new way, which would be adequate in a context so different from the Dutch setting. Unfortunately, his views did not shape the RCN mission policy for the first six or seven decades after 1895.

Whatever historical judgment we can have in this respect, I think that we need a more theological and therefore a more contextual approach of church polity. This implies that church polity should provide more room for diversity and plurality. Uniformity is not necessarily a legal virtue. Today variety, creativity and flexibility may be more important in order to make church polity serve the mission of the church. It all depends on basic ecclesiological views.

e. *Church polity and legal science*

Finally, what about the relation between church polity and legal science? I myself am a theologian, and I do not have a degree in law. I only did a very limited amount of research in legal philosophy and history of law, but I think that I profited a lot from it. In my view theologians and more specifically experts in church polity do need more juridical education. They should be *better* lawyers, should be more aware of the dynamics and potential of law.

This may sound paradoxical for people who are afraid of legalism. There is a certain suspicion that for church lawyers the only relevant criterion in any situation is that church order rules have been met in its most specific details. If so, it is all right. If not, you have a problem. Would not it be even worse, if they receive more juridical education? Would not that further conservatism and bureaucracy? It all has to do with a specific understanding of what 'law' is. In fact, I am convinced that a better understanding of 'law' prevents rather than furthers legalism and bureaucracy. It is a poor knowledge and sense of the dynamics of legal science that leads to either legalism, or — at the opposite side — the tendency to ignore church polity regulations. This is an unfruitful and potentially even dangerous alternative.

I have visited South Africa several times. What struck me was a major difference between the majority white and the majority black churches I met. In so-called white churches there seemed to be a tendency to ignore church law on the local level, sometimes with an appeal to the 'Reformed principle' of the autonomy of the local congregation. Nobody seemed to care too much about this. In so-called black churches, however, I felt a certain degree of legalism. In cases of conflict at the local level, for instance between a church council and a pastor, at some stage one of the parties involved would go to the civil court to seek justice.

Now, in South Africa the context plays a decisive role in this field. After the apartheid era, a new Constitution of the Republic of South Africa was adopted, with an impressive basis in human rights, over against any institution. If I am not mistaken this puts institutions like churches in a disadvantaged position in any conflict with citizens. Part of the church law research we really need to foster is the study of the relationship between church law and civil law. In this respect the contexts of churches in Indonesia, South Africa and The Netherlands, but even those of Western European churches — like those in The Netherlands, Belgium, France and Germany — are totally different.

In fact power is the issue here. Power is one of the main issues, both in church polity and in legal science. Power and law have a complicated mutual relationship. On the one hand it is law that determines power: a church order determines precisely what kind of powers a synod for instance has to force congregations to do something, or to overrule a decision taken on a classis level. Law defines and allocates power. On the other hand, power defines and determines law. Those in power can change the rules, at least as far as the rules make it possible (in a society under the rule of law), and sometimes even beyond that (in a dictatorial society). And, to make it a bit more complicated, those in power can use law as an instrument of power, especially if they know the rules in detail. It can happen that a church official abuses his position in order to gain power, and does so perfectly within the valid rules. Therefore, theology has to take the issue of power — including aspects like manipulation and violence — seriously, at least in the academic discipline of church law.

Legalism can paralyze church life. Church law as a theological discipline with a thorough understanding of the nature of the law, should be part of the answer. Law is not an eternal, unchangeable set of rules. It rather is a process in which a community seeks to organize its life in terms of its nature and mission in a specific context. Church law can play a positive and creative role in church life, if it is being taken seriously, not as a body of rules that are basically strange to the Spirit, but as a challenge to serve the Spirit also in terms of the way we organize the church in its structures.

### *Abbreviations and bibliography*

ASV: The Bible, American Standard Version.

CCCWKG: The Church as Community of Common Witness to the Kingdom of God. Roman Catholic-Reformed Dialogue (2007). In: Reformed World 57(2007)/2 and 3, 105–207.

CEV: The Bible, Contemporary English Version.

KJV: The Bible, King James Version.

MOE: Ministry — Ordination — Episkopé (2013). In: Bünker and Friedrich 2013, 15–95.

NMC: The Nature and Mission of the Church: A Stage on the Way to a Common Statement (2005). Faith and Order Paper 198, Geneva: WCC.

TCUC: Towards a Common Understanding of the Church (1991). Studies from the World Alliance of Reformed Churches 21. Geneva: WCC 1991.

Bibby, Reginald W. 2003. The Circulation of the Saints: One Final Look at How Conservative Churches Grow. Presented at the Annual Meeting of the Pacific Sociological Association. Pasadena — April 2003. Accessed September 24, 2010. http://reginaldbibby.com/images/circofsaints03.pdf.

Bronkhorst, Alexander J. 1947. Schrift en kerkorde: Een bijdrage tot het onderzoek naar de mogelijkheid van een 'schriftuurlijke kerkorde'. Den Haag: Zuid-Holl. Boek en Handelsdrukkerij.

Bünker, Michael, and Martin Friedrich (eds). 2013. Ministry, Ordination, Episkopé and Theological Education. Leuenberger Texte 13. Leipzig: Evangelische Verlagsanstalt.

Coertzen, Pieter. 2004. 'Decently and in Order': A Theological Reflection on the Order for, and the Order in, the Church. Canon Law Monograph Series 4. Leuven: Peeters.

DeMoor, Henry. 2010. Christian Reformed Church Order Commentary. Grand Rapids MI: Faith Alive Christian Resources.

Dombois, Hans. 1961. Das Recht der Gnade: Ökumenisches Kirchenrecht. Band I. Witten: Luther-Verlag.

Dombois, Hans. 1974. Das Recht der Gnade: Ökumenisches Kirchenrecht. Band II. Bielefeld: Luther-Verlag.

Dombois, Hans. 1983. Das Recht der Gnade: Ökumenisches Kirchenrecht. Band III. Bielefeld: Luther-Verlag.

Francis, Mark R. 2010. Ladislas Orsy's new book, Receiving the Council: Theological and Canonical Insights and Debates. Accessed September 24, 2010. http://www.praytellblog.com.

Gros FSC, Jeffrey, Harding Meyer, and William G. Rusch (eds). 2000. Growth in Agreement II: Reports and Agreed Statements of Ecumenical Conversations on a World Level. Faith and Order Paper 187. Geneva: WCC.

Gros FSC, Jeffrey, Thomas F. Best, and Lorelei Fuchs SA (eds). 2007. Growth in Agreement III: International Dialogue Texts and Agreed Statements. Faith and Order Paper 204. Geneva: WCC.

Hall, David W., and Joseph H. Hall (eds). 1994. Paradigms in Polity: Classic Readings in Reformed and Presbyterian Church Government. Grand Rapids MI: Eerdmans.

Janssen, Allan J. 2000. Constitutional Theology: Notes on the Book of Church Order of the Reformed Church in America. The Historical Series of the Reformed Church in America 33. Grand Rapids MI.: Eerdmans.

Kasper, Cardinal Walter. 2009. Harvesting the Fruits. Basic Aspects of Christian Faith in Ecumenical Dialogue, London — New York: Continuum.

Koffeman, Leo J. 2009. Het goed recht van de kerk: Een theologische inleiding op het kerkrecht. Kampen: Kok.

Koffeman, Leo J. 2014. In Order to Serve: An Ecumenical Introduction into Church Polity. Church Polity and Ecumenism: Global Perspectives 1. Zürich: LIT-Verlag.

Long, Edward L. 2001. Patterns of Polity: Varieties of Church Governance. Cleveland, OH: Pilgrim Press.

Meyer, Harding, and Lukas Vischer (eds). 1984. Growth in Agreement: Reports and Agreed Statements of Ecumenical Conversations on a World Level. Faith and Order Paper 108. Geneva: WCC.

Orsy, Ladislas. 2009. Receiving the Council: Theological and Canonical Insights and Debates. Collegeville, MN: Michael Glazier — Liturgical Press.

Reenders, Hommo. 2001. De Gereformeerde zending in Midden-Java, 1859–1931: Een bronnenpublicatie. Zoetermeer: Boekencentrum.

Torfs, Rik. 2004. Ideals and Canon Law Legal Framework. Accessed September 24, 2010. http://www.daimon.unimi.it/immagini/torfs.pdf.

# CONTEXTUALITY AND INTERCULTURALITY OF THEOLOGY

Volker Küster

The title of this essay refers to the *universality-particularity-dilemma* that is inherent to Christian faith. Its universal promise of salvation — often enough mutated into a universal truth claim, which was executed by violent means — has to always prove its relevance anew on the local level. This leads directly into an *identity-relevance dilemma*. For Christian faith to become relevant in a particular context, intercultural transformation processes are unavoidable, in which at the same time its identity has to be preserved. Since these processes do not only involve the encounter with cultures but also religions, they evoke an *exclusivism-inclusivism-dilemma*. Are people of other faith lost when they decide not to convert to Christianity, or are they already included in God's plan of salvation? Finally the existence of different historically-grown confessions and the cultural differences in world Christianity cause a *unity-plurality-dilemma*.

What will be exemplified in the following for theology applies to other dimensions of Christian faith as well. I understand theology as an open system that is involved in permanent interaction with its particular contexts and the Christian community at large. The same is true for other subsystems like liturgy and art (see Küster 2007) or, in the concrete case of the present volume, for church polity. The theoretical and terminological framework developed here can prove helpful also in the discussions around the contextual and intercultural aspects of these topics. The identity reconstructions of white settler communities of Dutch origin in South Africa or the US rely in their Christian foundations on the Synod of Dordt (see the contributions of Coertzen and DeMoor in this volume). At the same time the representatives of Indonesian Protestantism, a breed of Dutch colonialism, strive for emancipation from this frame of reference by including local legal traditions (see the contributions of Purwanto and Surjanegara in this volume).

I regard the four dilemmas mentioned above not so much as threats, but as creative tensions, of which we must be cognizant. They cause the ambiguity and fluidity of Christian faith that make our theological predicaments sound fragmentary and fragile. Reflection on the particularity and universality of Christian faith has found its expression in two closely-intertwined idioms: contextual and intercultural theology. As to contextual theology, I have deliberately chosen context as an umbrella term for the particular liberation theologies on the one hand, and inculturation and dialog theologies on the other. I opt for intercultural instead of inter-contextual when it comes to the universal dimension for three reasons: (1) liberation theologies already operate with universals like class, race or gender from their very beginning; (2) cultural renaissances and identity (re) constructions have only recently proven to build up strong agency against the hyperculture of global consumer capitalism and empire; and (3) culture has thus become a decisive factor in the interreligious, intercultural and interconfessional relations of Christian faith. Therefore the term intercultural theology connects well to the prevailing cultural studies discourse within the humanities.

Their development so far can be subdivided into three phases, which I sketch shortly in what follows (cf. Küster 2011). I speak of a contextual, intercultural and glocal turn, referring to a theoretical concept of cultural studies. At the same time this process can be compared to a pendulum that is swinging between the particular and the universal. In the 1970s it swung from the universal claims of Western academic theology towards the contextual theologies developing in the global South. This immediately triggered the search for an intercultural theology that could negotiate 'in-between' the different contexts — a project which took shape during the 1980s and allowed the pendulum to swing back to universal questions. With the end of the bipolar world order and the rise of globalization, the pendulum began to swing between the global and the local again in a process of permanent negotiation that makes theology turn glocal.

### *1. The* contextual turn*: The 'irruption of the Third World' and the theory of contextual theology*

The end of the Second World War and the reorganization of the world, especially the decolonization of Africa and Asia that went with it, caused the irruption of the Third World. In the wake of secular emancipation movements and cultural renaissances Christian intellectuals executed an epistemological break with the tradition of western academic theology and formulated contextual theologies. As adherents of the religion of the former colonizers, which was identified with western culture, they tediously struggled for a contextual Christian identity. In different ways they tried to demonstrate the relevance of the biblical stories and the Christian tradition for their own context. In situations of poverty and oppression the exodus, the story of God who led the people out of slavery, and the passion of Jesus Christ, God's presence in the suffering of the world, are paradoxical counter stories that unfold their power out of powerlessness. In the cultural-religious pluralism of Africa, Asia and Latin America the many faces of Jesus Christ become visible (cf. Küster 2001).

Contextual theologians in the second generation, including women, interweave the biblical stories with the stories of the local people. Human beings are always ensnared in stories; therefore this strategy turns out to be very effective. The generative themes of context, that according to Paulo Freire rule the life of a community in a given moment, and the generative themes of biblical stories, constitute a new web of meaning (cf. Lange 1982; Schapp 1985; Freire 1990). I describe this process as a hermeneutical circle between text and context, which has to be paced through again and again.

By moving forward the view is changing and opens new perspectives on the text, which accordingly open up new meanings. 'Text' does not only comprise the biblical stories but also their reception history in Christian tradition. The context is the variable that continuously changes; the text is the relational constant. It itself determines the limits of its interpretations. The text does not allow every-

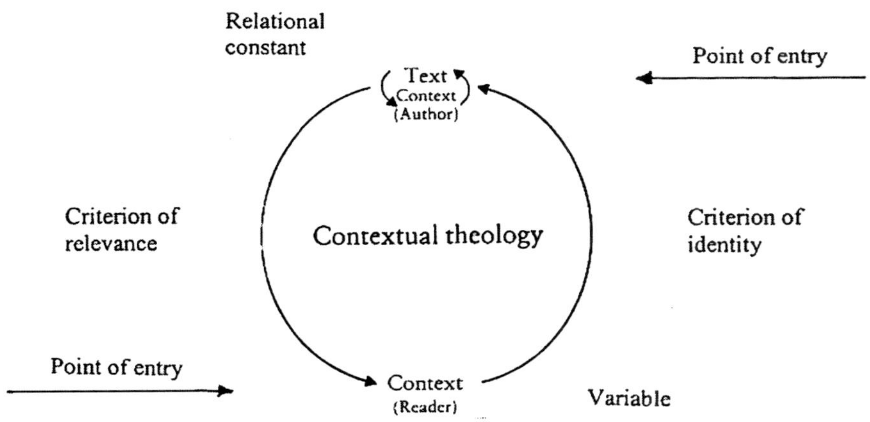


Fig. 1: *The hermeneutical circle*

thing; nevertheless it contains a richness of meaning that cannot be exhausted in a single interpretation. Accordingly there is also no 'one' sense of the text. At the same time the context is the relevance criterion and the text is the identity criterion of any contextual theology. This is an inner structure that is shared by all contextual theologies. Furthermore, contextual theologians apply a hermeneutics of suspicion not only against the various interpretations but also against the text itself. What are the ideological presuppositions and power relations involved in the hermeneutical process? Finally the diversity of contextual theologies has to prove itself in the ecumenical forum. This criterion of dialogue necessitates an intercultural theology that operates in-between the different contexts.

Thematically, two large schools of contextual theology can be distinguished: Latin-American liberation theology on the one hand, and the inculturation and dialog theologies of Africa and Asia on the other. Both have their predecessors. The catholic accommodation model thought it could control the interaction processes between Christian faith and culture and keep form and content separate like the kernel and husk of a nut. This static view that was shared by protestant indigenization theology and the evangelical translation models is challenged by the dynamics of the inculturation model. Form and content cannot be separated. If one peels off the layers of an onion, no kernel is left. While inculturation theologies may integrate elements of other religions, dialog theologies deal with the interaction processes between religious systems and people of different faith. With their revolutionary approach, liberation theologians distanced themselves from development theology and new political theology, which were in favor of evolution and reform.

In Africa and Asia however, there also emerged liberation theologies early on, such as Black theology of South Africa or South Korean Minjung theology (cf. Küster 2010A). Second generation liberation theologians in Latin America developed a theology of inculturation that took seriously folk Catholicism, the culture of the indigenous people and the descendants of the black slaves. Internationally, ecology, ethnic identity and the gender dimension emerged as new challenges. Not the least through the network structure of the Ecumenical Association of Third World Theologians (EATWOT), founded in 1976, contextual theologians, both male and female, are aware of the multi-dimensionality of their contexts (see www.eatwot.org).

*Table 1: Typology of contextual theology*

| cultural-religious type | socio-economic and political type |
|---|---|
| accommodation/indigenization / translation models (kernel-and-husk model) | development theology / new political theology (evolution; reform) |
| inculturation and dialogue theologies (onion model) | liberation theologies (revolution) |

contextual theologies:
cultural-religious, socio-economic and political, ecological
as well as gender dimension

## 2. *The* intercultural turn*: The encounter with 'the other' and the transformation of the universal*

Intercultural theology is originally a European project. Werner Ustorf characterizes it as "theological repentance of the north" (Ustorf 2008, 229, 243). At the beginning was the discovery of the 'other' theologies of the Third World by representatives of Western academic theology. At the same time Third World theologians have demonstrated, with EATWOT in an exemplary way, how a successful intercultural dialogue can be conducted, in spite of all set-backs and frustrations that also occurred during this process. The sympathizers in the West, however, were on closer view mainly professional border crossers (*Grenzgänger*) like missiologists or political theologians. They were committed to bridging the gap. Yet for most Western theologians, the first contact functioned as a sort of vaccination. Especially in Europe, theology today is executed as if contextual theologies had never happened. By contrast, for intercultural theology, the encounter with the cultural-religious other is of central importance. This is not about developing a new meta-system, but about seeking an adequate response to cultural-religious pluralism that necessitates a multi-functional and multi-perspectival approach, which shall be briefly introduced here:

### *Functions of intercultural theology*

Intercultural theology has at least four functions:

› *Heuristic function*: Intercultural theology develops a theoretical and methodological framework to tackle the encounter with the cultural-religious other. The interpretation of (hermeneutics) and communication with (communication theory) the other are oriented toward interdependency. At first contact, usually the attempt is made to translate the other into my own frame of reference and therefore a comparative approach is chosen. Sooner or later it comes to incommensurabilities, which can lead to conflict or dialogue.

› *Function of foundational theology:* Intercultural theology does not suspend the truth question; however, it presupposes that truth is always accessible only in a contextual way. By reflecting on the relationship between Christian faith and culture, by formulating a theology of religions, and by clarifying terminologies such as syncretism and fundamentalism or inculturation and dialog, it situates theology in the context of cultural-religious pluralism. It negotiates rules of dialog in intercultural discourse.

› *Anamnetic Function:* Intercultural theology collects and preserves contextual knowledge, while at the same time reinserting it into global theological discourse.

› *Ethical Function:* Intercultural theology not only cultivates an attitude of respect in the encounter with the cultural-religious 'other' but also intervenes in intercultural-religious conflicts.

*Perspectives of intercultural theology*

The multi-perspectival and multi-axial approach propagated by post-colonial feminist theologian Kwok Pui-Lan (see Kwok 1995; Kwok 2005) as well as the metaphor "Rahab's reading prism" coined by her African fellow-traveler Musa Dube (see Dube 2000, 123) are fitting descriptions for the mix of theories and methods applied by intercultural theology. I mention six such tools that I have been working with over the years, without claiming to be exhaustive:

› *communication theory*: Western missiologists tried in the 1950s to overcome the crisis of mission that had been smoldering since the time between the two world wars by introducing communication theory. Even if this approach has long been developed into a theory of intercultural communication, it is still prone to a certain one-sidedness that aims at an effective and adequate transmission of the message from the sender to the receiver (cf. Schreiter 1997, 33–39).

› *hermeneutics*: With the emergence of contextual theologies in the late 1960s and early 1970s, a hermeneutical turn took place that caused a change of perspective from the messenger of the gospel to the context of the receiver. In these theologies Christian faith and the respective local cultures and religions enter into dialog. The initial debates of demarcation in missiology between communication theorists and hermeneuts have already made way for the insight that both methods are not only compatible but also complementary: in order to understand I have to communicate and in order to communicate I have to understand.

› *postcolonial criticism*: The missiologists of the 1968 generation had already denounced the unfortunate entanglement of mission and colonialism. After the first generation of Third World Theologians reconstructed their identities as Christian intellectuals in post-colonial contexts, postcolonial criticism percolated from literary criticism into theology in the 1990s. According to postcolonial criticism, consciousness of asymmetric power relations is inherent in intercultural theology.

› *globalization theory*: At the same time, the dawning of the era of globalization symbolized by the fall of the Berlin wall and characterized by the end of the bipolar world order, the expansion of neo-liberal consumer capitalism and the compression of the world by new communication technologies, allowed the pendulum to swing again towards universal questions (cf. Schreiter 1997, 1–27). Postcolonial criticism's theory of culture is an important corrective for the globalization theories, which are socio-economically and politically oriented.

› *narrativity*: The emphasis that contextual theologies put on human experience, culminating in the statement "'We are the text' and the bible and the tradition of the Christian church are the context of our theology" (Chung 1990, 111), led to appreciation of narrativity. In the West for a short time a 'narrative theology' had been propagated, which however never really materialized (see Erbele-Küster 2009).

› *aesthetics*: With this revaluation of human experience and the stories that carry it, a broadening of theological genres has already been demonstrated. Stories, meditations or reviews appear alongside theological tracts. Literature, art and film become independent sources of theology. Aesthetics is indispensable for the methodological repertoire of intercultural theology (see Küster 2009).

### *The encounter with the other*

In earlier times my direct neighbor was the other and the distant neighbor was a stranger. Through migration and mass tourism as well as mass media, the new communication technologies and social media, this spatial differentiation has become obsolete. Still the factor of cultural-religious otherness remains—an otherness which neither Martin Buber with his tract *Ich und Du* (I and Thou, 1925) nor Emmanuel Lévinas with his in this respect often quoted book *Die Spur des Anderen* (The Trace of the Other, 1983) had in mind. This otherness is however the focus of intercultural theology.

When it comes to the appraisal of other religions, since the end of the 1980s the exclusivism—inclusivism—pluralism scheme has regularly been referred to. Non-Christians are thus either thought of as excluded from salvation if they do not convert to Christian faith, or as already included in God's plan of salvation. This exclusivism-inclusivism dilemma has its roots in the biblical texts and the ancient church. The pluralist option on the other hand is a postmodern theory that presupposes that all religions are equal ways to salvation. By having them converge in a point beyond theism/non-theism, however, it constructs de facto a sort of meta-inclusivism (cf. Hick and Knitter 1987).

Alternatively I propose similarity—alterity—plurality—relationality as another model constellation.

*Table 2: The encounter with the other*

| *similarity model* | *alterity model* | *plurality model* | *relationality model* |
|---|---|---|---|
| external: assimilation | inferior: barbarian | complementary | conflict |
| internal: self-awareness | superior: noble savage | diversity | dialogue |

- The *similarity model* has clearly inclusivist tendencies. Cultural-religious differences are eventually denied. The other basically resembles me; possible initial differences can be assimilated. Another version of this model sees the other always already present in one's own 'I': 'strangers are we to our self'.
- The *alterity model* is, despite what the name suggests, in the end also self-referential. The other is regarded both as inferior and stigmatized as barbarian (cf. exclusivism) or as superior, a 'noble savage', who then nevertheless represents the ideal of one's own society.
- The *plurality model* presupposes, alternatively, complementarity or radical diversity and shows a certain resemblance with the pluralist theology of religion.
- I personally prefer a *relationality model*, which suggests that there are 'overlaps' (*Überlappungen*) — commonalities as well as incommensurable differences — among the various cultures and religions (cf. Mall 1996, 38; Waldenfels 2006). Intercultural theology explores this contact zone that is characterized by dialog and conflict and not at all free from power structures. The other remains resistant to all attempts to be claimed. At the same time we make ourselves 'vulnerable' when we expose ourselves to it (cf. Margull 1992). Yet the attitude of respect for differences and borders created by intercultural theology invites the other to neighborology.

*3. The* glocal turn*: From contextualization to glocalization of theology*

Under the impact of globalization contextual theologies have undergone three significant transformations (see Schreiter 1997, 26f.):

- *Deterritorialization*: The first generation of contextual theologians was still presupposing the spatial limitation of their particular context. Through migration and the rise of a globally linked Diaspora, today contexts are deterritorialized.
- *Hybridity*: The initial essentialist concept of culture as present in theologies of inculturation is also under pressure. Migrants begin their travel with their home culture and religion as baggage. In their new home country they create hybrid identities. At the same time, in their countries of origin hybridizations take place under the impact of globalization.
- *Multiple Belonging*: Finally, belonging to one community that carries the particular contextual theology is also disintegrating. Human beings today develop simultaneous loyalties to multiple groups based on their circumstances of life and social networks.

While intercultural theology had in the beginning the function of crossing the borders and bridging the gap between the various contextual theologies, today they have become intercultural themselves. Intercultural theology explores the manifold interreligious, intercultural and interconfessional border crossings of Christian faith. It creates an attitude of respect and provides terminologies and methods to continue to dialogue, not only in an intra-disciplinary manner among the various theologies and theological disciplines, but also in an inter-disciplinary way. Contextual theologies on the other hand have created network structures themselves that have turned them into "global theological flows" (see Schreiter 1997, 15–21). The trend points from contextualization to glocalization.

### *4. Intercultural theology today*

Even if intercultural theology was initially oriented toward distant lands and initiated a change of perspective within missiology with the discovery of 'the other' overseas, its border crossing existence and the accompanying bridge building function could not remain one-way traffic for long. Desecularization, migration and multiculturality occurred on its horizon. What it has learned in distant lands was needed urgently at home.

On closer inspection, the territory of what is today Europe never was cultural-religiously homogenous. This is not only true for the time before Christianization. Even if Christianization was a success percentage-wise, Jews and Muslims have always been present as minorities at least in parts of Europe. In retrospect, the co-habitation of the three Abrahamic religions appears as a history of conflicts. Along with the expulsion of the Muslims during the Spanish reconquista, the Jews were forced to leave the country as well. During the crusades, which aimed at recapturing the holy city Jerusalem from the Muslims, pogroms among the Jews also occurred. The Jews were accused of being 'murderers of the Messiah'. The long tradition of Christian anti-Judaism led ultimately to the gas chambers of the Third Reich. After the European Jews had nearly been extinguished by the Nazi regime in the first half of the twentieth century, its second half witnessed the growing immigration of Muslims. The encounter with Islam is for Western Europeans the ultimate experience of the other, and not just since 9/11. The proverbial 'Turks in front of Vienna' (*Türken vor Wien*) (1529 and 1683) have engraved themselves deep into the cultural memory and have their repercussions in the actual Islamophobia.

Still, the Abrahamic religions determine the religious landscape of Europe (see Küster 2010B). The religions of Indian origin, Hinduism and Buddhism, by contrast are negligible numerically. After the concession, forced by the holocaust, that the 'Christian Occident' has accepted a Jewish-Christian legacy, the current recognition of the Muslim contribution, for instance to the transfer of antic knowledge, is pending. Even if a trialog has seldom taken place in Jewish-Christian and Muslim-Christian dialog, the position of the missing third party always has to be taken into account.

Whether immigrants entered the country as guest-workers more or less invited, or as inhabitants of the former colonies, or as refugees, European societies turned multicultural through migration soon after the end of the Second World War. The very word 'guest-worker' already suggests that immigration was originally not intended. The shortcomings of politics of integration gave rise all over Europe to populist right wing parties that demand assimilation to the particular 'lead culture' (*Leitkultur*), the eviction of illegal and delinquent migrants, and an end to immigration.

Methodologically and content-wise, intercultural theology is part and parcel of the cultural turn in the humanities. It performs a cultural-religious turn in theology, which at the same time will have repercussions in cultural studies, because it reinserts religions and religiosity into a discourse that for a long time has neglected them. Some even see a religious turn emerging. Intercultural theology opens up a cosmopolitan view, which thwarts the persisting Eurocentrism not only of theology. It always thinks from the perspective of the margins and decenters our thinking; socio-economically and politically through the option for the poor, as well as through the attitude of respect for the cultural-religious other. This complies with a theological argumentation based on the theology of the cross. Jesus has been crucified 'outside the gate' (cf. Ahn 1986). His 'vulnerability' has become a metaphor for the intercultural-religious dialog (cf. Margull 1992). Intercultural theology therefore destabilizes and subverts established discourses.

### *Bibliography*

Ahn, Byung-Mu. 1986. Draußen vor dem Tor: Kirche und Minjung in Korea. Theologische Beiträge und Reflexionen. Göttingen: Vandenhoeck und Ruprecht.

Buber, Martin. 1925. Ich und Du. Leipzig: Insel-Verlag.

Chung, Hyun-Kyung. 1990. Struggle to be the Sun again. Maryknoll, NY: Orbis Books.

Dube, Musa. 2000. Postcolonial Feminist Interpretation of the Bible. St. Louis, Missouri: Chalice Press.

Erbele-Küster, Dorothea. 2009. Narrativität. Accessed December, 11, 2013. http://www.bibelwissenschaft.de.

Freire, Paulo. 1990 [1970], Pädagogik der Unterdrückten: Bildung als Praxis der Freiheit. Reinbek bei Hamburg: Rowohlt.

Hick, John, and Paul F. Knitter (eds). 1987. The Myth of Christian Uniqueness: Towards a Pluralistic Theology of Religions. London: SCM Press — Maryknoll, NY: Orbis Books.

Küster, Volker. 2001. The Many Faces of Jesus Christ: Intercultural Christology. Maryknoll, NY: Orbis Books.

Küster, Volker. 2007. Christian Art in Asia: Yesterday and Today. In: Pongracz et al 2007, 28–43.

Küster, Volker. 2009. Gott/Terror: Ein Diptychon. Frankfurt am Main: Lembeck.

Küster, Volker. 2010A. A Protestant Theology of Passion: Korean Minjung Theology Revisited. Leiden: Brill.

Küster, Volker. 2010B. Indebted to Kinship: The Project of an 'Abrahamic Ecumene' Contested. In: Kuester and Speelman 2010, 163–180.

Küster, Volker. 2011. Einführung in die Interkulturelle Theologie. Göttingen: Vandenhoeck und Ruprecht.

Küster, Volker, and Gé Speelman (eds). 2010. Islam in the Netherlands: Between Religious Studies and Interreligious Dialogue. Münster: LIT-Verlag.

Kwok, Pui-Lan. 1995. The Bible in the Non-biblical World. Maryknoll, NY: Orbis Books.

Kwok, Pui-Lan. 2005. Postcolonial Imagination and Feminist Theology, Louisville, Kentucky: Westminster John Knox Press.

Lange, Ernst. 1982. Predigen als Beruf. Aufsätze zu Homiletik, Liturgie und Pfarramt, München: Kaiser.

Lévinas, Emmanuel. 1983. Die Spur des Anderen: Untersuchungen zur Phänomenologie und Sozialphilosophie. Freiburg/München: Alber.

Mall, Ram Adhar. 1996. Philosophie im Vergleich der Kulturen. Interkulturelle Philosophie — Eine neue Orientierung. Darmstadt: Primus-Verlag.

Margull, Hans Jochen. 1992. Zeugnis und Dialog. Ausgewählte Schriften. Ammersbek bei Hamburg: Verlag an der Lottbek.

Pongracz, Patricia C., Volker Küster, and John W. Cook (eds). 2007. The Christian Story: Five Asian Artists Today. London: Glies — New York: the Museum of Biblical Art.

Schapp, Wilhelm. 1985. In Geschichten verstrickt: Zum Sein von Mensch und Ding. Frankfurt am Main: Lembeck, 3rd edition.

Schreiter, Robert J. 1997. The new Catholicity. Theology between the Global and the Local, Maryknoll, NY: Orbis Books.

Ustorf, Werner. 2008. The Cultural Origins of 'Intercultural Theology'. In: Mission Studies 25(2008), 229–251.

Waldenfels, Bernhard. 2006. Grundmotive einer Phänomenologie des Fremden. Frankfurt am Main: Suhrkamp.

# THE RELEVANCE OF REFORMED CHURCH POLITY PRINCIPLES

## Revisiting the Concept

Mary-Anne Plaatjies van Huffel

### *1. Introduction*

The Reformed (or Presbyterian) system of church polity is employed by Reformed churches across the globe. This article intends to discern the fundamental principles of the Reformed church polity system. What does the concept entail? Can one talk of a set of principles confirmed by Reformed Churches across the globe? Are there valuable and valid norms, principles, that may help guide the action and behavior of Reformed churches? What composes the basis of Reformed church polity principles? Can a unique, universal set of principles be offered to which Reformed churches must adhere? A blurriness of different systems of church governance is evident among Reformed churches. This article will address the question how the principles of Reformed church polity should function in a culture characterized by anonymity and decreasing institutional commitment. Changes have taken place in the global South, in the context of the relation between churches and states during the past decades, as, for example in the transition from colonization to democracy and from modernity to postmodernity. Reformed churches in the global South are continuously challenged to reconsider their church polity in view of such changes. Revisiting the concept in order to strengthen and advance notions of Reformed church polity principles is needed.

It is problematic to obtain an overarching definition of Reformed church polity principles. The emphasis on principles tends to distinguish Presbyterian churches from other Christian churches. Etymologically, the term 'principle' comes from the Latin *principium*, meaning 'beginning', 'origin' or 'groundwork'. Principles are, therefore foundational, in some sense. Principles are assumptions, laws or rules, beliefs, standards, especially of good behavior, that have to be, or usually are to be followed. They represent a set of values or essential characteristics. Principles are fundamental truths or propositions that serve as the foundation for a system of belief or behavior or for a chain of reasoning. They can also be seen as fixed or predetermined policies or modes of action. On the one hand, principles require strict conformity to the letter of the law; while on the other hand, they promote natural justice. One should take into account the critique against the idea of a universal set of principles, which imply, for instance, that it is outdated to speak about Reformed church polity principles in a postmodern society.

Another way of putting the question is to ask: What is particular to Reformed church polity? Are these principles distinctively Reformed? For example, the parity of the clergy or the power of the local congregation or the unity of the church are not on their own account distinctive marks of Presbyterianism. Some of the principles which Reformed churches hold are common to other church governance systems as well. For example, Erastianism or Congregationalism holds similar principles (see Bouwman 2000, 28–31). The issue, therefore, in this article is not how Presbyterianism can define principles *vis à vis* Erastianism or Congregationalism.

The current presumption is that principles should be non-binding standards of good practice as well as guidance for implementation, which in turn can be adapted to the specific circumstances of Reformed churches worldwide, rather than a binding set of rules. The rejection of a fixed, universal and generalize-able set of principles is a characteristic of postmodernism and leads to diversity of interpretations of the principles of Reformed church polity. Whereas modernity was primarily concerned with principles such as identity, unity, authority and certainty, postmodernity is often associated with difference, plurality and skepticism. In a postmodern society one of the main questions will be: can Reformed churches still speak with authority and with certainty on issues like identifying marks (principles) of Reformed church polity? Interestingly Charles Hodge (1797–1878) more than a century ago asked the following question: what is essential to the existence of the principles of Reformed church polity, to which the attributes, the promises, the prerogatives of the Church polity belong? Hodge worked with the presumption that there are certain judicial principles that constitute the true idea of Presbyterianism. According to Hodge, fundamental principles underlie the constitution of the Presbyterian Church and its administration (see Hodge 1879, 119). For him the fundamental principles of our Presbyterian system are first, the parity of the clergy; second, the right of the people to a substantive part in the government of the Church; and third, the unity of the Church, in such sense, that a small part is subject to a larger and a larger to the whole (Hodge 1879, 119).

In this contribution I will first give a survey of how the issue of principles of Reformed church polity has been dealt with traditionally (cf. Bouwman 1928, Kleynhans 1985, Pont 1981, Spoelstra 1989). Second, I will discuss seven Reformed

Church principles. Finally, I will focus on the question whether these principles have been sufficiently incorporated in the church polity of the church of which I am a member, namely, the Uniting Reformed Church in Southern Africa (URCSA).

## 2. *Background of the formation of Reformed church polity principles.*

The basis of Presbyterian/Reformed polity is theological. At its heart, the polity of the church expresses Reformed theology. Historically five church polity systems can be distinguished: the Episcopal system (Roman or Papal), the Lutheran/Territorial system, the Independent or Congregational system, the Collegial system and the Reformed/Presbyterian system. These five systems of church polity differ in their ecclesiology, where the power resides, discipline, the organization of the church as well as the relationship between church and state. A Presbyterian form of church polity, in contrast to both Episcopal polities organized under governance by bishops (Roman Catholic, United Methodist, and Episcopal denominations) and Congregational polities organized under the governance of the local congregation (Congregational, Baptist) is organized under governance by elders. In other words, Reformed church government is elder-centered church government (cf. Beattie 2007, 1–8; Gray and Tucker 2004, 2–11; Engle and Cowan 2004, 73–98).

The notion of Reformed church polity principles is shaped by the work of reformers like John Calvin. He explicated the principles of Reformed church polity in his reformation in Geneva. The church, distinct from the state, has its officers and laws, and is therefore an administrative government of its own. In 1541, aided by the city council, he drew up the *Ordonnances ecclésiastiques* (see Calvin 1541). The council passed them on 20 November 1541. Calvin clarified the principles of Reformed church polity in his *Institutes of the Christian Religion,* especially in Book IV. A very considerable portion of that book is occupied with establishing these principles and pointing out their proper application to the regulation of ecclesiastical affairs. The Calvinistic system of church polity is based upon the following principles, which have exerted great influence in the development of Protestantism: (i) the autonomy of the church, or its right of self-government under the sole headship of Christ; (ii) the parity of the clergy as distinct from a *jure divino* hierarchy whether papal or prelatic; (iii) the participation of the Christian laity in church government and discipline; (iv) strict discipline to be exercised jointly by ministers and lay-elders, with the consent of the whole congregation; (v) union of church and state on a theocratic basis, if possible, or separation, if necessary to secure the purity and self-government of the Church (see Schaff 1882, 333–336). Johnson deduced the following as distinctive principles of this system of government (see Johnson 1900, 47–57):

1. The self-government of the church under the headship of Christ. Calvin believed that God in Christ is head of both church and state.
2. Ecclesiastical discipline of all the members of the church from the greatest to the smallest to be exercised by a parliamentary court consisting of ministers of the gospel and ruling elders. Calvin valued discipline as second only to teaching. Calvin formally sets forth the importance of discipline in his introduction to the discussion of 'The Discipline of the Church' (Calvin 1559, IV, 12). Calvin distinguished three degrees of discipline: private admonition, admonition in the presence of witnesses or before the church, and excommunication.
3. A consistory, or parliamentary court, consisting of elders of two classes, to exercise discipline.
4. The recognition and reinstitution of the New Testament ruling eldership (cf. Rom. 12: 8 and I Cor. 12: 28). Calvin reinstituted the New Testament office of the deacon. They were elected in the same manner as the elders.

Calvin rejected the organization of the medieval church as contrary to the New Testament. The *Ordonnances ecclésiastiques* stated that the ministers should choose someone suitable for the position as minister of the Word and should notify the government accordingly. It appears that in the *Ordonnances ecclésiastiques* the elders had no sitting on the meeting where ministers were called. Calvin later formally sets forth the importance of the participation of elders in the full governance of the church in Book IV his *Institutes*. Following his election, the minister had to take an oath of allegiance to the government according to a written form. Calvin laid great stress on the outward organization and order of the Church, but it was to be subordinated to sound doctrine and the inner spiritual life (see Schaff 1882, 333).

The organization of the Reformed Churches in the Netherlands owes a great deal to John à Lasco (1499–1560), a Polish Protestant evangelical reformer, who help to organize the Dutch refugee community in London. In his *Forma ac Ratio* (Form and Rationale) he mapped out the lines for polity and liturgy for the 'stranger churches' in London, based on Calvin's principles of church polity. This book possibly influenced John Knox's Scottish order which in turn was influential in Dutch Calvinist churches. This can be seen as the first step towards the contextualizing of the essential principles of Reformed church government.

The foundation of Reformed church polity was further developed at various ecclesiastical assemblies especially in the Dutch context. At the Synod of the Walloon Churches, held in Paris in 1559, the rule was formulated that 'no church may assume primacy or domination over another'. The implication is that in a church of Jesus Christ there is no room for domineering: a minister is not to lord it over another minister, nor a minister over consistory, nor consistory over consistory, nor elder over elder, etc. At the Convent of Wezel (1568) a group of Reformed brethren from the Netherlands also approved adjustments to Calvin's *Ordonnances ecclésiastiques*. The Convent of Wezel stated as the first article of its church order: "No church shall in any way lord it over other churches, no office-bearer over other office-bearers". The convent of Wezel paved the way for the organization of the Reformed Church in the Lowlands for more than two centuries and has influenced the church polity of the Reformed churches in the global South.

At the Synod of Emden (1571) adjustments to Calvin's *Ordonnances ecclésiastiques* were approved. The Synod of Emden emphasized among other matters the binding nature of decisions of synods. The synod also expressed the "no lording" principle in the first article of its church order. Art. 31 of the *Belgic Confession* (*Confessio Belgica*, CB) also affirms the 'no lording' principle. This principle was incorporated into the church order of Dordt. No lording over others is a fundamental principle that has characterized Reformed church polity until the present. Among ministers there is complete equality. In Presbyterian churches there is no such thing as clericalism (cf. Van Oene 1990, 3). Presbyterianism denies that all church power is vested in the clergy, and emphasizes that the congregants have a right to substantive participation in the government of the church. Furthermore, it denies that the apostolic office is perpetual. Christ committed his power in the first instance to the local congregation. The position of privileged priesthood is therefore redundant in a Reformed system of church governance. This principle serves to protect congregations and consistories from domineering individuals. Presbyterians find the locus of the church neither in the local congregation, as in a congregational polity, nor in a hierarchy of authoritative individuals, as in episcopal polity. No individual in the Reformed church governance system holds any authority in the church except by the call of the church.

The church order adopted at Emden was revised at the Synods of Dordrecht (1574 and 1578), Middelburg (1581), and The Hague (1586), before being adopted by the Synod of Dordrecht (or Dordt) (1618–1619). Although these synods took important decisions, and applied changes with a view to changing socio-political circumstances to the church ordinances, the old church organization of Emden, still remains, albeit in modified form. Not only the principles, but almost all the applications have been received and maintained in places far distant from Emden. It can therefore be claimed that the church order of Calvin has subsequently played a pivotal role in the formation of later Dutch church ordinances.

The Synod of Dordt 1618/19, moreover, granted certain powers to the government of the day as, for example, in the calling of ministers and included as well the regulation that the departure of a minister to another congregation of the church also required the approbation of the government. The government also had the right to attend by her deputies the meetings of the consistory, the classis and the synod.

On 1 April 1816 the *General Regulations (Algemeen Reglement)* for the management of the Dutch Reformed Church in the Kingdom of the Netherlands came into force. This set of rules replaced the *Dordt Church Order* and effected major changes in church governance in the Dutch context, such as a more centralized, top-down organizational structure and the loosening of the confessional bonds. Resistance to the *General Regulations* (1816) and to the associated hierarchical church governance system emerged in the Netherlands. It ultimately led to the Secession (1834) and the Doleantie (1886) (cf. Bos 1986, 70). According to Golverdingen, a complex of concepts was developed by A. Kuyper and F.L. Rutgers before, during and after the Doleantie: the independence of the local church, the character of the denomination, the nature of the authority of the major assemblies, the powers of the major assemblies in general, the deposition of elders, deacons and pastors, the proviso to appeal, and the authority of the major assemblies with regard to mismanagement (see Golverdingen 2001, 61–65).

Taking into account the historical development of Presbyterianism as well as the right of Reformed churches across the globe to adapt principles to varying conditions and circumstances, it seems clear to me that there are basic Reformed church polity principles that one can discern. Reformed churches and Presbyterian churches refer in different ways to principles in their respective church orders. For example, according to the Presbyterian Church in the United States of America (PCUSA), *The historic principles of Presbyterianism*, a document adopted by 195th General Assembly (1983) represents the explication of what Presbyterians believe (see HPP 1983, 1–15). These principles were written to describe the particular identity of Presbyterians and how that identity shapes the distinctive life of the church, holding in tension the need for diversity and the requirement for centrality of purpose and commonality of belief. The PCUSA affirms the following principles: that the several different congregations of believers, taken collectively, constitute one Church of Christ, called emphatically the Church; that a larger part of the Church, or a representation of it, should govern a smaller, or determine matters of controversy which arise therein; that, in like manner, a representation of the whole should govern and determine in regard to every part, and to all the parts united: that is, that a majority shall govern; and consequently that appeals may be carried from lower to higher governing bodies, until they be finally decided by the collective wisdom and united voice of the whole Church. For these principles and this procedure, the example of the apostles and the practice of the primitive

Church are considered as authority (CO-PCUSA, G-1.0400). Notwithstanding the above the PCUSA affirms the following historic principles of Presbyterian Church government and discipline:

1. The right of private judgment both for the individual or group within the church and for the church within the state. The right of private judgment is freedom from arbitrary laws, civil or ecclesiastical, which bind conscience.
2. Churches have the right to regulate their own internal affairs without government interference. Individuals, also, have the right to exercise private judgment within the decision-making processes of the church of which they are a part.
3. The church must have order in its life. Church officers function as representative members of governing bodies and exercise responsibility corporately.
4. Presbyterian polity provides a method for dealing with conflict. The processes assure that fairness and order accompany the decision-making and that differing points of view will be openly expressed. The diversity of the church is its best equipment for dealing with significant issues.
5. No church governing body may bind conscience contrary to Scripture.
6. The Holy Scripture defines the general character, qualifications, authority, and purpose of church officers but the church must interpret Scripture and establish the general rules by which it operates.
7. The rights of the minority are protected from the tyranny of the majority and, at the same time, the rights of the majority are protected from the paralysis of the intransigence of a minority (see HPP 1983, 1–15).

In the global South, for example the Reformed Churches in South Africa were influenced with the notions of church government by Bucer and Calvin as well as the development of church polity in the Netherlands (cf. Jonker 1965). The abovementioned principles codified in the global North informed assumptions in the global South about Reformed church polity, and can be discerned for example in the governance of the Uniting Reformed Church in Southern Africa. From the outset the Reformed churches in South Africa gave prominence to the principles of Reformed church governance, *inter alia* autonomy of the local churches, the confederative character of the denomination and the disciplinary power of the major assemblies.

### 3. *The foundational Reformed church polity principles*

Reformed church polity principles are directed toward the common good of the church. Seven church polity principles can be discerned to adjudicate the church polity and church governance of the Reformed Churches. These principles jointly link Reformed churches together as a family and entail the following:

self-government under the sole headship of Christ, the limited autonomy of the local congregation, the denominational tie serving the wellbeing of the church, the restricted power and responsibilities of ecclesial assemblies, the necessity and nature Christian discipline, the right to appeal, and the power of major assemblies with regard to misconduct. Reformed church polity is not constituted by holding one of these principles; it is in manifesting them all. I do not suggest hereby that the list of principles is comprehensive and I take into account that, in different contexts, emphasis is being put on different nuances of the principles. I, however, want to suggest the following as a probable list of Reformed church principles that may bind Reformed Churches together globally.

### 3.1 *Self-government under the sole headship of Christ*

One of the fundamental Reformed church polity principles is self-government under the sole headship of Christ. The church is described as the body of Christ and Jesus Christ as its only Head (CB, art. 29). Christ entrusted the ecclesiastical authority and legislative power to the offices. The church is a visible, organized body that recognizes Christ as the chief and only office-bearer of the church (cf. Jonker 1965, 1–10, Spoelstra 1989, 102). Christ uses people for the leadership of his Church on earth and instituted the offices and ministries.The officers of a governing body are temporary and limited. The authority exercised by those holding office in the church is delegated by Christ. This principle is an explicit exclusion of all Erastianism, because the latter system gives the state authority over the church. The authority of all ministerial office therefore rests upon Christ. All authority exercised in the church is received from Christ, the only Head of the church. The church is called into existence through the Word and Spirit. Christ exercises dominion over His Church by His Word and Spirit. The institution of the church took place by the King of the church itself. Christ is the only Legislator and grants to the church its rights and does not cede his power to any secular authority (Calvin 1559, IV, 9.1).

### 3.2 *The limited autonomy of the local congregation*

A second basic principle of the Reformed church governance is the recognition of the limited autonomy of local congregations. The authority of the local congregations is restricted by a common confession and church order. The local congregation is organized by the voluntary association of a number of believers. Reformed church polity recognizes the right of every other church, or association of particular churches, to establish its form of polity and terms of communion for itself, and recommends all to exercise mutual forbearance towards each other (see Hopkins 1878, 68).

A local congregation consists of a number of professing Christians, with their offspring, voluntarily associated for divine worship and godly living, agreeably to the Holy Scriptures, and submitting to a certain form of government (see Stephens 1907, 18). Membership in the church is voluntary. One is not forced to become a member, nor is one compelled to remain a member. The principle of the limited autonomy of the local church goes back to the very beginning of the history of the Reformed churches. Each local congregation is autonomous with the right of self-governance, but is restricted in that the local churches cannot stand on their own, but must unite on the basis of their confession. In the presbyterial-synodical system congregations are always in relation to each other. Failure to maintain the principle of the limited autonomy of the local congregation leads to hierarchy.

The local congregation is, however, a complete church, *ecclesia completa,* and is thus in principle independent of other congregations or churches (see Bouwman 2000, 19). The local congregation is, in itself, a complete manifestation of the body of Christ and is subject to Christ the head of the church (Matt. 16:18–19). The church is the visible representation of the kingdom of God, living according to the laws of Christ (see Bouwman 1928, 70). The authority that Christ, as head of his church, gives to his church resides in the church council. Ecclesiastical power in the local congregation is exercised through these legitimate officers. The church councils, also called consistories or sessions, as the visible representative government of God's kingdom, have general oversight of the local congregation in the preaching of the gospel, the administration of the sacraments, and the exercise of Christian discipline (see CB, art. 29). Reformed churches are governed by judicatories usually composed of ministers, elders and deacons. Calvin vests the self-government in the Christian congregation, and regards all the ministers of the gospel, in their official character, as ambassadors and representatives of Christ. Christ uses people for the leadership of his Church on earth. All the offices in the church are ordained by Christ who rules the congregation through the special offices in the church (Matt. 16:13–19, 18:15–20, John 20:21–23) (see Bouwman 1928, 67). These office bearers form the church council.

Traditionally in Reformed church polity, the church council has been seen as the only continuing assembly. Because Presbyterian governance is through teaching and ruling presbyters, all three offices must be instituted in the local congregations. No church can have only a minister of the Word. Besides the minister there must be elders, and in a number of cases also deacons who with the minister constitute the church council. De Jong warns that violation of these principles can lead either to independent church governance or to hierarchy (see De Jong 1918, 157).

3.3 *The denominational ties serve the well-being of the church*

The notion that no Reformed congregation stands by itself is also one of the fundamental principles of Reformed church polity. In a Reformed tradition, a very close bond exists among churches (see Van Dellen and Monsma 1954, 26). The unity of the church is expressed in mutual relationships. The church is divided into many separate congregations which require mutual counsel and assistance in order to preserve the soundness of doctrine, the regularity of discipline, and the prevention of infidelity, error and immorality. The churches of the federation, although distinct, voluntarily manifest their unity by means of a common confession and church order. There is a spiritual obligation to seek and maintain the federative unity of the churches by formal bonds of fellowship and cooperation. Among churches belonging to the federation, three assemblies are recognized: the church council, the presbytery and the synod.

The word 'federation' has as its main component the Latin word *foedus*, meaning 'covenant'. Federation is a covenant among these churches. Entrance into, remaining in and departure from a federative relationship is strictly a voluntary matter (see Van Oene 1990, 3). No church can or may be compelled to take this step nor can a church be prevented from breaking with the federation. According to Voetius, denominational ties or federative relationships do not belong to the essence or being of the church (see Bouwman 1937, 148). It rather serves the well-being of the church. Federative relationships are appropriate for the proper ecclesial community and for mutual edification. The several neighboring congregations are not independent, but are united under a federation. Within a federation of churches, each congregation has a limited autonomy. The federation serves to prevent both hierarchy and independent church governance. It is there only to help, not to take matters out of the hands of the minor assemblies. In some Reformed churches, as for example in URCSA, a congregation that decides to break with the federation is perfectly free to do so and no ecclesiastical assembly can prevent it. A congregation may through its church council withdraw from the federation at any time. Voetius emphasizes that the voluntary consent is not only a basis, but that it is a prerequisite for the establishment and practice of the federation (see Voetius 1888, IV, 120; cf. Bouwman 1937, 148). It is however out of order for a congregation to withdraw from the presbytery without first obtaining the consent of the presbytery. The only proper method of dissolving the relation between a presbytery and a church desiring to become an independent body is for that church to withdraw, declining the further jurisdiction of the presbytery, and the presbytery to record its withdrawal as required (Bittinger 1888, 33). Reformed churches embrace accountability in denominational relationship. If a church persistently violates the agreement as laid down in the church order, all the federation can do is to expel that church from this federation, meanwhile offering assistance to those members of that church who want to remain faithful (see Van Oene 1990, 2).

### 3.4 *The restricted power and responsibilities of ecclesial assemblies*

Reformed church polity is based on the interdependence of governing bodies. A fourth fundamental principle of Reformed church polity is that the executive, legislative and judicial power in the Church is bestowed in both the minor and major assemblies. The rights of the local congregation cannot be bypassed nor usurped by a major assembly. Therefore all power mentioned above can be exercised only by church courts and in no case by individual officers (see Hodge 1879, 120). There are four degrees of courts in the Presbyterian churches. These are the church council, the presbytery, the synod and the general synod. Church councils are permanent bodies while presbyteries and synods are temporary. The church council (minor assembly) is composed of the teaching and ruling presbyters of a particular church; Presbyteries are conventions of an equal delegation of the ministers and church council members within a larger area.; a synod is composed of several presbyteries in a geographical area and is the intermediate governmental unit responsible for the mission of the church throughout its region. The synod exercises limited supervisory authority over both presbyteries and congregations. The general synod is the highest judicatory of the Reformed Church and exercises an appellate supervisory power over the acts, proceedings, and decisions of the lower assemblies.

Member churches meet together in major assemblies (presbyteries and synods) to manifest ecclesiastical unity. Major assemblies are composed of delegates from churches in a certain region. According to Voetius, the power of the major assemblies is delegated (*potestas delegata*; see Voetius 1888, 122, 174–178). The authority of church councils on the other hand is original. Major assemblies preside over minor assemblies, or determine matters of controversy which arise therein. In all assemblies only ecclesiastical matters shall be transacted, only in an ecclesiastical manner. The term 'major' is the equivalent of 'broader' and does not indicate a higher rank. The term 'major' or 'broader' indicates rather that in an assembly more churches are represented than at the 'minor' assembly. Major assemblies are therefore not super-consistories and the term 'minor assembly' does not imply a lower rank (see Van Oene 1990, 132). The duties and powers of the major assemblies are limited to the agreement among the churches in the federation. In most Reformed churches, for instance, the general assembly or synod does not have magisterial authority. While governing bodies have certain authority, power, and responsibility, authority and power are limited by the provisions of the church order, confessions and Scripture. A major assembly shall deal ordinarily with those matters which concern its churches in common or which could not be finished in the minor assemblies. Ordinarily, a major assembly would therefore not be allowed to declare a matter admissible if it could have been accomplished in a lower assembly. The major assembly, according to De Jong, may only take decisions on matters in dispute in local churches in order to solve matters intractable by the minor assembly; otherwise the major assembly acts outside its competence (see De Jong 1918, 158). Major assemblies must concentrate on those issues which are common to all congregations within their purview. Failure to recognize the authority of the major assemblies leads to an independent form of church governance. Major assemblies do not constitute a permanent institution that is higher in rank than and has authority over the churches that are represented at it, or over the constituent minor assemblies.

Major assemblies are deliberative in character. The delegates do not represent the interests of their individual congregations, but represent rather the congregations of a certain region as a whole. This principle guards against congregationalism. The church is not a democracy, where everything is decided by the popular voice (see Hodge 1879, 3). In URCSA, for instance, the synod is charged with certain duties and powers: *inter alia* the Synod has power to receive and issue all appeals, complaints, and references, that are regularly brought before it from the presbyteries, and to decide finally in such cases all questions that do not affect the doctrine or constitution of the Church, provided that cases may be transmitted to judicial commissions as prescribed in the church order.

### 3.5 *The necessity and nature of Christian discipline*

To exercise discipline is another fundamental principle of Reformed church polity. Jesus entrusted to the church the keys which open and close the Kingdom of God, namely, the power to bind and to dissolve, to forgive sin and to hold the sinner accountable (cf. Matt. 18:15–20). Discipline is one of the two keys of the kingdom of heaven. The other one is the proclamation of the Gospel.

Discipline entails the exercise of authority by the church over its members, officers and judicatories. According to Stephens, discipline is the exercise of authority, and the application of the system of laws, over a church's members, officers and judicatories (see Stephens 1907, 42). The end of discipline is the maintenance of the truth, the vindication of the authority and honor of Christ; the removal of offences; the promotion of the purity and edification of the Church and the spiritual good of offenders (Bittinger 1888, 43–44). The purpose of admonition and discipline is the salvation of the penitent, to restore those who err to faithful obedience to God and full fellowship with the congregation and to maintain the unity, the purity and holiness of the church of Christ. The censures to be administered by the church council are admonition, rebuke, suspension or deposition from office, suspension from the communion of the church, and, in the case of offenders who will not be reclaimed by milder measures, excommunication (Calvin 1559, IV, 11.1). The discipline exercised in the church concerns both doctrine and conduct. Moreover, discipline is to be exercised jointly by ministers and elders with the consent of the whole congregation.

### 3.6 *The right of appeal*

A sixth foundational principle of Reformed church polity is the right of appeal. An appeal is an investigation to ascertain whether a minor assembly erred in its decision. The decisions of such assemblies are settled and binding among the churches unless they are contrary to Scripture, the Reformed confessions, or the adopted church order (Calvin 1559, IV, 8, 9, 10). If anyone complains that he or she has been wronged by the decision of a minor assembly, or that an injustice has been made during the hearing, or that the decision of a minor assembly was incorrect or faulty, he or she has the right to appeal to the major assembly. Assemblies and church members may appeal to the assembly next in order if they believe that injustice has been done or that a decision conflicts with the Word of God or the church order. The major assemblies cannot institute judicial process and can consider such only on review, reference or complaint or appeal from the presbyteries (see Hodge 1879, 251).

The church has a right to receive, hear, resolve and decide references, appeals and complaints, including questions of doctrine or discipline, following constitutional procedures, and to advise and to assume original jurisdiction for adjudication on matters from church sessions where their authority cannot be exercised. All proceedings of the church council, the presbytery, and the synod are subject to review by, and may be taken to, a superior judicatory, by general review and control, reference, complaint, or appeal (see Stephens 1907, 3). The majority governs and consequently appeals may be referred from lower to higher judicatories, till they be finally decided by the collected wisdom and united voice of the entire Church (see Stephens 1907, 107). Minor assemblies may petition major assemblies by overture. Church councils, if convinced that they cannot comply with a decision of a major assembly because it does not agree with the Word of God, cannot be compelled to do so. If a church council refuses to comply with the final decision of the Synod (if the matter decided upon at the major assembly has been lawfully placed before it by way of a church council's request or an appeal), the dissenting congregation is no longer eligible for membership in the federation; by common consent the churches have agreed to abide by the decisions of a major assembly. In reviewing the proceedings of a minor assembly the major assembly shall determine whether the proceedings have been regular and in accordance with the church order, if the proceedings have been prudent and equitable, and if the lawful injunctions of a major assembly have been followed. If necessary, the major assembly may direct the lower assembly to reconsider and correct an irregularity or resolve a delinquency. A decision may not be executed pending an appeal. The church council should suspend further action until a final verdict has been reached at a general synod. The whole process must be suspended until all possibilities of appeal have been exhausted (cf. Stephens 1907, Bouwman 1937).

Major assemblies have the duty of oversight and the right to review and jurisdiction over minor assemblies. Stephens rightly states that it is not competent for an assembly to revise the proceedings of a previous assembly in a judicial case (see Stephens 1907, 116). Disputed matters of doctrine and discipline may be referred to a major assembly for adjudication. Governing bodies of the church have no civil jurisdiction or power to impose civil penalties. They have only ecclesiastical jurisdiction. Adjudicated matters are the only areas where the major assemblies may make decisions that are settled and binding when the appellate process has been exhausted. Advice and counsel of major assemblies is not binding upon the churches unless settled by adjudication. The general synod has no right to refer the final decision of any matter affecting the doctrine of the church to an inferior judicatory (see Stephens 1907, 116). The general synod's judicial decisions are final and obligatory in all similar cases (see Hodge 1879, 271). Hence, there can be no appeal from the decision of the general synod. Its decision is final (see Stephens 1907, 116).

All ecclesiastical assemblies of URCSA are bound to abide by the agreement laid down in the church order. The major assemblies of URCSA have the authority to determine matters of controversy upon reference, complaint or appeal. If any church member of URCSA complains that he/she has been wronged by the decision of a minor assembly, he or she has the right to appeal to the major assemblies. Until a decision is made upon such appeal, the church member must conform to the determination and judgment already passed. The General Synod of URCSA receives and issues all appeals, complaints, and references that affect the doctrine or constitution of the church, and are regularly brought before it from the lower judicatories; provided, that cases may be transmitted to the Permanent Judicial Commission of the General Synod as prescribed in the church order. Except in cases involving doctrinal and constitutional questions, a regional synod of URCSA is the final court of appeal. A regional synod has power of final decision in all questions that do not affect the doctrine or constitution of the church. A regional synod does not have original jurisdiction over either ministers, as does a presbytery, or over the elders and communicants, as the church council has. The general synod of URCSA has no authority to reverse the judicial acts of a former general synod or even the regional synods including cases of such palpable errors as would manifestly tend to obstruct the substantial administration of justice. Hence major assemblies of URCSA are obliged to take effectual care that minor assemblies observe the church order.

*3.7 The power of the major assemblies with regard to misconduct*

Taking all the above principles into account, the question remains: What happens in the case of misconduct or in cases where there are difficulties in the minor assembly of such a nature that apparently they are unable to solve? What happens if a minor assembly does not bring a matter to a major assembly? Do the major assemblies have the right to initiate action or would that necessitate hierarchy? Voetius answered affirmatively on the question of the binding force of the synods in the case of mismanagement or gross misconduct (see Voetius 1888, IV, 134; cf. Bouwman 1937, 196). Hodge, Bittinger and Stephens concur. The Reformed Church in America (RCA) for example makes provision in its church order that a classis shall have the authority to supersede a consistory in the administration of a local church when, in its judgment, there are conditions in that church which make it unable to fulfill the functions of a local church as these are defined by the classis (CO–RCA, art. 7, sec. 12). According to Hodge, the general synod may cite synods to appear and answer charges of irregularities in doctrine, government or discipline, and disown those which have departed from the standards of the church (see Hodge 1879, 272). If a judicatory is, at any time, well advised of any unconstitutional proceedings of a lower judicatory, the latter shall be cited to produce the records, and to show what it has done in the matter in question; after which, if the charge is sustained, the whole matter shall be remitted to the lower judicatory, with directions as to its disposition, according to Stephens (see Stephens 1907, 101). According to Hodge, if the presbytery refuses to dissolve a pastoral relation in the case of misconduct, the decision may be reversed by synod on complaint (see Hodge 1879, 253).

*4. URCSA practice*

During the past decades a deviation of the above mentioned principles took place in URCSA. For example, the major assemblies of URCSA gradually usurped power in order to make decisions on such matters as church unification, property rights and even the confessional basis of the church without giving the minor assemblies the opportunity to participate in the decision-making process. Consideration should be taken of the neglected Reformed church polity principle that give major assemblies in case of maladministration, impuissance, heresy or schism the right to intervene in the governance of the local congregation and to implement their decisions in minor assemblies. I submit that the superior judicatory should be able, if well advised of such neglects, omissions, or irregularities on the part of the inferior judicatory, to require the lower judicatory to produce its records and should be able either to proceed to examine and decide the entire matter as completely as if proper record had been made, or it shall cite the lower judicatory and proceed as in the next preceding section.

Over the past decade, numerous cases have emerged in URCSA in which judicatories have neglected to perform their duty, and by which neglect, corrupt or unconstitutional practices may have been allowed to gain ground, offenders of a gross character may have escaped discipline, some part of their proceedings may have been omitted from the record or not properly recorded, the accused failed to appear before the judicatory, or the presbyteries failed to issue the records for review to the synod in the case of appeal cases. This practice leads to unnecessary delays in appeals. According to Bittinger, if it has been ascertained that the citations, ordered at the last meeting, have been duly served on both the appellant and the respondent, the minor or major assembly should proceed to the investigation of the business assigned for trial (see Bittinger 1888, 8). In the absence of records for review, the higher judicatory may require it proceeding, either immediately or at a specified time, as circumstances may determine. When a major assembly learns of an irregularity or delinquency of a minor assembly, it must require the minor assembly to produce appropriate records and take proper action in order to preserve the purity, peace and good order of the church.

No provisions are made in the URCSA's church order when a judicatory whose judgment has been appealed fails to submit its records. Currently the major assemblies of the URCSA, however, have no power to intervene directly into the affairs of minor assemblies, *inter alia* to take the initiative with regard to implementation of the decisions with regard to disposition or suspension. Taking into account Voetius notions of the power of synods in the case of mismanagement or gross misconduct, it is my supposition that such a judicatory should be censured and the sentence appealed shall be suspended until a record is produced on which the issue can be fairly tried. In cases in which the lower judicatories have been directed so to do and have refused or neglected to obey, higher judicatories should institute a judicial process (cf. Bouwman 1937, Voetius 1888).

## 5. *Conclusion*

Reformed church polity principles have progressed from the initial days of being a concept related to church-state relationships to a concept that is central to the governance of Reformed churches globally. This article has proposed several fundamental principles of the Reformed church polity system. Principles indicate our starting points, our basic convictions. Understood in this way, a principle expresses more than a personal preference. Principles illuminate reality. The above principles point Reformed churches toward behaviors and attitudes that assist them in the appropriate governance of the church. We should take both the conditional nature and the immutable nature of some of these principles into account.

In my view, Reformed church polity principles are not outdated concepts and should not be left behind as modern ideas that do not fit with the postmodern schemas and representations of governance. Theoretical foundations of objectivism, constructivism and postmodernism have thus far had minimal influence on the principles of Reformed church polity. We should also admit that these principles cannot cover all facets of ecclesial life. The idea of Reformed church polity principles will continue to be a contested concept within the field of church polity. One cannot view them as a set of principles which is confirmed unanimously by Reformed churches across the globe. However these principles are being embraced by many Reformed churches globally. The principles provided above are therefore guidance and suggestions to Reformed churches in their church governance. This article suggests principles which may help to guide the actions of Reformed churches. It also represents a common basis that Reformed churches can consider as essential for the development of good church governance practices.

The authority of principles like the power and responsibilities of ecclesial assemblies has become increasingly problematic in a postmodern era. Even in a postmodern world a body of rules, principles, or standards accepted as axiomatic and universally binding is needed. The Reformed system of government calls for continuity with and faithfulness to the heritage which lies behind the contemporary church. However, one should take the diversity of the structures, histories and mission contexts, developments and experiences of the different Reformed churches worldwide into account. The juridical character of Reformed church polity should be expressed from a global perspective in order to underscore the many fundamental values that Reformed churches share with regard to self-government of the church, the autonomy of the local congregation, denominational ties, the power and responsibilities of ecclesiastical assemblies, Christian discipline, the right of appeal and the power of the major assemblies with regards to misconduct. I suggest that there is a uniformity of principles to which Reformed churches across the globe can agree. I submit that all Reformed churches should adhere to the minimum set of Reformed church governance principles.

## *Abbreviations and bibliography*

CB: Confessio Belgica (Belgic Confession) (1561).

CO-PCUSA: The Constitution of the Presbyterian Church (U.S.A.). 2009. Louisville: Office of the General Assembly.

CO-RCA: The Book of Church Order of the Reformed Church in America. 2011. New York: Reformed Church Press.

HPP: The Historic Principles of Presbyterianism. In: Report of the special committee on historic principles, conscience, and church government of the General Assembly (1982) of The United Presbyterian Church in the United States of America. 1983. Louisville: Office of the General Assembly.

URCSA: Uniting Reformed Church in Southern Africa.

Beattie, Frank A. 2007. Companion to the Constitution: Polity for the Local Church. Westminster: John Knox Press — Geneva Press.

Bittinger, Benjamin F. 1888. Manual of Bylaws and usage. Philadelphia: Presbyterian Board of Publication.

Bos, Frans L. 1986. Toetssteen voor allen. Oud licht over nieuwe kerkrechtelijke vragen. Rotterdam-Zuid: Boekencentrum.

Bouwman, Clarence. 2000. Spiritual Order for the Church. Kelmscott: Premier Printing.

Bouwman, Harm. 1928. Gereformeerd Kerkrecht: Het recht der kerken in de praktijk. Part One. Kampen 1928/1934. Kampen: De Groot Goudriaan. Unabridged third edition.

Bouwman, Marius. 1937. Voetius over het gezag der synoden. Amsterdam: S J P Bakker.

Calvin, John. 1541. Ecclesiastical Ordinances. In: Schaff 1882, 333–336.

Calvin, John. 1559. Institutes of the Christian Religion. Two volumes. Edited by John T. McNeill. Translation Ford Lewis Battles 1960. Philadelphia: The Westminster Press — London: SCM.

De Jong, Jan. 1918. Verklaring van de Kerkenordening van de Nationale Synode van Dordrecht van 1618–1619: College voordrachten van prof. dr. F.L. Rutgers over Gereformeerd Kerkrecht. Rotterdam: Drukkerij Libertas.

Engle, Paul E., and Steven B. Cowan. 2004. Who Runs the Church? Four Views On Church Government. Grand Rapids Mi: Zondervan Publishing.

Golverdingen, Marinus. 2001. De strijd om het kerkrecht in de Gereformeerde Kerken in Nederland van 1926 tot 1944. Apeldoorn: Theologische Universiteit.

Gray, Joan S., and Joyce C. Tucker. 2004. Presbyterian polity for church officers. Louisville: Geneva Press.

Hanko, Herman. 1963. Notes on the Church Order. Grand Rapids Mi: Protestant Reformed Church Press.

Hodge, J. Aspinwall. 1879. What is Presbyterian Law? Edinburgh: Thomas Nelson and Son.

Hopkins, Samuel M. 1878. Manual of church polity. Auburn: W.M.J. Moses Publishing House.

Jonker, Willem D. 1965. Om die regering van Christus en sy kerk. Pretoria: Unisa.

Johnson, Thomas C. 1900. Johan Calvin and the Genevan Reformation: A Sketch. Richmond, VA: The Presbyterian Committee of Publication.

Kleynhans, Ewert P.J. 1985. Gereformeerde kerkreg. Deel I, II and III. Pretoria: NGK Boekhandel.

Pont, Adrianus D. 1981. Die historiese agtergrond van ons kerklike reg. Pretoria: NGK Boekhandel.

Schaff, Philip. 1882. History of the Christian Church. Volume VIII: Modern Christianity. The Swiss Reformation. Grand Rapids Mi: Eerdmans.

Spoelstra, Bouke. 1989. Gereformeerde kerkreg en kerkregering: Handboek by die kerkorde. Hammanskraal: Teologiese Skool Hammanskraal Pers.

Stephens, John V. 1907. Presbyterian Government. Nashville, Tenn: The Cumberland Press.

Van Dellen, Idzert, and Martin Monsma. 1954. The Church Order Commentary, being a Brief Explanation of the Church Order of the Christian Reformed Church. Grand Rapids Mi: Zondervan Publishing.

Van Oene, Willem W.J. 1990. A practical guide to the Use of the Church Order of the Canadian Reformed Churches. Winnipeg: Premier Publishing.

Voetius, Gisbertus. 1888. Kerkrechtelijke Verhandelingen. Translated from 'De Politica Ecclesiastica' of Gisbertus Voetius with preface by dr F L Rutgers (ed.). Amsterdam: J.A. Wormser.

# THE DEMOCRATIC CAPTIVITY OF THE CHURCH

Joseph D. Small

The Presbyterian Church (U.S.A.) — PCUSA — voted in 2010–2011 on three dramatic proposals to amend its constitution: (1) to replace the Form of Government in its *Book of Order* with an entirely new document, (2) to remove the constitutional prohibition against ordaining persons not living 'either in fidelity within the covenant of marriage between a man and a woman, or chastity in singleness', and (3) to approve inclusion of the *Confession of Belhar* in *The Book of Confessions,* a collection of Creeds, confessions, and catechisms that constitutes the church's doctrinal standards.

Amending the PCUSA constitution requires a majority vote by a general assembly and ratification by the church's presbyteries. A majority of the 173 presbyteries is required to approve proposed amendments to the *Book of Order*, while approval by two-thirds of the presbyteries is required to amend *The Book of Confessions.*

Following acceptance by the 2010 General Assembly, the presbyteries had seventeen proposed amendments before them. Fourteen were minor adjustments, and were approved overwhelmingly. However, close votes on the three major issues exposed deep fissures within the PCUSA. The new Form of Government, passed overwhelmingly by the General Assembly (468–204) was narrowly approved by the presbyteries (52%–48%). While many factors contributed to the close vote of the presbyteries, discussion and debate reflected divergent appraisals of the denomination's direction and varying levels of trust in denominational leadership. The close vote on ordination standards in both the General Assembly (373–323) and the presbyteries (53%–47%) was the fifth vote in fifteen years on ordination standards, and was a milestone in the four decades of contentious debate on the place of gay and lesbian persons in the church. However, as with previous votes on ordination standards, the 2010–11 vote did more to exacerbate disagreement than to resolve it. Addition of the *Confession of Belhar* in the church's confessional standards passed easily in the General Assembly (525–150) but failed to gain approval by the necessary two-thirds of the presbyteries (62%–38%). The denial of Belhar reflected confessional and theological confusion in the church as well as the judgment of many that the vote had been rushed. All of these margins would have been comfortable victories, even landslides in politics, but they are disturbingly narrow when matters of the church's faith and order are at issue.

A subtext in the recent constitutional amendment process is the extent to which the PCUSA has become captive to American democratic political procedures in making decisions on fundamental matters of ecclesial faith and order. The church's legislatively-driven practice of reducing complex issues to simplified alternatives, and then pressing for hasty votes, accompanied by the political maneuvering of partisan organizations, has produced a winners/losers climate in the church, widening theological, ethical, ecclesial, and psychological gaps. Voting's winners (both past and present) assert that 'the church has spoken' even when nearly half of the church dissents. Losers of votes on controversial matters are often aggrieved by the inflated claims of winners, leading to increased discord within the church. For decades, split votes on particularly contentious issues have resulted not in their resolution, but in deepened division. The church's decision-making processes have come to emphasize disagreement rather than confirm concord.

### *Presbyterian Disestablishment*

The gradual disestablishment of the church is the context for its democratic captivity. Presbyterians appear prominently in lists of North America's 'mainline' Protestant churches, the denominations that developed from the sixteenth century Protestant Reformation and arrived early in North America: English Puritans and other independents in New England, Dutch Reformed in New York and New Jersey, Anglicans in Virginia, Scotch-Irish Presbyterians in Pennsylvania and the Carolinas. These groups became the Congregationalists, Presbyterians, Reformed, Episcopalians, and (later) Methodists that dominated the religious, civic, and cultural life of the United States for 350 years.

Historically, Presbyterians, Episcopalians, and Congregationalists were the elite mainline churches. They were influential out of proportion to their numbers, over-represented among Presidents, members of Congress, Supreme Court justices, and judges. Together with the Dutch Reformed, Presbyterians and Episcopalians were prominent in industry and finance. But now the mainline churches are all in decline — in numbers, but more significantly, in eminence and influence. Sociologists and cultural commentators refer to them now as 'sideline', 'oldline' and 'offline' churches. The marginalization of the historic mainline churches is a pervasive reality that shapes contemporary Presbyterian identity.

Social historians identify three distinct disestablishments of the church in

North America: *legal disestablishment* in the eighteenth century, *civic disestablishment* in the nineteenth century, and *cultural disestablishment* in the twentieth century. It is the cultural disestablishment of the church that has been especially painful and bewildering to the mainline (cf. Small 2010).

Some of the original British colonies embraced state sanctioned and state supported churches, but their *legal disestablishment* was well under way by the time of the 1776 revolution. Independence from English rule was accompanied by independence from religious hegemony. Legal disestablishment of the churches did not abolish their standing in American society, however. It left intact the civic and social dominance of the mainline Congregational, Presbyterian, and Episcopalian churches. For most of the nineteenth century schools, hospitals, charities, and other social institutions were shaped by the mainline churches. But the civic preeminence of these churches weakened as waves of nineteenth century immigration brought Catholics, Jews, and other Protestant groups to the United States. Religious proliferation was broadened by the emergence of American-born denominations such as the Disciples of Christ and numerous free and holiness churches, as well as the Mormons and other non-Christian groups. This led to the *civic disestablishment* of all churches, but especially of the old mainline. Since no church or family of churches was the majority church, none could assert civic dominance; all churches were immersed in the new reality of denominational pluralism.

Through all of this, however, a comprehensive cultural establishment of the churches endured. The United States remained a 'Christian nation'. Conceptual, social, and cultural establishment endured long after legal and civic establishments were only memories; Christianity and Americanism were merged in a unified national religiosity. However, during the second half of the twentieth century, pervasive social change in the United States effectively distanced a dramatically altered American culture from the churches. By the end of the century, the old mainline churches were marginalized, previously marginal evangelical churches were reluctant and ineffective social players, and religion generally was relegated to private life. The half century from 1960–2010 was an era of the rapidly accelerating *cultural disestablishment* of the churches.

Simply put, Christianity is no longer integral to American society and its churches are no longer shapers of American culture. Causes of the churches' cultural disestablishment are complex, the product of multiple forces over long periods of time. Nevertheless, the reality of cultural disestablishment is conspicuous in the contemporary religious landscape: Christianity is now but one of the many religious communities that have found a home in America, and churches are no longer accorded social status in the culture. Christian churches are only one choice in a profusion of religious options; increasingly, American piety is 'spiritual, but not religious'.

The disestablishment of the church in North America differs from the process of secularization in Europe. Americans remain a 'religious people' who profess faith in a god, are confident of that god's providential care, and anticipate special divine interventions in their lives. Polls consistently show that over 90% of Americans believe in 'god', and that over 80% consider themselves 'christian'. But American religiosity is theologically diffuse and not necessarily connected to a *community* of faith. Religion itself is internalized, and the churches remain relevant to American religiosity only to the extent that they provide spiritual goods and services to enhance personal well-being. What Ingolf Dalferth says of Europe is beginning to become evident in the United States: "Both inside and outside the various churches, the ever more pervasive mood is that of living in an age of epilogue, of fading memories, of a futile clinging to yesterday. God, many believe, has had his time, and here at the end of the second millennium that time seems to have run out.... The influence of the churches is unmistakably diminishing, and the objections of Christians increasingly fade away unheard. One no longer expects much of Christians, at least not regarding anything determinative for today" (Dalferth 1996, 127ff.).

The profusion of religious options, coupled with American privatism that relegates religious faith to the realm of personal choice, has made it difficult for American Christianity to understand its new context theologically. It is uncertain about how to view the great world religions, puzzled by the emergence of non-traditional spiritualities, and ambivalent about once certain theological affirmations. The churches are bewildered by cultural indifference to Christian religion, and confounded by the churchlessness of more and more people... including the church's own children.

While cultural disestablishment affects all Christian denominations, its impact on the old mainline churches is dramatic. Evangelical, holiness, and pentecostal churches were never legally or civically established. Ethnically cohesive bodies such as the various Lutheran churches were not fully engaged in the civic life of the society. Catholics and Jews experienced prejudice and discrimination in Protestant America, and had to swim against the cultural stream. Since these groups always understood themselves as living in various degrees of tension with American society, the culture's movement away from the churches came as only a mild surprise. It is the mainline churches that were particularly ill prepared for their failure to maintain a central place in national life.

Not long ago, American churches (which Protestants used to call, more modestly, 'denominations') asserted their superiority over other churches.

Reformed churches considered synodical forms of church governance faithful to Scripture (and consistent with American democracy) while episcopal forms were clearly borrowed from Roman culture (and consistent, of course, with Old World monarchies). And, Reformed church sacramental practice (decent and in good order) was superior to both Catholic superstition and free-church neglect. And, Reformed church commitment to the 'transformation of culture' was more consistent with the gospel (and American values) than other churches' attempts to dominate culture or to separate from it. This was all Presbyterian mythology, of course. But we were not alone, for other churches possessed their own folklore, often casting Presbyterians in the scoundrel's role. In any case, churches experienced themselves over against other churches.

Thankfully, unpleasant denominational triumphalism is a receding memory for most mainline churches in North America. It has been replaced by unprecedented openness to one another, characterized by cordial albeit shallow relationships at every level of church life. This new openness is partially comprised of bourgeois American tolerance, postmodern uncertainty, and confessional minimalism, but it also represents a genuine willingness to recognize each other as authentic expressions of the one church of Jesus Christ. Yet the decline of denominational triumphalism has not dispelled the myths that once fueled it. Two characteristic Presbyterian myths endure in ironic forms.

### *The Myth of Transformation*

The first myth lives in the residue of former civic and cultural establishment. It was given influential expression in H. Richard Niebuhr's mid-twentieth century book, *Christ and Culture* (Niebuhr 1951). Niebuhr set out a typology of the relationship between Christianity and the social order: Christ *against* culture, the Christ *of* culture, Christ *above* culture, Christ and culture in *paradox*, and Christ *transforming* culture. In spite of Niebuhr's disclaimers, the book seems to imply preference for the concluding type, Christ transforming culture. In any event, Presbyterians readily adopted Niebuhr's terminology, applying it to the church's responsibility to bring about social transformation consistent with the church's values.

Presbyterian rhetoric maintains the belief that the church possesses theoretical and practical wisdom that can be brought to bear on social and political issues, providing specific policy guidance to governments and other social institutions. The assumption is that recipients of PCUSA advice can be led to make legislative and executive decisions embodying the church's commitments. Thus, general assemblies regularly adopt numerous social policy statements which are embedded in the programs and budgets of church agencies. The agencies then cite the church's social policy in urging governmental institutions to legislate the policies into law. The church's commitments are not limited to words, of course, for it also believes that the character of its life and the shape of its mission contribute to societal transformation: "The Church of Jesus Christ is the provisional demonstration of what God intends for all of humanity" (CO-PCUSA 2009, G-3.0200). In all of this, however, the church assumes that it occupies a position (*above culture*?) from which it can view society objectively in light of the gospel, bringing precise wisdom to bear on complex, politically charged issues, thereby contributing to Christ's transformation of culture.

The irony of this Presbyterian myth is two-fold. First, the church continues to believe, against all evidence, that political institutions are interested in, much less influenced by, Presbyterian statements on public policy. There was a time when the church's voice mattered; that time is rapidly receding into the mists of civic and cultural disestablishment. Even so, the church continues to pursue a strategy of attempting to influence political and social institutions. An unfortunate consequence of the church's preoccupation with speaking to social and political institutions is its neglect of efforts to foster serious, sustained discussion of ethical and moral issues *within* the church. The result is that the church's policy statements are regularly ignored by the church's membership as well as by government officials. A second irony is evident in the church's failure to recognize the extent of its own acculturation. Imagining itself as the transformer of culture, it is blind to the myriad ways in which the culture has transformed the church. Two examples of the church's assimilation to American culture point toward a more pervasive reality.

### *Justice*

The church's work for social transformation centers on justice. Justice has been a priority goal of the PCUSA for decades, and denominational justice programs are widely supported and generously funded. In all of this it is assumed that the meaning of 'justice' is self-evident to everyone. What the church means by justice seems self-evident only because it expresses widespread popular assumptions within modern American democracy. In concert with democratic assumptions, the church grounds *justice* in the assertion of personal and group *rights*. The Declaration of Independence's 'unalienable rights... to life, liberty, and the pursuit of happiness' is assumed to cover all circumstances—all people and groups possess absolute rights that must be recognized. Of course, in many circumstances one assertion of rights is likely to conflict with another assertion of rights, and so 'rights' quickly becomes an adversarial dispute between rival claims. Appeals for rights-based justice are then made on the basis of *fairness*.

Any failure to accede to the assertion of rights by a person or group must be rectified, and fairness is the presumed standard that will determine a just outcome. But since fairness is in the eyes of opposing plaintiffs, it is assumed that justice must ultimately be determined by recourse to legislative or judicial procedures. The pursuit of rights-based justice too easily becomes a zero sum game.

Scripture and Christian tradition have much to say about justice, and the church's responsibility to do justice and to seek justice is clear. However, Scripture and Christian tradition do not equate God's justice with fairness, and they do not assume that justice is established through the adjudication of competing rights. Justice/righteousness — Hebrew *tsedeq*, Greek *dikaiosune* — has more to do with relationships than with rights, covenants than with laws, peace than with verdicts, communion than with adversarial conflict. Reading customary American concepts of justice into biblical texts is a category mistake.

'Justice' is not a simple, self-evident concept. Alasdair MacIntyre's inquiry draws attention to "the intimidating range of questions about what justice requires and permits, to which alternative and incompatible answers are offered by contending individuals and groups within contemporary societies". He goes on to say that "underlying this wide diversity of judgments upon particular types of issues are a set of conflicting conceptions of justice, conceptions that are strikingly at odds with one another in a number of ways" (MacIntyre 1988, 1). The church's acceptance of American democracy's prevailing assumptions about justice blocks its capacity to discern distinctive Christian contours of justice and to live them out in faithfulness to God, and in witness to American society.

### *Marketing*

A second example of the church's transformation by American society is the pervasive influence of commodified, consumer-oriented, market-driven culture on Christian faith and practice. Positioned within American society as a voluntary association, the church is unable to resist becoming a consumer commodity in the American marketplace. Like other churches, the PCUSA — denominationally and congregationally — spends time and energy determining how to market itself, employing management consultants to devise media campaigns and attempting to sell itself as a creative and effective provider of religious goods and services. Inevitably, this places it in competition with other churches for market share in a declining demographic.

Whether skillfully or clumsily, American churches market themselves, their institutional selves, by promoting brand awareness based on the promised fulfillment of needs. Far from proclaiming the gospel, the churches proclaim themselves, without a hint of discomfort or embarrassment. The dangers are obvious.

The focus of marketing is the consumer, and its strategy is to tailor the product to appeal to the consumer's real or imagined needs and desires. The church, then, is tempted to smooth out the rough edges of the gospel in order to present itself as an appealing commodity in the religious marketplace. However, by presenting itself as commodity, the church may be seen as simply one more product in a cultural sea of goods and services. Vincent Miller speaks of "consumer capitalism's insatiable hunger for marketable stuff, which creates a world where everything is transformed into a commodity that can be brought to market, exchanged, and consumed: selves, others, culture, religion" (Miller 2008, 77). When the church presents itself as a religious commodity, it is in danger of becoming lost in the mall of America. What may be less obvious is that it is only a short leap from the commodification of the church to the commodification of God. The progression from choosing a church, to choosing a religion, to choosing a god, leads directly to "I determine what God is" (Dalferth 2000).

*The Myth of Democratic Polity*

In all of this, Presbyterian Church polity has shown itself to be a contributor to its own transformation by the culture. Its polity has not provided a catalyst for faithful thinking about the shape of the gospel and the ways in which the gospel frees the Christian community from captivity to liberal democracy's values and procedures. Simply put, the current practice of Presbyterian polity exacerbates the effects of democratic captivity. Because the PCUSA suffers from an ecclesiological deficit — the absence of a shared understanding of the nature and purpose and mission of the church — the practice of its polity mimics the state rather than expressing the character and quality of Christ's body.

It is a fundamental Presbyterian myth, once celebrated openly but now residing in the church's collective subconscious, that American representative democracy was patterned after Presbyterian polity. It was claimed that church sessions, presbyteries, synods, and the general assembly provided the template for representative town councils, municipal and county boards, state legislatures, and the national Congress. It was all a pleasant fiction, of course, both historically and conceptually inaccurate. And, like many pleasant fictions, this one had an underside; it concealed the extent to which the church's polity has been shaped by the assumptions and practices of the American political system.

Sociologist James Davison Hunter details an important twentieth century development in American culture: "the politicization of nearly everything... the turn toward law and politics — the instrumentality of the state — to find solutions to public problems" (Hunter 2010, 102). The church is not immune to politicization; in fact, the mythology of its alignment with the American political system makes it especially susceptible to the framing of ecclesial life in legislative and juridical categories. Moreover, as with the practice of politics in the United States, the politicized PCUSA has come to interpret its life through the filter of partisan beliefs, values, ideals, and associations. The bipolarity of democracy American style has strengthened the growth of a two-party Presbyterian system that openly conducts political campaigns in electoral, legislative, and judicial contests.

Although the democratic captivity of the church pervades the entire exercise of Presbyterian polity, it is most evident in the way polity operates when critical issues are in play at the general assembly level. Historically and philosophically, the church's polity has been understood as the means to secure, if not full agreement, at least a willingness to live with the outcome of polity's operations. But the current capacity of Presbyterian polity to reach meaningful consensus or amicable acquiescence on issues before the church has been diminished.

The church's captivity to legislative and regulatory procedures is symbolized by novel terminology that was adopted in the mid 1980's. Sessions, presbyteries, synods, and the general assembly had been called judicatories. While sometimes understood as 'courts of the church', the term 'judicatory' did not denote a judicial court in a legal system, but rather an assembly to inquire into significant matters and reach considered conclusions. Judicatories had been evolving in tandem with democratic institutions, however, and so the church replaced 'judicatory' with a new, politicized generic term: 'governing bodies'. Quite apart from the gracelessness of the expression, it conveyed the rapidly accelerating notion that the purpose of presbyters was to govern the church — to direct, regulate, and manage the affairs of the institution. The expectation of governance affected polity at all levels of the church, but especially at the general assembly.

The PCUSA, acting as a good democratic institution, made it clear that the primary responsibility of general assemblies is to do the business of voting on legislative and procedural proposals placed before it. Meetings are conducted according to *Robert's Rules of Order*, a widely-used organizational guide to 'constructive and democratic' parliamentary procedure designed to ensure 'fair and orderly meetings and conventions' (www.robertsrules.org). General assemblies are understood to be legislative meetings designed to conduct business efficiently, according to schedule. The premium placed on legislative procedure is evident in the pre-assembly briefing for committee leaders and staff. The three day leadership briefing is devoted almost exclusively to training in matters of procedure. Attention to the substance of proposals before the assembly is virtually absent. This guarantees that general assembly debate is dominated by procedure rather than substance.

Legislatively driven agendas are designed to end debates on contested theological and moral issues by enacting one side into church policy and ecclesiastical law. 'One side' of the reductionist 'two sides', must be enacted because democratic voting procedures always reduce an issue to this or that, yes or no, up or down, in or out. C.P. Snow observed that "[T]he number 2 is a very dangerous number. Attempts to divide anything into two ought to be regarded with much suspicion" (Snow 1964, 9). Dividing complex theological, ethical, and moral matters into two trivializes them and renders them substantively unresolvable. Even the best intentioned church discussions reinforce polar divisions by guaranteeing a voice to 'both sides of the issue'... as if any issue worth discussing has only two sides. The simplified division of substantial concerns into two opposed alternatives is further degraded by the expectation that the way to choose between them is by majority vote. Commitment to democratic legislative procedures presses toward dualisms on every matter, reductionist alternatives reduced to stark choice.

The church imagines that general assemblies can decide complex theological, ethical, and moral issues by counting votes. While voting always produces winners and losers, it can work reasonably well in political arenas where winning and losing is the assumed outcome, even the name of the game. Voting works best, however, in situations where differences are encompassed within broad consensus regarding aims, so that balloting is about the best means to achieve those aims. Voting does not work well in situations of intractable polarity (witness the United States Congress) or when fundamental issues of faith and life are at stake. What have church votes on contended theological and moral issues produced besides narrow victories for one side or the other? The aftermath of voting is the absence of reception, and an ecclesial landscape littered with continuing legislative maneuvers, invocation of parliamentary rules, judicial appeals, trials in church courts, and the departure of congregations and ministers.

To make matters worse, having been reduced to two sides, issues are further diminished by the use of slogans, often 'rights' and 'justice' at one pole, and 'biblical authority' and 'Christian morality' at the other; or, negatively, 'racism' and 'homophobia' at one pole, 'liberation theology' and 'relativism' at the other. Contending sides understand that slogans and epithets are necessary because governing bodies do not have time to learn about and consider the issues before them. All complexity and nuance is lost as church assemblies vote up or down on 'justice', or 'the Bible', without ever asking, *Whose Justice? Which Rationality?* (MacIntyre 1988) or, *Whose Community? Which Interpretation?* (Westphal 2009). General assemblies do not ask because they have been called into session to do legislative business, not theology.

The ability of general assemblies to explore faith and faithfulness is weakened by their composition — they are gatherings of strangers. Two hours of mandated 'group building exercises' do not create levels of mutual understanding and responsibility, and the compacted assembly schedule does not create space for deep discernment and careful consideration of substantive theological, ethical, moral, and ecclesiological matters. PCUSA general assemblies consist of over seven hundred commissioners, half ministers and half elders, ninety percent of whom have never been to a general assembly. They meet for one week — two days of preliminary procedural matters, two and a half days of committee meetings (to which commissioners are randomly assigned by computer) and two and a half days of plenary voting on hundreds of proposals — only a fraction of which they have read, let alone studied. Commissioners vote, adopt legislation and make rules, and then return home with no continuing responsibility for the actions they have taken.

The American democratic procedures that have shaped the practice of Presbyterian polity were developed for ongoing legislative and judicial bodies, not for a one-week-and-done meeting of persons unfamiliar with both the matters at hand and each other. Legislators and judges work together over time, becoming familiar with one another and the issues before them. While this does not guarantee good results, especially when intense partisan differences prevail, democratic procedures assume both familiarity with issues and the time necessary to consider them. Neither assumption applies to the PCUSA general assembly.

*Beyond Captivity?*

What would decision-making in the church look like without forced choice majority voting? There are no easy answers to the question, but the dysfunction of Presbyterian polity, particularly at the national level, suggests two possibilities. The recently adopted Form of Government made a number of important and promising polity changes. One of the most promising changes was replacing 'governing body' terminology for sessions, presbyteries, synods, and the general assembly with the term 'council'. The new term 'council' is evocative, implying a shift in emphasis away from directing and regulating an institution toward the possibility of thoughtful deliberation on matters of the church's faith and faithfulness. 'Council' evokes images of Nicaea, Westminster, Barmen, and Belhar rather than the United States Senate.

The general assembly, as a council of the church, is composed of presbyters, half of whom are called 'teaching elders' and half of whom are called 'ruling elders' (historic Presbyterian terms for ministers and elders that have been recovered in the new Form of Government). When they come together in council, they do not leave behind their essential calling; they are still ordered ministers with responsibility for teaching the Faith and for 'ruling out'—measuring fidelity to the gospel in the church. This suggests that a general assembly could be a primary ecclesial space for teaching and learning, discernment and mutual accountability, rather than a vehicle for voting and legislating. Councils are not pressed for time in order to decide something; they take time for study, discussion, and prayer so that they may discern the leading of the Holy Spirit, the mind of Christ, the will of God.

There are no easy answers to the question of how decision-making beyond the forced choice majority voting might occur in the church, but a brief account in Stanley Hauerwas's memoir, *Hannah's Child* is suggestive. While at Notre Dame, Hauerwas was a member of a Methodist church whose pastor wanted to move the congregation to weekly celebration of the Eucharist. After considerable study, the church board met to discuss the matter. The board seemed to be on board, so Hauerwas moved that it be put to a vote. The pastor, who had been quiet up till then, suddenly declared: 'You will not vote on this issue'. Hauerwas was startled; wasn't this just what the pastor had worked for? But the pastor reminded the board that the Eucharist is about the unity of the church. If the celebration of the Eucharist were determined by a majority vote, unity would be betrayed. Anyone in the congregation who had reservations needed to be heard first, and if there was strong dissent, the church would have to wait (see Hauerwas 2010, 141).

I am less impressed by the details of the story than by its spirit. All too often, when a majority vote determines the matter, the unity of the church is betrayed. Presbyterian votes on contended theological and moral issues often fall within the 55%–45% range. Can it be said that the *church* has decided anything when nearly half of the church dissents? The solution does not lie in so-called 'consensus methods of decision-making' or in 'super majorities', for these only perpetuate the notion that decisions must be made and that legislation is the appropriate means of settling matters of faith and morals in the church. Decisions to change or not to change significant elements of the church's faith and life take time (an un-American concept).

Time is a problem for general assemblies, however. They cannot meet for years (Westminster, Vatican II) or months (Nicaea). However, as the PCUSA's national council (general assembly) it could engage regional councils (presbyteries) and local councils (church sessions) in protracted consideration of fundamental matters. Organs of Presbyterian polity would then work in concert, over time, to engage the whole people of God in substantive matters of faith and morals before the church. It would require far more than a change in terminology, however, for such a shift to occur. The precondition for the church's release from its bondage to democratic legislative procedures is to say 'no' to the current reductionism and division that have characterized the politicized church. Brazilian theologian Rubem Alves expresses the seemingly counter-intuitive reality that the word leading to hope is 'No!' "To negate means to reject the ultimate validity of the current state of affairs", Alves writes. "The consciousness then projects itself in the direction of the future, giving birth to hope" (Alves 1969, 13).

A second possibility for a new way of determining issues of faith and life lies in saying 'no' to an odd feature of the PCUSA's hyper-democratic method of decision-making: it always acts in isolation from other churches. The PCUSA presses forward on significant theological, moral, and ecclesiological matters without even consulting other churches, including its international partners and those in the United States with which it is in 'full communion'. The church's formal commitment to ecumenical engagement would be enriched by attending to theological and moral matters in meaningful consultation with other churches.

The Groupe des Dombes' latest contribution to ecumenical thought, *'One Teacher': Doctrinal Authority in the Church,* affirms that authority in the church belongs to the whole people of God. The document also recognizes the difficulty of according an appropriate place for the exercise of this authority in actual church polity. Nevertheless, *'One Teacher'* notes that the churches cannot simply adopt every form of democratic debate, for they must give space that allows decisions to mature. A vital aspect of the space needed for decisions to mature grows from refusing to act as independent theological and moral agents. *'One Teacher'* asks "that all churches agree to share in the debate regarding problems of faith and morals which are raised in a new way, acting together to take decisions in common whenever possible, and accepting the gospel principle of mutual correction" (Le Groupe des Dombes 2010, 143).

PCUSA general assemblies are not universal councils of the church, but they can set agendas and shape deliberations in concert with other churches and their councils. American churches face many of the same questions; each would be enriched by the others as together they engaged in mutually accountable exploration of Christian faith and life. The churches share theological, moral, and ecclesiological concerns that go beyond present disputes. Moreover, American churches could realize that their mutual consideration of vital issue would be enhanced by consultation with sister churches that live the faith outside of the American context. Saying 'no' to American provincialism could bring hope for life within the one holy catholic apostolic church.

These two possibilities suggested by a terminological change in the church's constitution do not, of themselves, deal comprehensively with the democratic captivity of the church. Unfortunately, it may be that old procedures will be poured into new terms, so that councils will simply act as governing bodies under a different name, and openness to other churches will continue to be confined to the occasional welcome of token ecumenical guests. However, the (narrowly approved) adoption of a new Form of Government presents the PCUSA with an opportunity to recover the originating vision of a polity that serves the gospel rather than regulate the institution.

### *Beyond the Presbyterian Church*

The democratic captivity of the church is not unique to the PCUSA. It is also a reality, *mutatis mutandis*, in mainline Protestant denominations generally and, increasingly, in other American churches. While the details of PCUSA life are distinct, they are not parochial, but pervasive. Democratic procedures were instituted and employed by churches for good and faithful reasons. However, they have developed in concert with American political and legal culture so that they now play out the least attractive and most unhelpful features of legislative partition, partisan politics, litigious interaction, and perpetual discord.

The PCUSA is currently experiencing its fourth schism in less than a hundred years. The Episcopal Church and the Evangelical Lutheran Church in America (and the Southern Baptist Convention) are also in schism. While the roots of these splits are deep, the precipitating cause has been majority voting on procedural, legislative, and regulatory matters in democratically constituted governing bodies. Fatefully, reliance on democratic procedures to decide the matters has enabled the churches to avoid the root causes themselves.

Liberation from democratic captivity does not lie in churches' abandonment of democracy, but rather in its restoration of the ministry of the whole people of God. Expanded and extended attention to matters of Christian faith and life is needed throughout the churches to broaden and deepen the *sensus fidei*. This can then lead to a *sensus fidelium* that is genuinely inclusive rather than the victory cry of momentary majority.

### *Abbreviations and bibliography*

CO-PCUSA: Presbyterian Church (U.S.A.). Book of Order. Louisville: Office of the General Assembly (2009).

PCUSA: Presbyterian Church (U.S.A.).

Alves, Rubem A. 1969. A Theology of Human Hope. New York: Corpus Books.
Dalferth, Ingolf U. 1996. Time for God's Presence'. In: Volf et al. 1996, 127–141.

Dalferth, Ingolf U. 2000. I Determine What God Is! In: Theology Today, 57(2000)/1, 5–23.

Hauerwas, Stanley. 2010. Hannah's Child: A Theologian's Memoir. Grand Rapids Mi: Eerdmans.

Hunter, James Davison. 2010. To Change the World. Oxford: Oxford University Press.

Le Groupe des Dombes. 2010. 'One Teacher': Doctrinal Authority in the Church. Grand Rapids Mi: Eerdmans.

MacIntyre, Alasdair. 1988. Whose Justice? Which Rationality? Notre Dame: University of Notre Dame Press.

Miller, Vincent J. 2008. Consuming Religion: Christian Faith and Practice in a Consumer Culture. New York: Continuum.

Niebuhr, H. Richard. 1951. Christ and Culture. New York: Harper and Brothers.

Small, Joseph D. 2010. Presbyterian Disestablishment. In: Small and Rosenthal 2010, 163–175.

Small, Joseph D, and Gilbert S. Rosenthal (eds). 2010. Let Us Reason Together: Christians and Jews in Conversation. Louisville: Witherspoon Press.

Snow, Charles P. 1964. The Two Cultures and a Second Look. Cambridge: The University Press. 2nd edition.

Volf, Miroslav, et al. (eds). The Future of Theology: Essays in Honor of Jürgen Moltmann. Grand Rapids Mi: Eerdmans.

Westphal, Merold. 2009. Whose Community? Which Interpretation? Grand Rapids Mi: Baker Academic.

# EMERGING MISSIONAL ECCLESIOLOGY IN THE DUTCH REFORMED CHURCH IN SOUTH AFRICA AND CHURCH POLITY

Nelus Niemandt

## *Introduction — from Christendom to missional*

How does a denomination such as the Nederduitse Gereformeerde Kerk (NGK; Dutch Reformed Church; DRC) in South Africa transform from a Christendom church to a missional church (see Guder 2000, 6–18 for a more comprehensive description of Christendom)? How does a church that benefited from a position of privilege and power transform into a missional church? How does the focus shift from what the church *does* to what the church *is*? How can the missional character of the church be expressed in its polity?

This challenge is explored by investigating the policy decisions and church polity of the General Synod of the DRC. It is possible to study this problem as an example of 'congregational studies' (see, for example, Brouwer 2009, 19, 397–439; Hendriks 2004; in the South African context: Niemandt 2010A). This study, however, will approach the problem by investigating policy decisions of the General Synod of the DRC and the interplay between missional ecclesiology and church polity. Whereas congregational studies might be described as a bottom-up process, this will be more of a top-down study process, recognizing that the life and identities of congregations are significantly influenced by church polity. This study is done from a missiological perspective, claiming that all theology has to be missiological (see Bevans 2010, 10; Flett 2010, 295), but it acknowledges the importance of a multi-disciplinary approach and thus recognizes the role of theological disciplines such as church polity, church history and practical theology. It is especially done with a profound appreciation of the relation between ecclesiology and church polity and the grounding of church polity in ecclesiology (see Koffeman 2009, 13, 17).

*The emergence of a missional ecclesiology*

The hypothesis of this study is that a missional ecclesiology is emerging in the DRC and that this is such a defining development that it must be reflected in church polity.

This emerging missional ecclesiology must be understood in the context of a missional renaissance (see McNeal 2009, 1–4) that is visible in the deliberations of international ecumenical events, as well as in the contemporary missional church conversation (see Van Gelder 2008, 2). A missiological and ecclesiological shift has occurred since the middle of the twentieth century and this has influenced the DRC (see Anderson 2008, 167; Guder 2000, 15–23).

The term *missional church* gained prominence in the work of the Gospel in our Culture Network (GOCN) and with works such as *Missional church: A vision for the sending of the church in North America,* edited by Darrell and *Church-Next* by Eddie Gibbs, as well as through the growing interest in the so-called emerging church movement (see Guder 1998, Gibbs 2000, Gibbs and Bolger 2005; Jones 2008; McLaren 2000 and 2001). The works of Lesslie Newbigin as well as *Transforming Mission* by David Bosch played an important role in laying the groundwork for a new approach to mission (see Newbigin 1995, 29; Bosch 1991). It is difficult to capture a dynamic and emerging concept such as missional church in a single definition, and Roxburgh and Boren correctly warn that there is no missional formula that provides a magic pill for entering missional life (see Roxburgh and Boren 2009, 24). For the sake of clarity a few definitions might be useful:

› A missional church is "a community of God's people that defines itself, and organizes its life around its real purpose of being an agent of God's mission to the world. In other words, the church's true and authentic organizing principle is mission" (Hirsch 2006, 82).
› "The missional church perspective understands that congregations are created by the Spirit and that their existence is for the purpose of engaging the world in bringing God's redemptive work in Christ to bear on every dimension of life" (Van Gelder 2008A, 44).
› Granberg-Michaelson defines missional church from a denominational point of view: "A missional church places its commitment to participate in God's mission in the world at the center of its life and identity" (Granberg-Michaelson 2008, 267).

The important ecumenical events in 2010 recognized this important shift towards a missional ecclesiology. Edinburgh 2010 identifies the core conviction that the church is missionary in its very nature—a mission flowing from God's calling and sending (in: Kim and Anderson 2011, 180). Lausanne III (2011) states in the

*Cape Town Commitment* that God calls his people to share his mission: "Our mission is wholly derived from God's mission, addresses the whole of God's creation, and is grounded at its center in the redeeming victory of the cross". The message from the Uniting General Council of the World Communion of Reformed Churches (WCRC) recognizes the calling of the church to participate in the mission of the triune God and that the church is sent out "to love and serve the Lord, called to communion and committed to justice" (WCRC 2010, 62). The section report on mission says: "The missional identity and engagement of the churches and of our communion is the *raison d'être* (reason for being) of WCRC, is essential to its Reformed identity, and therefore, must be reflected in its structures, use of resources and programmatic actions" (WCRC 2010, 164).

There seems to be ecumenical consensus on the missional nature of the church — a shift from a church-centered mission to a mission-centered church.

*A turning point in developing a missional ecclesiology*

A new missional ecclesiology is also developing in the DRC. Saayman distinguishes four eras or waves of extraordinary mission endeavor in the DRC in his *Being Missionary — Being Human. An overview of Dutch Reformed Mission* (see Saayman 2007). Although he refers to important policy decisions of the DRC in 1998 — see The *Rule for the Missions/Witness of the Church*, Rule 18 (CO-NGK 2002, 94-98) and the 2002 *Declaration* by the General Synod (see CO-NGK 2002, i) — he does not recognize this developing missional ecclesiology and sees the 'fourth wave' as an outward focused missionary activity directed to 'the ends of the earth'. This fourth wave is more comprehensive than Saayman grasps and there is a clear indication of an emerging missional ecclesiology in the policy decisions of the Dutch Reformed Church.

The 'birth' of a new missional ecclesiology can be traced back to the 2002 General Synod of the DRC, when synod decided to ask its commission focusing on congregations to study the issue of a practical congregational ecclesiology (see NGK 2002, 542). This request was extended in 2004 (see NGK 2004, 444). This represents a turning point in the deliberate formulation of a missional ecclesiology, as the preceding synods acknowledged the importance of congregations in the mission of the church, but did so exclusively from the more conventional approach of the churches' mission work. It was (and still is) described in article 53 of the *Church Order* as part of the chapter entitled 'The Work of the Church', as follows (see CO-NGK 2002, 21, CO-NGK 2007, 23):

> 53.1 Mission is the saving act of the triune God, Father, Son and Holy Spirit, to the world, by which He, through his Word and Spirit, gathers for Himself a community out of the entire human race.

Through this congregation

› God causes his Word to be proclaimed to the fallen world,
› He brings about the communion of the saints out of all nations and
› He enables the ministry of service to be rendered to the world in need,
› He causes his command to protect and manage creation to be given visible expression, and
› His justice is proclaimed to society and the world.

By these means He causes his kingdom to come until the end of time.

53.2 Through missions the church ministers the gospel in all its dimensions to people outside the church.

53.3 Mission is the vocation of every member as well as the congregation. Where the extent and other circumstances of the work require it, missionary work is undertaken within the broader church structures of presbytery and synod.

The Rule for the Missions/Witness of the Church, Rule 18, gives a more detailed description of the mission work (CO-NGK 2002, 94–98). Rule 2.1.2 states that it is the duty of the church council "to motivate and equip the congregation to be involved with the saving work of God to the world as a missionary congregation". Although the particular wording—'missionary congregation'—might suggest an approach that can be categorized within the broader concept of missional church as defined above, a close study of these rules (by-laws) clearly reveals it to be an approach that can best be described as a classic, colonial understanding of mission work as missions. The English translation of the rule, perhaps unintentionally, used the term Rule for the *Missions*. It is still understood as the work of a few—a missions committee (rule 2.1.2)—on behalf of the whole congregation. Mission is understood primarily as something the church does, under the heading of 'The Work of the Church', and reflects much of the colonial, propagandistic paradigm of mission (see Van Gelder 2008A, 40).

### *The contours of an emerging missional ecclesiology*

A closer look at the study process that focused on the formulation of a practical congregational ecclesiology, as well as at other policy decisions by the General Synod of the DRC, reveals the contours of an emerging missional ecclesiology (see Niemandt 2010B, 92–103 for a more comprehensive description). It includes the following aspects that I will elaborate below:

The understanding of the church as life in the Trinity—the theological reflection on the relational Trinity influenced a new emphasis on relationships and community in the description of the church's missional identity;

› A conscious missional identity based on the DRC's Reformed identity;
› The rediscovery of the importance of the Missio Dei—the DRC's calling to participate in God's mission;

› The missio Dei leads to the missiones ecclesiae. The church is understood as missional by its very nature;
› A renewed theological interest in the Kingdom of God;
› A renewed commitment to Africa and to the healing of South Africa, paving the way for a focus on local communities.

*Church is life in the Trinity*

One of the most basic assertions of missional ecclesiology is that the church participates in the reality of God's presence and activity in the world. Reflection on missional church starts with the Trinity, for Trinity introduces us to a sending God who is a missionary God (see Van Gelder and Zscheile 2011, 6; Bosch 1991, 390). The DRC was also influenced by the profound shift in Trinitarian thinking, starting with Karl Barth, who reclaimed a theological understanding of God's Trinitarian self-revealing (see Guder 2000, 19; Flett 2010; Dekker 2011, 25, 148–151). This Trinitarian thinking was expanded by the missionary conference in Willingen (1952) that is described by Flett as the first ecumenical expression of the Trinitarian grounding of missionary activity (see Flett 2010, 154).

The DRC is characterized by its Reformed character and history. Among other implications, this means that the church is understood from its life in the Triune God. The 2002 General Synod put it in clear terms: "Through Christ, the church is committed to the Triune God of the Bible — Father, Son and Spirit. We believe the church belongs to the Triune God and exist in union with God. The church is the people of God, the body of Christ and the Temple of the Spirit. Everything we are and do — our identity, our mission and our ministry — are determined by this relationship. This is the most basic principle in being God's church. This God is the Triune God who revealed himself in the Old and New Testaments as Father, Son and Spirit" (NGK 2002, Addendum A8.1).

*Church Order* Article 53.1 states: "Mission is the saving act of the Triune God, Father, Son and Holy Spirit, to the world, by which He, through his Word and Spirit, gathers for Himself a community out of the entire human race" (CO-NGK 2002, 21 and CO-NGK 2007, 23).

The 2004 General Synod says the foundation of a congregation is the Trinity and recognizes that this understanding has important implications for ecclesiology (see Niemandt 2010B, 96; NGK 2004, 35).

At the 2011 General Synod, the DRC accepted a policy document as the basis for further discussion on missional ecclesiology (see NGK 2011A, 131). In this document, mission is understood as an activity of the Triune God, Creator, Savior and Redeemer for the sake of the world and in which the church is privileged to participate. This formulation is a clear indication of the shift in the missional ecclesiology of the DRC, and places the development within a clear understanding of the life of the church as a life in the Trinity.

### *A missional and Reformed identity*

An important policy document on the church's Reformed identity was accepted by the 2007 General Synod. It states: "The church exists through the grace of God and belongs to God. We belong to God. The church is God's gift to the world for the sake of the world. The calling of the church can be described as sent by God and thus being missional. The church is essentially in the world and directed towards the world" (NGK 2007, 14).

In the 2011 policy document entitled *Missional Ecclesiology*, the identity of the church is described as Reformed and missional (see NGK 2011A, 131). This echoes the section report on mission of the WCRC where the missional identity and engagement of the church are described as essential to its Reformed identity (see WCRC 2010, 164).

### *The Missio Dei — to participate in God's mission*

The theme of *missio Dei* is one of the most important motifs in missiological reflection in the last fifty years (see Bosch 1991, 389–393; Koffeman 2009, 186; Guder 2000, 20). God is a missionary God who sends the church into the world. It is not the church which 'undertakes' mission; it is the *missio Dei* which constitutes the church (see Bosch 1991, 519). In this understanding, mission begins with the entry of the Triune God into creation, especially in the incarnation of Jesus Christ, and the sending into the world of the Holy Spirit (see Schreiter 2010, 15). It shifts the agency of mission from the church to God, and the understanding of mission from being church-centric to becoming theocentric (see Van Gelder and Zscheile 2011, 6). The church's very nature is missionary (see Guder 2000, 20).

In a discussion document that was tabled at the 2002 General Synod, the following description is noteworthy: "In the twentieth century it was clearly grasped that the church does not exist for its own sake, but that the church is sent to serve and help others. The church serves God's mission (*missio Dei*) in this world. Therefore each and every congregation is a missional congregation" (NGK 2002, Addendum A8.1).

The 2007 report tabled at the General Synod states that the *missio Dei* defines the essence and substance of the church. The church focuses on the world and is directed towards the world, because the church does not exist for the sake of its members or itself (see NGK 2007, 44–56).

The 2011 document on missional ecclesiology asserts the *missio Dei* as basis for the church. The church is mission and participates in God's mission, because it cannot do otherwise. The church was created and born for this — the church is the fruit of God's mission and exists to participate in and be of service to this mission. The *missio Dei* is at the core of being church. Missional church describes the very essence of being church: to participate in God's mission (see NGK 2011A, 132).

### *The* missio Dei *leads to the missiones ecclesiae*

Mission is a movement of God to the world and the church is an instrument for that mission. Our missionary activities are only relevant insofar as they reflect participation in the mission of God. "The *missio Dei* is the *missio ecclesiae*" (Flett 2010, 291). The New Testament writings do not explicitly command the church to do mission; they assume that mission is what these communities were all about (see Guder 2000, 52). Koffeman understands this fundamental movement to the world as an expression of the catholicity of the church: it defines the church and constitutes its credibility (see Koffeman 2009, 187).

The groundwork for a missional understanding of the DRC was laid in the important policy document *Church and Society* (*Kerk en Samelewing;*), where the church is described as a missional community (see NGK 1986, 11).

The 2002 General Synod received a report on ecclesiology where 'twentieth-century insights' into ecclesiology were shared with the synod (see NGK 2002, Addendum A8.1). The church does not exist for its own sake, but to participate in God's mission and to serve others: "The church serves God's mission in this world — therefore each congregation is a missional congregation".

The 2011 document on missional ecclesiology declares: "The church is missional and participates in God's mission because it simply cannot do otherwise. This is exactly why the church exists — the church was created for this very purpose. The *missio Dei* leads to the *missiones ecclesiae*. The church is the fruit of God's mission and participates in the continuation of that mission. This is the heart of the church. Mission defines the essence of the church" (NGK 2011A, 132).

The church is a missional church and must be defined, described and ordered from its mission to the world. Mission defines the essence of the church; therefore it ought to determine the teaching, liturgy and confessional nature of the church.

### *The kingdom of God*

*Missio Dei* theology is closely related to the Kingdom of God. Flett draws attention to the important contribution of Hartenstein in the understanding that neither the church nor mission holds priority (see Flett 2010, 126). Both are called to the kingdom of God. God's mission is the coming Kingdom (see Guder 2000, 35–39). The work of God in his creation is larger than the mission of the church or the church (see Van Gelder and Zscheile 2011, 4). We should, however, not understand the relationship between church and kingdom as if the church is a mere impoverished example of the kingdom. Although the church might be imperfect, it lives in the knowledge that the kingdom has not as yet arrived and that the church cannot be the kingdom in its fullness (see Dekker 2011, 83).

In the DRC, the 2004 discussion document reminds the church that God uses his church in bringing about his kingdom, but that God also uses other organizations and people who are now Christians to accomplish his mission (see NGK 2004, 36). In the 2007 policy document on Reformed identity, the DRC asserts that faith is not only about church. The kingdom is broader than the church and the church is a sign of expression of the kingdom. Believers are called to set up signs of the kingdom and to live in such a way that they testify to the reign of God. Kingdom living is evident in everyday life and can be described as earthy and natural (see NGK 2007, 14, 16). The 2007 Statement of Calling says: "Called as believers, we are salt for the earth and light for the world. We are servants of God's coming Kingdom" (CO-NGK 2007). The 2011 document on missional ecclesiology has a chapter on the relation between missional church and God's kingdom and understands the ultimate goal of the church's witness as being an instrument in service to the new dispensation of God's kingdom (see NGK 2011A, 133).

The issue is captured by Bevans when he says that there cannot be an ecclesiology that does not understand the church's essence in relation to the commitment to the preaching and witnessing of God's present and coming reign (see Bevans 2010, 10).

### *A renewed commitment to Africa and to the healing of South Africa*

Building on the work of Barth, Flett observes that to serve God is to live in service to the world (see Flett 2010, 273). The church cannot exist in the world without calling people out of it and inviting them to participate in God's work and service.

The 2002 General Synod issued a Declaration, reflecting on the synod. The following is significant: "We commit ourselves anew to our continent, and in particular to Southern Africa. We are distressed by tragic stories of the most terrible forms of violence, the tremendous extent of poverty and famine, the consequences of the Aids pandemic, and the lack of respect for people, animals and the environment. We too are implicated. General Synod extends its sympathy to the many victims. We want to make a difference. Therefore we commit ourselves to work with others to find solutions for our society. As a church we offer our help at every level. We assure the government of our intercession and our commitment to serve the community" (see CO-NGK 2004, i).

The 2007 General Synod issued a Declaration of Calling in which it acknowledged the DRC's calling as being 'part of God's body in Africa' (see CO-NGK 2007).

The 2011 report on missional ecclesiology has a section on the missional church and ministry to communities (see NGK 2011A, 136). A missional church has a missional diaconate. It focuses on the problems and issues in the world, and on the distress of individuals and families, communities and countries and continents. A missional church ignites change. The aim of a missional diaconate is to participate in God's transformation of communities and the society at large.

### *Conclusion*

One cannot but conclude that a new missional ecclesiology is establishing itself in the DRC. The 2011 policy document *Missional Ecclesiology* was the culmination of a study and discernment process that developed over nearly nine years. It can be described as more than the mere contours of an emerging missional ecclesiology. It is a significant development in DRC ecclesiology and polity and is itself a full-fledged ecclesiology.

### *Missional ecclesiology and church polity: a case study*

To what extent did this emerging ecclesiology influence church order during the 2011 General Synod? Church polity serves the church and must reflect the identity, calling, life and order of the church. It is the architecture of the life of the church (see Dingemans 1987, 9). In his eloquent discussion of Karl Barth, the *missio Dei* and the church, Flett argues that the community is Christian only insofar as it is missionary; and that the missionary act is the concrete form of divine and human fellowship (see Flett 2010, 296). Therefore a failure to refer to mission at every level or the lack of dogmatic attention to the purpose for which the Christian community exists, is unthinkable. Taking his argument further, one would expect a full-fledged ecclesiology to be reflected in the church order, since the church is missional by its very nature and church polity expresses the identity and nature of the church. This is one of the challenges facing the church: how can the missional character of the church be expressed in its polity (see Koffeman 2009, 191–192)? Granberg-Michaelson describes the question 'what does it mean to be Reformed and missional?' as an important confessional challenge faced by the Reformed Church in America (RCA) (see Granberg-Michaelson 2008, 277). This is of particular importance since the question of mission is not found in the major confessional documents of Western Christendom before the early twentieth century (see Guder 2000, 10).

The commission that prepared the 2011 policy document on missional ecclesiology made recommendations on possible changes to the DRC church order. It referred to the Preface of the 2004 *Kerkorde* where it is claimed that the foundation has been laid for new structures and methods of operating that will give expression to the calling of the Dutch Reformed Church in Africa and South Africa (CO-NGK 2004, iii). It was clearly a case of the commission making a case for the restructuring of the church order that would facilitate a missional understanding of the church. The most important recommendations concerned articles 1, 9 and 10 of the *Church Order.*

*Article 1*

Article 1 describes the confession and order of the DRC: "The Dutch Reformed Church is based on the Bible as the holy and infallible Word of God. The doctrine which the Church confesses in agreement with the Word of God, is expressed in the Forms of Unity as formulated at the Synod of Dordt in 1618-19, namely the thirty-seven articles of the *Belgic Confession*, the *Heidelberg Catechism* and the five *Canons of Dordt*" (CO-NGK 2007, 1). The recommendation was to add the following as an introduction to article 1: "The Dutch Reformed Church is called to participate in God's mission in this world. The church proclaims the ministry of reconciliation and salvation in Christ to all people". This is similar to articles found in the church orders of other Reformed churches. The Presbyterian Church ( U.S.A.) — PCUSA — states in its article 1: "Christ calls the Church into being, giving it all that is necessary for its mission to the world, for its building up, and for its service to God. Christ is present with the Church in both Spirit and Word. It belongs to Christ alone to rule, to teach, to call, and to use the Church as he wills, exercising his authority by the ministry of women and men for the establishment and extension of his Kingdom". The Protestantse Kerk in Nederland (PKN) combines its commitment to its confessional base with a description of the calling of the church and congregations in its article I-2: "Living by God's grace in Jesus Christ, the church fulfills its mission to listen to the word of God and to proclaim it". Article I-8 describes the church as "sent to the world, and called to the ministry of reconciliation, the church witness through preaching and service salvation in Christ" (CO-PKN 2004, 3; see also Koffeman 2009, 193).

The report on missional ecclesiology recommended a statement on both the confessional and missional nature of the church, as is the case in the RCA (see Granberg-Michaelson 2008, 263-282). In the words of Dingemans, the apostolate and confessional nature are part and parcel of the nature of the church, the inside and outside of the same issue (see Dingemans 1987, 20). The 1951 *Church Order* of the Nederlandse Hervormde Kerk in The Netherlands placed the article on the missional nature of the church before the article on the confessions, because it understood true confession as a reaction to the movement in mission (see

Dingemans 2000, 247). The DRC report concludes by calling upon the General Synod to respond in a creative way to the growing insights into the nature of the church: "This requires a process of obedient listening, discernment to understand where God is working and what God wants to do" (see NGK 2011A, 141).

The document on missional ecclesiology was very well received and approved as a discussion document that must be integrated with current policies and the church's understanding of its diaconal service (see NGK 2011B). However, the General Synod did not approve the abovementioned changes to article 1 of the *Church Order*, following a recommendation by the 2011 Interim Committee on *Church Order* (a committee that functions during the General Synod and makes recommendations on all reports that have implications related to church polity) that it must not be used as an introduction to article 1 'because Article 1 describes the foundations of the DRC and not its calling'. It is clear that the Interim Committee on *Church Order*, and the General Synod in following its advice, did not understand the proposed change, since it was not intended to describe the calling of the church but its missional foundation. (It must, however, be mentioned that the new Executive of the General Synod decided in November 2011 to prioritize missional ecclesiology as one of the most important issues in the DRC.)

The hypothesis of the present paper is that the church order of the DRC does not, as yet, reflect or facilitate a missional ecclesiology in the DRC. This hypothesis is based on the conviction that the identity and nature of the DRC as a Reformed church ought to be described in two concepts: (1) the missional nature of the church and (2) the confessional character of the church. Dingemans summarizes the calling of the church in two fundamental concepts: the mission (*apostolaat*) and confessions of the church (see Dingemans 1987, 19). Article 1 (which describes the foundation of the DRC) only refers to the confessional character and basis of the DRC and lacks the important missional characterization. Perhaps Koffeman is correct in his statement that the classical Reformed definition of the *notae ecclesiae* was determined by the context of the reformation and therefore lacks any reference to the missional character of the church (see Koffeman 2009, 190–191; see also Guder 2000, 10). The confessions of faith and old church orders have nothing of the church's missional essence in their scope. Our present-day context as well as developments in missional theology challenge the church to express its missional character in church polity (see Koffeman 2009, 192).

### *Article 9*

Article 9 describes the office or ministry of the Minister of the Word. The 2007 *Church Order* formulates article 9.4 as follows: "In a congregation a minister accepts particular responsibility for preaching and serving the sacraments.

Together with the other offices the minister is responsible for: the prayer ministry, worship services, teaching and equipping, edification of the congregation, the congregation's ministry in the world, leading and organizing the congregation, exercising Christian love and discipline, pastoral care. Church councils, in conjunction with the minister, discern how this calling and these responsibilities are exercised, in line with particular gifts, and incorporate it in an employment contract" (CO-NGK 2007, 5–6).

The commission recommended two additions to article 9.4: 'discernment and church planting'. 'Discernment' was proposed, because "discernment is the first act of mission" (NGK 2011A, 133). Swart makes a convincing argument that discernment, as a core practice of Christian leadership, seeks the movement of the Triune God in relationship with all of creation (see Swart 2008, 87–115). The motivation to add 'church planting' to the responsibilities of the Minister of the Word was to add this essential aspect of missional church to the responsibilities of ministers. The report stated that church planting is the discipline to form new faith communities as a way of participating in God's mission and to serve as an expression and sign of God's kingdom (see NGK 2011A, 138).

The General Synod eventually accepted the recommendation of the Interim Committee on *Church Order* that these two additions not be accepted. Perhaps one can conclude with Koffeman's reference to a report of the Netherlands Council of Churches, where the report pleads for a fundamental reimagination of the office of Minister of the Word, that 'the world needs a type of Christian and missional church that calls for a fundamental rethinking of the office of minister' (see Koffeman 2009, 205). In this sense, the General Synod failed its own calling, as stated in the 2007 Statement of Calling. In that particular statement, the DRC recognized its calling as a missional church, called and sent to make a difference in the world and to serve communities.

### *Article 10*

Article 10 regulates the territorial principle and states: "A Minister of the Word may not perform any official duties (Article 9) within the boundaries of another congregation without the permission of its church council". The report recommended that the article be scrapped from the church order. In the motivation of this recommendation, the commission referred to the importance of church planting. Dekker calls it 'community formation' (*gemeenschapsvorming*) (see Dekker 2011, 159f.). The commission understood the scrapping of article 10 as a step toward facilitating church planting, especially in a culture where the identity of people is not determined as much by their geographical location as by the network of social cultures that define modern culture. Koffeman says that a church that identifies with the *missio Dei* cannot do otherwise than facilitate an orderly way to facilitate community formation (see Koffeman 2009, 201).

At the DRC General Synod in 2011, the Interim Committee on *Church Order* amended the proposal to scrap article 10 completely and the synod eventually accepted the following formulation and change to article 10: "A Minister of the Word may not perform any official duties (Article 9) amongst the members of another congregation without the permission of its church council". The amendment was motivated as a change in the geographical limitations on the work of a minister of the Word. This change will facilitate church planting. During the debate on the issue in the General Synod it was clearly stated that this change should facilitate work among people who are not members of the DRC regardless where they live. It constitutes a deconstruction of the territorial principle and ought to facilitate the formation of different configurations of communities (see Koffeman 2009, 201).

### *Can missional ecclesiology change church polity?*

The reframing of a denominational system, or to use Dingemans's concept, the redrawing of the architecture, is complex and requires an adaptive change (see Roxburgh 2008, 77). The report on missional ecclesiology stated that a kenotic approach is necessary for the church to embrace its missional identity (see NGK 2011A, 136). *Kenosis* lies at the heart of a missional theology. Self-sacrifice for the sake of those to whom the Spirit is sending the church is the only way to follow Christ. Forney states that church governance is created out of and for specific contexts (see Forney 2008, 55). God's mission takes different forms in different times and places and changing contexts, therefore a solution-orientated drive typical of denominationalism must be abandoned and a dynamic relationality embraced (see Forney 2008, 56).

The problem with church polity is that it tends to drift towards a typical default position of denominational polity, namely to focus on matters of organization and function rather than on the nature of the church and ecclesiology. The missional conversation has reintroduced a focus on the essence of the church and the nature of the church as being missional (see Van Gelder 2008A, 42). The recommendation to expand articles 1 and 9 and to scrap article 10 of the DRC church order was to reflect the missional nature of the church as well as facilitate missional praxis. The introduction of missional language was intended to be helpful for theologically framing the conversation and facilitating transformation (see Roxburgh 2008, 79). Research has shown that the introduction of a new missional language changes congregations (see Niemandt 2010A). The question is whether the report on missional ecclesiology succeeded in changing the language of the General Synod of the DRC. Although diffusion of change takes time (see Roxburgh and Romanuk 2006, 79–108), the decisions on articles 1, 9 and 10 suggest that the General Synod has not, as yet, fully embraced a new missional theology. Yet, a new language is beginning to echo in the denomination.

The most important aspect, however, is the fundamental reframing of imagination. A missional ecclesiology calls for a rethinking of many basic assumptions about the church and church polity, and a new language to facilitate the reimagination in changing contexts. This asks for a radical reframing of the imagination concerning what is possible through the Spirit. As Swart concludes: "Christian leadership as *imaginatio Trinitatis* is shaped by the theological reality of a communion ecclesiology rooted in the life of the Triune God and socially embodied in the cultural flows of the world" (Swart 2008, 114).

I have already stated that the problem with denominational polity is that it tends to focus on matters of organization and function rather than on the nature of the church and ecclesiology. What Granberg-Michaelson says about the RCA is true for Reformed denominations generally: "We need to examine and rework our polity, because it is clear that the way we are presently functioning is not empowering the missional engagement of our congregations" (Granberg-Michaelson 2008, 281). Everything the church is and does must be missionary. A missional polity must compel and guide the church/denomination beyond itself to participate in the activity of the Triune God in the world. This raises the question: how can missional polity be formulated to guide churches and denominations beyond themselves to participate in the activity of the Triune God in this world, and how can that formulation be supported by a more dynamic interpretation of the discipline of church polity?

## *Abbreviations and bibliography*

CO-NGK 2002: Nederduitse Gereformeerde Kerk. 2002. Die Kerkorde van die Nederduitse Gereformeerde Kerk. Wellington: LuxVerbiBM.

CO-NGK 2004: Nederduitse Gereformeerde Kerk. 2004. Die Kerkorde van die Nederduitse Gereformeerde Kerk. Wellington: LuxVerbiBM.

CO-NGK 2007: Nederduitse Gereformeerde Kerk. 2007. Die Kerkorde van die Nederduitse Gereformeerde Kerk. Wellington: LuxVerbiBM.

CO-PKN 2004: Kerkorde en ordinanties van de Protestantse Kerk in Nederland inclusief de overgangsbepalingen. Zoetermeer: Boekencentrum.

NGK 1986: Nederduitse Gereformeerde Kerk. 1986. Kerk en Samelewing. 'n Getuienis van die Ned. Geref. Kerk soos aanvaar deur die Algemene Sinode van die Ned. Geref. Kerk.

NGK 2002: Nederduitse Gereformeerde Kerk. 2002. Agenda van die Algemene Sinode van die Nederduitse Gereformeerde Kerk 2002. October, 2002.

NGK 2004: Nederduitse Gereformeerde Kerk. 2004. Agenda van die Algemene Sinode van die Nederduitse Gereformeerde Kerk 2004. October, 2004.

NGK 2007: Nederduitse Gereformeerde Kerk. 2007. Agenda — Deel 1 van die Algemene Sinode van die Nederduitse Gereformeerde Kerk 2007. Junie, 2007.

NGK 2011A: Nederduitse Gereformeerde Kerk. 2011. Agenda vir die 14de vergadering Algemene Sinode van die Nederduitse Gereformeerde Kerk 2011. 10–14 Okt, 2011.

NGK 2011B: Nederduitse Gereformeerde Kerk. 2011. Handelinge van die 14de vergadering Algemene Sinode van die Nederduitse Gereformeerde Kerk 2011. 10–14 Okt, 2011.

RCA: Reformed Church in America

WCRC 2010: World Communion of Reformed Churches. Proceedings of the Uniting General Council 2010. Grand Rapids Mi, United States, June 18–28, 2010.

Anderson, Daniel R. 2008. Missional DNA of the Evangelical Lutheran Church in America. In: Van Gelder 2008, 166–197.

Barrett, Lois Y. (ed.). 2004. Treasure in Clay Jars: Patterns in Missional Faithfulness. Grand Rapids Mi: Eerdmans.

Bevans, Stephen B. 2010. From Edinburgh to Edinburgh: Towards a missiology for a world church. In: Kalu et al. 2010, 1–11.

Bosch, David J. 1991. Transforming Mission: Paradigm shifts in theology of mission. New York: Orbis.

Brouwer, Rein. 2009. Geloven in gemeenschap: Het verhaal van een Protestantse Geloofsgemeenschap. Kampen: Kok.

Dekker, Wim. 2011. Marginaal en missionair: Kleine theologie voor een krimpende kerk,. Zoetermeer: Boekencentrum.

Dingemans, Gijs D.J. 1987. Een huis om in te wonen: Schetsen en bouwstenen voor een Kerk en een Kerkorde van de toekomst. 's-Gravenhage: Boekencentrum.

Dingemans, Gijs D.J. 2000. De stem van de Roepende: Pneumatheologie. Kampen: Kok. 4th revised edition. 2005.

Flett, John G. 2010. The Witness of God: The Trinity, Missio Dei, Karl Barth and the nature of Christian community. Grand Rapids Mi: Eerdmans. Kindle edition.

Forney, David G. 2008. Living in the city—journeying outside the gate. In: Van Gelder 2008, 46–74.

Gibbs, Eddie 2000. ChurchNext: Quantum changes in how we do ministry. Downers Grove: InterVarsity Press.

Gibbs, Eddie, and Ryan K. Bolger. 2005. Emerging churches: Creating Christian community in postmodern cultures. Grand Rapids Mi: Baker Academic.

Granberg-Michaelson, Wesley. Insights into becoming a missional denomination. In: Van Gelder 2008, 263—282.

Guder, Darrell (ed.). 1998. Missional church: A vision for the sending of the church in North America. Grand Rapids Mi: Eerdmans.

Guder, Darrell. 2000. The continuing conversion of the church. Grand Rapids Mi: Eerdmans.

Hendriks, H. Jurgens. 2004. Studying Congregations in Africa. Wellington: NetAct.

Hirsch, Alan. 2006. The forgotten ways: Reactivating the Missional Church. Grand Rapids Mi: Brazos.

Jones, Tony. 2008. The new Christians: Dispatches from the Emergent frontier. San Francisco: Jossey-Bass.

Kalu, Ogbu U., Peter Vethanayagamony, and Edmund Kee-Fook Chia. 2010. Mission after Christendom. Emergent themes in contemporary mission. Louiseville: Westminster John Knox.

Kim, Kirsteen, and Andrew Anderson (eds). 2011. Edinburgh 2010: Mission Today and Tomorrow. Oxford: Regnum.

Koffeman, Leo J. 2009. Het goed recht van de kerk: Een theologische inleiding op het kerkrecht. Kampen: Kok.

Lausanne III. 2011. Cape Town Commitment: The Third Lausanne Congress on World Evangelization, Cape Town, 16-25 October 2010.

McLaren, Brian D. 2000. The church on the other side: Doing ministry in the postmodern matrix. Grand Rapids Mi: Zondervan.

McLaren, Brian D. 2001. A new kind a Christian: A tale of two friends on a spiritual journey. San Francisco: Jossey-Bass.

McNeal, Reggie. 2009. Missional Renaissance: Changing the scorecard for the Church. San Francisco: Jossey-Bass.

Newbegin, Lesley. 1995. The Open Secret: An introduction to the theology of Mission. Grand Rapids Mi: Eerdmans. Revised edition.

Niemandt, C.J.P. (Nelus). 2010A. '5 Years of missional church'. Missionalia. 38 (2), 97–413.

Niemandt, C.J.P. (Nelus). 2010B. Kontoere in die ontwikkeling van 'n missionêre ekklesiologie in die Nederduitse Gereformeerde Kerk—'n omvangryker vierde golf. In: Nederduitse Gereformeerde Teologiese Tydskrif 51(2010)/3–4, 92–103.

Roxburgh, Alan J. 2008. Reframing denominations from a missional perspective. In: Van Gelder 2008, 75–103.

Roxburgh, Alan J. and M. Scott Boren. 2009. Introducing the missional church: What it is, why it matters, how to become one. Grand Rapids Mi: Baker.

Roxburgh, Alan J. and Fred Romanuk. 2006. The missional leader: Equiping your church to reach a changing world. San Francisco: Jossey-Bass.

Saayman, Willem. 2007. Being Missionary—Being Human: An overview of Dutch Reformed Mission. Pietermaritzburg: Cluster Publications.

Schreiter, Robert. 2010. Mission from the ground up: Emergent themes in contemporary mission. In: Kalu et al. 2010, 12–24.

Swart, Jannie. 2008. Christian Leadership as Communion Imagination in the Public Networking of Organizational Companionship. In: Journal of Religious Leadership, 7(2008)/2, 87–115.

Van Gelder, Craig, (ed.). 2008. The missional church & denominations: Helping congregations develop a missional identity. Grand Rapids Mi: Eerdmans.

Van Gelder, Craig. 2008A. An ecclesiastical Geno-Project: unpacking the DNA of denominations and denominationalism. In: Van Gelder 2008, 12–45.

Van Gelder, Craig, and Dwight J. Zscheile. 2011. The missional church in perspective: Mapping trends and shaping the conversation. Grand Rapids Mi: Baker Academic. Kindle edition.

# LOCAL AUTONOMY IN A SECULARIZED SOCIETY

Harm G. Dane

### *Introduction*

In this contribution I want to draw attention to the central position of the local congregation in Reformed church polity. My thesis is that this central position hinders the church in its central mission task, due to profound social changes and patterns of church membership. First, I will give a short introduction to the present situation of the Protestant Church in the Netherlands (Protestantse Kerk in Nederland; PCN). Second, I will give a brief historical sketch of the background to the centrality of the local congregation in both the Reformed Churches in the Netherlands (*Gereformeerde Kerken in Nederland*; RCN) and the Netherlands Reformed Church (*Nederlandse Hervormde Kerk*; NRC) which united together with the Evangelical-Lutheran Church in the Kingdom of the Netherlands (*Evangelisch-Lutherse Kerk in het Koninkrijk der Nederlanden*; ELC) in 2004 to form the PCN. Third, I intend to make some remarks about modern society and its influence on people, which will lead to reflections about the changing nature of local congregations and the consequent inability of the church to react to these social changes. In suggesting another pattern of church polity to address this challenge I draw on the example of a national supermarket chain. Finally, I will give some suggestions for further investigation.

### *The Protestant Church in the Netherlands in modern society*

The church polity of the PCN is based on the autonomy of the local congregations. Church law is very clear about this: directly after its first article — on confession, tradition and the mission of the church — article II clearly states that the church is made up of local congregations. Only after this are the tasks and duties of congregations, the classis and other supra-local structures described in detail.

This concentration on local autonomy is not surprising given the heritage of the PCN. In the process of unification the NRC and especially the RCN insisted on the importance of the autonomy of local congregations. In my capacity as the last general secretary of the RCN I was deeply involved in discussions about the unification process and read about the hesitations and complaints arising from a fear of the loss of local autonomy. It is remarkable that many of these fears were linked with financial independence and the ownership of church property.

It is not history alone that played a part in the decision-making regarding the new church's policy; it was also an answer to strong anti-institutional sentiments in the wider society. In society—and among church members—there is a deep mistrust of large organizations and institutions, whether it be government, political parties, labor unions or churches. People prefer to live with informal relations that are appropriate for their particular phase of life or because of specific tasks to be accomplished. We live in what has been termed a 'network society'.

In the meantime the process of secularization continues. The number of church members in the PCN continues to decline; over the last decade the average loss was over 60,000 people per year. All congregations have to deal with fewer members, lower income and the challenge of continuing parish life with fewer elders and volunteers. Consequently, local congregations have to consider a future with less professional pastoral support, closing and selling church premises, concentrating on fewer activities, uniting parishes, etc. All this is taking place at the same time that there is a deep felt need to consider new ways to reach people who have no contact with the gospel or who are alienated from the church.

These three elements—a smaller church, local autonomy and a new missionary necessity—form the basis of my central question, namely whether the focus on local autonomy of congregations is an appropriate approach for the church in an increasingly secularized society.

### *Short history of local autonomy in the rcn*

The plea to maintain local autonomy within the RCN, though rooted in the Reformed church tradition (*Dordt Church Order*), can also be understood as a strategic answer by Abraham Kuyper to the problems he had when he organized the RCN at the end of the nineteenth century. Kuyper broke with the NRC in 1886 and formed the RCN in 1892, following an earlier separation from the NRC in 1834.

On the one hand, Kuyper insisted on the importance of a strong, theologically-based socio-political movement to counter the dominant liberalism of his day. For him the RCN was an important instrument in achieving political goals, e.g., formal Christian schools, Christian social organizations (labor unions, welfare, health etc.). On the other hand, he had to build up the RCN throughout the Netherlands from small beginnings. In many local contexts small groups of people with little formal education and from lower classes had left the NRC. Only a few had some organizational experience and it proved impossible to establish a central organization. So Kuyper relied on the available resources and capabilities of these few men (sometimes women) in local congregations to finance the new church. It was also important to develop a strong theological unity among the members and the dispersed congregations, with the aim of establishing a strong soci-political movement. Due to these limitations, Kuyper used other means to build up the new church. He started a national newspaper and a Christian weekly in which he explained his theological convictions and political ideas. He founded a university to educate theologians and intellectuals and he founded a political party, the first one in The Netherlands.

Within the church he created a stable network of leading intellectuals in the *deputaatschappen,* the church commissions who advised classes, provincial synods and the general synod of the church on all manner of theological and social questions. These *deputaatschappen* formed the theological backbone of the RCN, taking custody and control of the theological unity of the RCN. After 1945, several *deputaatschappen* were given a budget and developed an important role in building classis, regional and national movements in different spheres, e.g., youth work, mission and social welfare. It was understood that this work was necessary to grow the church on supra-local levels as a consequence of social changes after World War II.

This small sketch highlights the reality that the RCN's focus on local autonomy was restricted to financial, organizational and pastoral concerns. The church's theological and social ideology was centralized with local congregations having little opportunity to develop their own policies. It is important to remember this when thinking about whether local autonomy is appropriate for being a missional church in today's context.

### *Local autonomy in the NRC*

The NRC was the established national protestant church of the Netherlands since the Reformation, earlier known as *Nederduitse Gereformeerde Kerk.* So it comes as little surprise that since the Reformation the medieval situation of isolated parish communities continued and became part of the *Nederduitse Gereformeerde Kerk.* This situation has endured for several centuries. "Our Church lived and lives in the twentieth century as though it has to operate in the seventeenth-century world" (Kraemer 1945, 44). Although institutionally it was the national church, there were significant theological and spiritual differences between local congregations.

After World War II there was a growing awareness of the importance of local communities within the church; these were too important to be left in isolation as only an institutional part of the national church. This was true for two main reasons. First, the national church had become more important to everyday national life. Second, the local congregation had taken on a more important role as an instrument of Christian education. Stimulated by Hendrik Kraemer among others, it was evident that membership in a national church was insufficient for growing discipleship and faithful participation in church and civic life. At the end of World War II Kraemer introduced the idea of 'congregation building' *(gemeenteopbouw)* to highlight the importance of the local congregation as the manifestation of church in society alongside the national church in relation to state and nation, and as the most important context for educating church members in the Christian faith and its value in everyday life and civic participation (see Kraemer 1945).

These two sketches of the RCN and NRC make clear that the local autonomy of congregations was not a quality in and of itself but was related to the situation and challenges in which the church was working. Furthermore, local autonomy is not an isolated quality but is an element in relation to other aspects of church polity and governance.

### *Fluid Society*

Whole libraries have been written in recent years about changes in modern society and the impact on religion. While I cannot give an overview here, it is helpful to explore some aspects in order to understand the tension between modern society and protestant church polity.

First, the fragmentation of society into different elements—e.g., economics, juridical, education, and private (see Habermas 1987)—means the isolation of church and religion. A consequence of this fragmentation is the impact on individuals who live fragmented lives throughout the day, as for example, at work, at home, politically, in relationships, etc. So, religion no longer provides an overall orientation to life but is one orientation alongside many others by which people may choose to live. More importantly, people develop different identities to cope with these different spheres.

The famous claim by French philosopher Lyotard that the time of big stories is over is often used to characterize post-modernism. A consequence for the church has been the rejection of meta-narratives, big stories, so that all religions, philosophies and life-orientations have equal status. No longer can a dominant theology claim to be absolutely true and no clerical authority is above criticism. This means that being a Christian is no longer a matter of tradition or habit, but rather a matter of choice and conscious decision.

The dismantling of the welfare state in many European countries throughout the 1970s created a liberal cultural climate that insisted on self-reliance and personal responsibility—'be yourself'—and on each person showing responsibility for 'writing your own biography'. Ulrich Beck introduced the term *risk society (Risikogesellschaft)* to demonstrate that modern governments can no longer guarantee a safe and prosperous life for their citizens (see Beck 1986). Each person must instead take care of themselves. At the same time, flexibility in the labor market develops, so that people change jobs more frequently and can no longer assume that a job is for life. There are increasing divorce rates and the exponential growth of information technology, with permanent information flows and connections with people around the globe based on shared interests. These and other developments show that lives no longer pass by in life-long patterns, but are subject to dramatic and unexpected changes. These realities prompted Zygmunt Bauman to speak of the 'fluid society' in which social structures and patterns of relations do not endure but are characterized by being temporary (see Bauman 2000; Bauman 2004). Consequently, people no longer rely on social institutions, because institutions are fixed structures that do not move with rapid social change and personal life. Another consequence is the fluid identity of people. Everyone needs to have an open mind to manage new situations and to identify the environment that meets personal need. Mental needs constantly change with age, changes at work and home, family situations and religious conviction or spiritual outlook. In such a fluid society with fluid individuals we have to consider the future shape of the church.

### *The objective and subjective community*

As we have already established, the PCN consists of local congregations. But in reality the local congregations are not the most basic entity of the Protestant Church; the individual members of local congregations are. All congregations consist of members; congregations consist of individuals who have been baptized, confessed their faith and live in a defined local area. So, congregational membership (and therefore membership in the PCN) is formally determined by objective facts and the congregation is defined as the sum of these objective members, i.e., those living in the neighborhood, the baptized and/or converted. While this definition of a local congregation is valid from an ecclesiological perspective, it does not easily fit with modern society.

De Jong states than a local congregation can be understood in three ways: as an organization, as a social movement and as a social community (see De Jong 2008). These three are intertwined and difficult to separate, nonetheless each has different ways of operating, different cultures and behaviors, different goals and ideas, and different formal and informal leaders. Every member of the local congregation is inclined to be more involved in one of these aspects than the other two. In addition, many congregational conflicts and tensions can be understood through the lens of these three different social phenomena, with members displaying different expectations and values.

This threefold sociological approach to the congregation is interesting when considered alongside the anti-institutional atmosphere in society. Increasingly people are not interested in the congregation as an organization (and even less interested in the large central organization of the national church structures), and they are less interested in formal objective membership. People belong to a congregation because they enjoy what is on offer in that context; they feel at home with a particular style of worship, preaching or a congregation's social program. New people joining are not asked whether they are baptized or converted but merely if they would like to join the congregation, participate in its activities and pay a contribution towards making parish life possible.

In short, we can see a shift from an objective approach to church membership, which had dominated our understanding, to a more subjective approach. In the first instance, congregations have become social communities.

From the Middle Ages until the eighties of the last century, the local congregation was a fixed geographical community. Where an individual lived was the determining factor in where that individual worshipped. This was a very objective criterion and everyone accepted other members because of this criterion. Theologically-speaking, we did not choose each other but we were gathered by and around Scripture. Sociologically-speaking, an individual geographical location determined the congregation one belonged to.

This situation no longer exists. Christians choose the congregation they want to belong to, not on the objective criteria of where they live but the subjective criteria of where they feel at home. So the congregation has become a community of choice, based on the decision of each member to belong to that specific congregation. This shifting pattern has deep consequences for the internal cohesion of local congregations, as has been pointed out by Nauta (see Nauta 2006). In the 'objective congregation', membership is not a matter of personal decision and the whole congregation is not the result of a number of those personal decisions. The congregation finds its *raison d'être* within itself and this is the condition for an individual to become a member. Members accept the rules of the congregation, the decisions made by the minister and elders, etc., as long as one does not succeed in changing them. This is significantly different from current patterns of 'subjective congregations' where membership is based on choice.

The identity of members in the 'objective congregation' is based on the congregation they belong to; in the 'subjective congregation' the character of the congregation is based on the members' identity, the choices they have made, the people they want to become. It is not difficult to see how the character of the congregation formed by choice is founded on feelings of well-being and social harmony. When individuals no longer feel at home in that congregation they leave and find one better-suited to their individual spiritualities and needs. But more importantly, the subjective congregation has a strong tendency to maintain the church for the homogeneous group that already attends, keeping the environment comfortable and familiar. New people will be accepted into the group on the condition that they accept the existing social atmosphere. Radical change is unwelcome because it disturbs the congregation's cohesion and those who disturb it find themselves excluded.

This might sound like a rather negative evaluation of the modern congregation, but it is intended to be descriptive. For those belonging to the congregation they have chosen, it is a place and community of inspiration, faith, comfort, social interaction and activities. These congregations play an important role for many people, so there is good reason to support them in their mission in a secular society. But is this pattern of church life the most appropriate way to communicate the gospel in a secular society? Are these congregations capable of reaching out to people totally alienated from church and gospel? And from a different perspective: are we not overloading these congregations with unrealistic expectations to be the change agents of the church in meeting the challenges of modern society?

In summary, the local congregation is thought of as being defined by geographical boundaries but in fact a congregation increasingly defines its own spirituality, as do the people who choose that specific kind of congregation. The objective basis of the local congregation has changed to a subjective desire for people to belong to the community. This subjective basis is an obstacle to change and to the people who do not want to change their spiritual home. Conversely, as soon as there is tension and conflict over change, people decide to move to another community. It is clear that under these circumstances the instruments of social control and pastoral discipline do not work. Both responses confirm the tendency to comfort those who belong to the congregation and to form a closer circle together.

*The challenges of the church in modern society*

It is generally agreed that the church in Western Europe is increasingly weak while at the same time people are increasingly interested in personal spirituality. Although the churches have a lot to offer an individual spiritual quest, the church struggles to connect with this search. The desire for spirituality has different aspects: for knowledge, experience, life guidance, social interaction and personal support. But all these aspects need to be translated into different kinds of service for these diverse groups of people. A growing group of older people who had left the church in their youth, young people who have never shown interest in the church, young parents struggling to raise their children, stressed managers, disorientated people, etc. are all seeking meaning, support, transcendence and spirituality. Yet the church fails to make significant contact with them. Every local congregation has its weekly sermon on Sunday morning, a mix of education, experience, direction for Christian living, but what occurs in those contexts is largely only comprehensible to those who belong and are familiar with the rituals, language and music. This kind of sermon does not fit modern people's search and I think it is unrealistic to expect local congregations to explore all the experiences of church relating to religious, spiritual experiences, social cohesion and support in everyday life. Therefore, we must seek other ways to bridge the gap between society and church.

### *An example of change: the supermarket company*

Is there anything that the church can learn from developments in society? Are there other organizations looking to make contact with new clients? I will share one example that has inspired me; and I apologize in advance for any technical organizational language. The church does not need to be afraid of taking principles from secular organizations, as the church has often borrowed schemes and methods from the wider society.

My example is of the large supermarket Albert Heijn in The Netherlands (see Strikwerda 2008). This large supermarket chain is present throughout The Netherlands, known familiarly as AH, and it has a substantial share of the total grocery market. All local supermarkets are largely independent enterprises, responsible for making a profit in their locality. But at the AH head office it was discovered that a whole section of people (mostly young people) never entered their local AH supermarket. Their individual lifestyle, shopping needs and the time available all meant that they never used their local AH. So the head office decided to develop ways of reaching this specific group of people without losing their regular client base. They could have decided to re-organize the local supermarket chain, develop new products etc. They did not choose this route. Instead they developed a new AH market solution, to be developed by new local operators in new locations: railway stations. The layout, design, products available, etc. all make it clear that this is an AH store. Furthermore, customers of the railway 'AH-to-go-shops' as they are known, will more easily use their local AH supermarket as they become accustomed to AH products.

AH has succeeded in winning a new set of customers not by improving or changing the existing formula or markets, but by starting a new wing of the same core organization. In management language this is called 'multidimensional control'. Using this language, one could say that the protestant church is characterized by mono-dimensional governance: everything is expected from a single formula, namely the local congregation. In response to the dominant anti-institutional atmosphere in modern culture there is a tendency in the church to strengthen this mono-dimensional governance. There is little interest in local congregations for church policy, nor is there any great interest in national or regional levels of the church. All energy is concentrated on the local congregation. It is easy to justify this concentration with ecclesiological and theological arguments. But as we saw previously, we must remember that in the protestant tradition local autonomy was never an exclusive or isolated approach of church policy. In the history of the RCN the *deputaatschappen* can be understood as a realization of multidimensional governance in the church long before the management concept developed.

*Next question: the relationship between baptism and church membership*

To be clear, I do not have a solution to the problem I have identified. My thesis is that the challenge to the church in modern Europe cannot be addressed by retaining the belief that the heart of the church beats in the local congregation. A local congregations is of great value to those who are involved, but it is overcharged when we place on it the expectation that it will reach out to all those who are alienated from church and gospel. We have to develop new governance structures that will allow the national church to shape new programs and activities to reach people who are currently beyond the reach of local congregations. We have to develop activities based on different levels of experience, understanding, ethics and social welfare, and a range of activities for different social categories at local, regional and national levels. This is what I term 're-inventing the church', realizing that this has significant implications for church policy. When we stop focusing on local congregations we have to address many questions about responsibilities, finance and membership.

That last item — membership — is last but not the least. Membership in the PCN is now exclusively related to membership in a local congregation. But this same local congregation is a barrier for many people, representing an in-crowd, and unattractive to join, even though they might be interested in the experience, knowledge and professional skills of the church. Another aspect of church membership is the one-to-one connection between the sacrament of baptism and the socio-juridical membership of the faith community. That is to say, many people have been baptized without being a church member any longer; but this does not undo the act of baptism. And although the church order says that baptism can only be performed once, many people want to be baptized again when they become a member of a new community or when they, as adults, are fully aware and make a conscious choice. So in reality, baptism and church membership do not share a one-to-one connection since membership has to do with choice and participation on a temporary basis because of personal biography, social regularities and other factors. Increasingly people like to belong and participate in a community without being baptized, not knowing whether they will be connected with that community for a lifetime or not. Or it is because they only want to participate in a specific local congregation without being part of a national institutional church.

All these questions cannot be solved overnight. For this reason, I suggest a long-term research project to develop models and proposals which will shape a church appropriate for the next decades. The geographically-defined congregation which determines church life according to patterns from the Middle Ages is no longer appropriate for the mission challenges of our modern society. Respect for the tradition and all the theological arguments used to sustain this pattern of church cannot be an obstacle to finding new ways of making contact with people currently beyond the reach of the church as we know it, though never beyond the reach of the gospel. And in the history of the church we can find good examples of active church policy on other than the local level.

## *Abbreviations and bibliography*

PCN: Protestant Church in the Netherlands (Protestantse Kerk in Nederland).
RCN: Reformed Churches in the Netherlands (Gereformeerde Kerken in Nederland).
NRC: Netherlands Reformed Church (Nederlandse Hervormde Kerk).
ELC: Evangelical-Lutheran Church in the Kingdom of the Netherlands (Evangelisch-Lutherse Kerk in het Koninkrijk der Nederlanden)

Bauman, Zygmunt. 2000. Liquid Modernity. Cambridge: Polity Press.

Bauman, Zygmunt. 2004. Identity: Conversations with Benedetto Vecchi. Cambridge: Polity Press.

Beck, Ulrich. 1986. Risikogesellschaft: Auf dem Weg in eine andere Moderne. Frankfurt am Main: Suhrkamp Verlag.

De Jong, Gert. 2008. Doen alsof er niets is: sociologische gevalsstudie over een kerkelijke gemeente als dynamische configuratie. Wageningen: Ponsen en Looyen BV.

Habermas, Jürgen. 1987. Theorie des kommunikativen Handelns: Handlungsrationalität und gesellschaftliche Rationalisierung. Frankfurt am Main: Suhrkamp Verlag. 4th edition.

Kraemer, Hendrik. 1945. De Roeping der Kerk ten aanzien van de wereld en van het Nederlandsche volk. 's-Gravenhage: D.A. Daamen's Uitgeversmaatschappij NV.

Nauta, Rein. 2006. Paradoxaal Leiderschap: Schetsen voor een psychologie van de pastor. Nijmegen: Valkhof Pers.

Strikwerda, J. (Hans). 2008. Van unitmanagement naar multidimensionale organisaties. Assen: Van Gorcum.

# REFORMED MINISTRY

## Lifelong Calling or Interchangeable Profession?

Rein Brouwer

The theme of this contribution is a possible change in the perception of the office of the minister. The question explored is what the consequence might be of the development of 'interim ministry' as a professional specialization for the way we perceive the office of the minister as a lifelong calling closely connected to a local congregation. After some introductory notes on the monastic roots of the proximity principle in protestant church orders, the article proceeds with a description of interim ministry as a fledgling phenomenon in the Protestant Church in the Netherlands (PCN). After that, some results of an empirical research project on interim ministers and the meaning of 'trust' in the relationship between interim minister and congregation are presented, followed by an exploration of normative notions in the empirical data. The article closes with some thoughts on a possible change in perception of the ministry.

### *I*

In the Rule of Benedict, we read of the 'gyrovagi'. The *gyrovagi*, the 'Wanderers' or 'Landlopers', as a class of monks "who keep going their whole life long from one province to another, staying three or four days at a time in different cells as guests. Always roving and never settled, they indulge their passions and the cravings of their appetite.... It is better to pass over all these in silence than to speak of their most wretched life" (Verheyen 1935). That is why Benedict established a rule for *Cenobites*, who are the most steadfast class of monks. Being steadfast, staying at the same place for a prolonged period of time, is seen as a monastic quality. '*Stabilitas de perseverantia*' (RSB 58, 9) is what is expected of a novice. In fact, it is one of the three things that, according to the Rule, a new monk promises following a twelve-month period of trial: "*Suscipiendus promittat de stabilitate sua et conversatione morum suorum et oboedientia*" ('Let him who is received promise stability, the conversion of morals, and obedience', RSB

58, 17). Obedience and 'stabilitas' are at the centre of monastic life. In another chapter, the Rule identifies the enclosure of the monastery and the stability in the community as the workshop in which the monks operate the spiritual arts with diligence (RSB 4, 78). 'Workshop' is a rather modern sounding word but it is the translation of the Latin *officina*, which is familiar to *officium*, meaning function, duty, ministry, office. The 'officina' is the place where we exercise and operate our 'officium'. In other words, staying at the same place, *stabilitas loci*, and holding on, *perseverantia*, is the holy space in which we practice our ministry, our office.

It should not come as a surprise if there would be an historical link between the monastic vow of stability and the way the Reformation perceived the localization of the office of the minister in the congregation. The *Church Order* of the Protestant Church in the Netherlands (PCN) still prescribes that ministers live within the boundaries of the congregation (CO-PCN, ord. 3-16-3). Of course, there are exceptions to the rule, but the exceptions emphasize the rule. Even the part-time minister is obliged to live within the vicinity of the church, if possible (CO-PCN, ord. 3-17-4). The *General regulation for the minister's salary* requires the church board to provide the minister with a suitable house to live and work within the boundaries of the congregation. In return, the minister has the right and the obligation to make use of this place during the time of his incumbency (GRMS, art. 10-1/2). Again, there are specific reasons why the church board can relieve the minister of this privilege. Nevertheless, in general, the basic assumption of the PCN church order is the close proximity of the minister and the congregation, i.e. the parish house and the church building.

Leo Koffeman confirms this 'proximity-principle' in his theological introduction to church law. He states that the most central ecumenical and church law question is that of office (see Koffeman 2009, 137ff.). In essence, he writes, church law is about office, even within the presbyterial-synodical system. From a theological perspective, the legitimacy of office is related to the ministry of the Word and the Sacraments, and that brings it in close proximity to the local congregation. The office exists in a unique way, but only as far as it is linked to the local faith community. Koffeman dares to rejuvenate the concept of Christ-representation for the ordained office in the protestant church, but he also mentions that the ministers and the congregation together are the expression of God's presence in the church. So, no matter how the office of protestant minister develops in response to a changing society and church, the ordained office is located in concrete communities of faith and is warranted by the ministry of the Word and the Sacraments to the local faithful who have called this minister.

According to the 1982 Faith and Order report on *Baptism, Eucharist and Ministry*, the ordained ministry should be exercised in a personal, collegial and communal way (BEM/M 1982, 26). The churches that seek for *koinonia* in the World Council of Churches converge on the importance of the local communion. "The intimate relationship between the ordained ministry and the community should find expression in a communal dimension where the exercise of the ordained ministry is rooted in the life of the community and requires the community's effective participation in the discovery of God's will and the guidance of the Spirit", according to the BEM report. From this 'rootedness in the life of the community' the office should also be collegial in order to represent the different concerns of the community. Furthermore, the office should be personal, representing as it does the presence of Christ among his people. All three adjectives point in the direction of the local congregation. Of course, there are metropolites, popes, bishops, moderators, deans, chaplains, and other judicatory officials, but they all are exceptions to the rule. The rule is that the office is local. The ecumenical convergence of BEM underlines Koffeman's statement on the linkage between the office and the local faith community. Both Koffeman and Faith and Order presume the 'proximity principle'. The *stabilitas loci* is still alive, even in a non-monastic Reformed context. What does this mean for the growing interest in interim ministry, now that the way interim ministry is developing within the PCN does not quiet fit with the *stabilitas loci*?

*II*

An 'interim minister' in the PCN is not a 'retired minister' who is helping out. Neither is he or she a 'classical counselor' or a 'minister under contract' or 'consultant' who guides and advices a congregation during the absence of an incumbent minister. 'Interim ministry' is a new specialization within the ministry of the PCN. Currently there are about thirty ministers doing interim work in our church. Some of them are fulltime interim ministers, others parttime, sometimes in combination with a regular ministry in a congregation. Eight of these interim ministers are in denominational service, and recently the General Synod decided to increase that number. They are 'managed' by a staff member of the Denominational Service Center of the PCN. Whenever a church board decides to hire an interim minister, they either negotiate with an independent interim minister, or they contact the Denominational Service Center of the PCN and contract one of the eight 'official' interim ministers. Part of the agreement is the job specification and the duration of the contract. On average the interim minister remains in the congregation for about a year. When the interim minister is asked to guide, advice, and support the congregation during a vacancy period, this will take no more than six months to a year, for ten or twenty hours a week. But it is not unusual that there be some postponed maintenance to take care of. In most cases there is some work to be done on congregational structures and responsibility, on decision making processes, on identity formation, and on communication. In these situations, interim ministers tend to stay in a congregation for more than one year, sometimes nearly two years. That is certainly the case when there is also grief and mourning over loss (death of a pastor, steep decline of membership and resources, radical reconstruction of the congregational structure, a conflict or crisis). In general, however, the interim minister is a temporary shepherd, taking care of business as usual, and trying to stabilize the feelings of insecurity and uncertainty that come with the in-between time.

The USA literature on interim ministry refers to five developmental tasks: coming to terms with history, discovering a new identity, transition to new leadership, renewing the relationship with denominational partners, committing to a new future and new leadership (see Gripe 1997; Nicholson 1998; Mead 2005). These tasks are specifically focused on guiding a congregation through the transition from one minister to another. In most USA churches it is obligatory for a congregation in transition to have an interim. Engaging a transitional minister is part of the church polity. Dutch interim ministers, however, are not transitional ministers in the USA sense of the word. They do not specifically manage the transition process from one minister to another. It is better to see them as facilitators of the transition and not as managers of the transition; they just pave the way. This perception is supported by the lack of a specific regulation in the church order of the PCN.

Interim ministers are in the service of the denomination (CO-PCN, ord. 3-28), but there is no specific article, regulation, or ordinance that legalizes the interim ministry. Article 37 of the *General Regulation for the Minister's Salary* might be the formulation that comes closest. It is about 'acting ministry in another congregation'. It regulates the payment for the auxiliary services of a minister from another congregation, and also the quantity of time of the commission, namely no more than one third of a fulltime job (GRMS, art. 37, 'Acting ministry in another congregation'). Interim ministers, however, perform their auxiliary services in a congregation more than fifty percent of the time. Furthermore, the General Regulation in any case is intended for ministers called by and connected with a local congregation. So, article 37 of the General Regulation was not invented for interim ministers in denominational service. The thought behind it was probably simply to find a way for a local minister with some spare time on his hands to engage with a nearby congregation that could use some help. According to the manager of the interim ministers (email August 2011—RB), article 37 is a possible legal sanction, in absence of a better regulation, but in fact it is not. Introducing a denominational minister in a local context who is doing more than just some auxiliary work, who is actually replacing a minister, stretches the intention of this article. As a consequence, a sufficient legal regulation does not exist. We have a specialized ministry operating, paid for by the church members, but not warranted by the order of the church.

One can assume that this is not the first example of church polity not backed up by church law. However, this could be dealt with rather easily. Church lawyers could design a new *General Regulation for the Interim Ministry*, according to CO-PCN ord. 3-22 ('Ministers in General Service'), consisting of the following sections: I. General definition, II. Formal training and permanent education, III. Competency, IV. Admission and commission, V. Congregational contract, VI. Mobility Management (Denominational Service Centre), VII. Special arrangements, VIII. Final Provisions. One of the sections should include an article signifying the interim minister as a minister in denominational service who enters a contract with a local church council on the provision of services for an agreed-upon period of time.

The moment this little legal imperfection is smoothed out, there would no longer appear to be a problem. The work of the interim ministers is effective, and the congregations are grateful for what these interim ministers do in times of uncertainty.

*III*

In the following, interview material will be offered that was gathered as part of ongoing research on interim ministry (the interviews are cited as IM1, IM2, and so on). The main questions of the research project are what interim ministers do that makes this ministry so special, and which understandings of 'trust' are involved in the working agreement between minister and church session. Eight interim ministers were interviewed in the summer of 2012.

Before offering some clues about the answer to these questions, let me say a few words on the research strategy. Practical theology is a hermeneutics of lived faith, and practical theologians research practices of faith. 'Practice' is used here in the way sociologist Pierre Bourdieu uses the notion of 'habitus' as 'regulated improvisation': "subjective but not individual systems of internalized structures, schemes of perception, conception, and action" (cited by Smith 2008, 217 n. 2). Practices are culturally-shaped and embodied patterns of behavior, borne by social groups over time. Practices are always meaningful, intentional and theory-laden. Practices of faith derive their meaning from the life of God in his Son Jesus Christ through the Holy Spirit. That is why practical theologians work with an empirical methodology to obtain a clear perspective on practices. However, this research strategy is integrated within a theological framework because we are looking at practices of faith. For my research, this means two things: first, trying to get an empirical hold on the practices of interim ministers; and second, asking the question 'what do these practices mean from a theological perspective?' The theological perspective is explicitly framed by the concept of 'trust'. 'Trusting someone' means that someone is trustworthy to me in a certain situation, that the other person has my best interests at heart (see Hardin 2006). The implication is that trust presupposes my assessment of the trustworthiness of the other person. I need to know the other's intentions in order that I can trust him. From social scientists we learn that trust is a relational concept. However, there is also a theological quality to trust. God trusted us with his love, visible in Jesus Christ, the image of God. In Jesus God became vulnerable, and through God's vulnerable trust we are able to trust each other (see Strunk 1987). Both these perspectives—the social scientific and the theological—come together in the interpretation of the empirical material from the interim ministry research.

Trust is a central concept in thinking about congregational ministry. From experience we know that trust between a congregation and its minister is built up over the years. It takes some time to develop a relationship of trust that is strong enough to set a process of congregational transformation in motion. So, how does trust work for interim ministers who are dropped into a congregation and leave within six to twelve months? From the interviews with the different interim ministers, three clusters of trust were induced: an objective, a situational, and an operant cluster of reasons why people find interim ministers trustworthy.

The *objective* reasons are given with the interim ministry. People trust interim ministers because they are working in the service of the church, they are vested with an office, their involvement is provisional, and they are independent from the congregation, and vice versa. Next, there can also be an intuitive understanding, a sort of instant intimacy between people. Several interim ministers testified that this intuitive 'click' is a large part of their success.

A second cluster of reasons occurs with the *situation*. Interim ministers are sometimes dealing with complicated situations. People are fed up with what has been happening, they are longing for someone from outside to set them straight, to pick up the pieces, and to start a healing process. At the outset, interim ministers are trusted with the responsibility of changing the congregational situation. One respondent said that "they trust him, because they were tired with all the games they played. They could not admit to each other that something was wrong and needed to be fixed. Only when someone is coming from outside, then...he takes the sting out of the problem, so they can move on" (IM2).

A third cluster of reasons has to do with how the interim ministers *operate*. Reporting on what people give them as feedback, the interim ministers told me that they are visible, open to critique, providing space for difference of opinion and constructive criticism, and being there for people, understanding them, encapsulating their expectations.

So, three clusters of reasons why people trust the interim minister can be recognized: objective, situational, and operant. In all these cases trust is closely linked to how an interim minister synchronizes with a congregation. Of course, congregations are the clients of the interim minister, and the customer is king, but the data also show how the interim ministers intentionally attend to the congregation and its development. A congregation puts itself and its difficulties trustingly into the hands of a minister who is no more than a temporary passer-by. On the reverse side, the interim minister responds in an ethical and pastoral way, respecting the congregation as subject of its own flourishing. Some quotations from the interviews"It is my job that they reach their own objectives" (IM1).

› "I am giving them back their own organization" (IM1).
› "I am not the owner of the process. I only present them with the tools. They have to do it themselves" (IM8).
› "It is not my congregation, but Christ's. I am just a passer-by, although I feel responsible" (IM8).

Part of the interim ecclesiology is that interim ministers see themselves as servant ministers. We might call it 'ethical leadership' or 'servant leadership' (see Northouse 2004), being sensitive to the interests, needs and concerns of the church board. It is their office to be a responsible and involved minister. Nevertheless, at the same time it is temporary, they are passing by; they will not be tied up. The Denominational Manager states, rather proudly, that a good interim minister starts withdrawing the moment his job has begun. Interim ministry seems above all to be an exercise in letting go. These ministers are not in it for their own interest, they say. That is one reason why people trust them. Their objective is development owned by the majority of the congregation.

› "I don't mind what the church board decides, as long as they make decisions the right way for the congregation"(IM1).

*IV*

Interim ministers facilitate the congregational process. Their own normativity or theology does not seem to play a role. Even when there are theological differences, an interim minister should be able to do the job. Nevertheless, the empirical data show that normativity is present in everything they do. Some data from the interviews (italics mine, RB).

› "I always look at how things can function different and *better*" (IM1).

- "It is difficult to be totally impartial. You want to support the ones who put in something *good*....When is something 'good'? That is decided by the church board. They are the ones that have to work with it" (IM2).
- "He mentions a situation in which people got annoyed very quickly. That is not *helping* the process and that is why he intervenes" (IM5).
- "Sometimes it can be difficult at the beginning when you know from the information and the conversation that the question they are raising is not the *right* one. They are talking about a symptom, not the real issue" (IM6).
- "Making them talk about what is *at stake* is a golden opportunity for the interim minister" (IM6).
- "Impartial means that they work it out together in order to continue in a *constructive* way after I am gone" (IM7).
- "It is *essential* that they can express their pain. Telling the story will relieve them, so that they can breathe more freely" (IM7).

Words like 'at stake', 'good', 'better', 'right', 'constructive', 'helping', and 'essential' betray a normative stance. There is a norm, a standard, which functions as a guiding principle. Interim ministers adjust themselves to different situations. They attend to the questions a congregation is dealing with. They connect to the spirituality and polity of a congregation. However, there are also some objective criteria for what is good for the congregation or what is essential for congregational life. There are two dimensions to the normativity of interim ministers. Firstly, normativity is colored by a theological discourse. An example:

- "The congregation is the body of Christ. My role is to perceive what is functioning healthily and what not. My main focus is on the healthy part, because that is what we can use. Most of the time we focus on what is dysfunctional. However, we had better confirm what is going well; otherwise, you are stuck with the part that is ill. Next, you try to make what is ill healthier. What is healthy is decided by 'what is our reason for existence?' The congregation is not a social club; it is not there for self-preservation. Let us at least talk about God; back to the essence!....When I become superfluous, and the congregation healthier, then I have done a good job" (IM1).

Another interesting example:

- "A sensible minister understands a congregation's development. When a minister keeps doing his own thing, he ends up in conflict. That will bring him into a situation in which he does not fit in the congregation anymore. As a minister, you have to be aware of staying close to the congregational development. That is the way to remain meaningful to them. A minister has to anticipate the developments. The Holy Spirit is doing something with the church. The sort of church we have now, has no...well, let me be careful. Practice shows...what is the meaning of the church, and closely connected to this, what is the meaning of the gospel for our contemporary society? The structure of the church has to be in correspondence with the changing society, so that the gospel can move on" (IM2).

We have already seen the second dimension of the interim minister's normativity in the interview data. The criterion is not only what is in accordance with ecclesiology or church polity, or with a faith discourse. There is also an intrinsic normativity to the interim minister's office. The congregation is the subject of its own process of change and flourishing, which is another dimension of normativity. The process itself is important as part of the trust-construction. Of course, the process is not separated from the content. The development of the congregation has to do with becoming 'church' in a changing society. However, a significant emphasis is put on going along with the congregation, helping it finding their way, supporting its unfolding destination. It is the role of the minister to attend to this process. Trust is built by safeguarding the process.

*V*

This is how we educate our future ministers, and this is what practical theologians teach when they talk about church development. However, the perception of the ministry as predominately servient, provisional, process-oriented, functional, and with no strings attached, could be detrimental to the authority of the office, and to trust in the office. A church board could expect their next incumbent minister to be as attentive and constantly conscientious as the interim. However, how does one endure this for more than four years? Moreover, what if a church board is tempted to trust their minister as long as he encapsulates only their interests and moves on as soon as they get bored with him? Of course, I amplify and exaggerate to make a point. It would be interesting to learn from church boards and congregations who have experience with interim ministers if their perception of the ministry and the ministry office has changed, and in what way.

Is interim ministry the exception to the rule, or does the interest in interim ministry bring out a fundamental shift in the perception of the ministerial office: a shift from a life-long calling to a chain of temporary contracts; a shift from being a minister tied to the local situation to detached denominational service; a shift from holding on as a minister, persevering in difficult times, enduring the evil days and the years in which you will say, "I don't enjoy life anymore" (Ecclesiastes 12:1), to rounding off because it no longer works; a shift from trust that builds up over time and has proven to stand the test of time to trust that lasts as long as the job takes; a shift from authority based on an indefinite congregational calling to a limited contract? One can assume that such a shift will have consequences for a change in church polity. One such possible change could be that all ministers end up in denominational service in order to lease them to local congregations for different commissions, for a short time or a long time, part-time or full-time. The result could be a greater distance between the local congregation and the professional minister.

In any case, a minister, part-time or full-time, temporary or incumbent, is always a servant of the Word. Doing interim work without regularly leading worship in the congregation one works with can strengthen the impression that the ministry is merely managing crises rather than guiding the congregation spiritually. It is not necessary in the PCN, as it is in USA churches, for the interim minister to be present every Sunday. But connecting the congregational process to the reading of Scripture in the midst of the congregation underlines the authority of office. That is why an interim minister should lead in congregational worship once every month or two months. That should be part of his job description. It would be very interesting to research differences between those congregations whose process includes the spiritual presence of an interim minister and those whose does not. Research results so far indicate that guiding the congregation spiritually is essential for a fundamental transformation.

Further research is needed to corroborate this thesis, and to confirm the spiritual backbone of the (interim) minister's office and authority.

## *Abbreviations and bibliography*

BEM: Baptism, Eucharist and Ministry. Faith and Order Paper 111. Geneva: WCC (1982).

CO-PCN: Church Order of the Protestant Church in the Netherlands.

GRMS: General Regulation for the Minister's Salary of the Protestant Church in the Netherlands.

PCN: Protestant Church in the Netherlands (Protestantse Kerk in Nederland).

RSB: Regula Sancti Benedicti. Accessed November 6, 2012. www.osb.org.

Bass, Dorothy, and Craig Dykstra (eds). For Life Abundant: Practical Theology, Theological Education, and Christian Ministry. Grand Rapids Mi: Eerdmans.

Gripe, Alan G. 1997. The Interim Pastor's Manual. Louisville: Geneva press. Revised edition.

Hardin, Russell. 2006. Trust [Key Concepts in the social Sciences], Cambridge: Polity Press.

Koffeman, Leo J. 2009. Het goed recht van de kerk: Een theologische inleiding op het kerkrecht. Kampen: Kok.

Mead, Loren B. 2005. A Change of Pastors ... And how it affects change in the congregation. Herndon: Alban Institute.

Nicholson, Roger S. (ed.). 1998. Temporary Shepherds: A Congregational Handbook for Interim Ministry. Herndon: Alban Institute.

Northouse, Peter G. 2004. Leadership: Theory and Practice. London: Sage Publications.

Smith, Ted A. 2008. History, Practice and Theological Education. In: Bass and Dykstra 2008, 214–240.

Strunk, Reiner. 1987. Vertrauen: Grundzüge einer Theologie des Gemeindeaufbaus. Stuttgart: Quell Verlag. 2nd edition.

Verheyen, Boniface OSB. 1935. Rule of St. Benedict. Translation. Atchison: Abbey Student Press. Accessed November 6, 2012. www.kansasmonks.org. 8th edition.

# FUNDAMENTAL HUMAN RIGHTS IN CALVINIST CHURCH POLITY

## An Orientation

Johannes Smit

### *Orientation*

The question whether fundamental human rights should be appropriated by the church is a controversial issue in contemporary church polity. Especially from the Roman Catholic Church tradition questions are being asked about the church's commitment to fundamental human rights (see Provost and Walf 1992). A basic argument is that the church contradicts itself when fundamental human rights are promoted by the church for civil government but not embraced for internal use by the church (see Koffeman 2007, 269).

In evangelical church polity in Germany, a decades-long discussion on the possible adoption of fundamental human rights by the church for internal use has led to at least one church community's adoption of a catalogue of fundamental human rights in its church order. This case indicates however an isolated development; the general point of view seems to be that fundamental human rights are a category of state law and not of church polity.

In Reformed church polity the discussion has, to my knowledge, not really started yet. Some advocates of fundamental human rights in the church simply state that fundamental human rights are a reality in the church and anybody who disagrees must prove the opposite (see Koffeman 2007, 274). On the other hand, from a Calvinist point of view, as legal historian John Witte states: "It is one thing for religious bodies to accept the freedom and autonomy that a human rights regime allows. This at least gives them unencumbered space to pursue their divine callings. It is quite another thing for religious bodies to import human rights within their own politics and theologies. This exposes them to all manner of unseemly challenges" (Witte 2007, 340).

This article contributes to the discussion from the viewpoint of Calvinist church polity. A clarification at this early stage may be useful. The aim of this article is to give a short overview of a positive evaluation of fundamental human rights in the church from the German evangelical contexts, and to pose some questions which should in my view be considered in the discussion from the Reformed tradition's point of view. It does not pretend to evaluate all viewpoints in Germany, but simply examines what in the broader context may be seen as an isolated development in an ongoing discussion.

The term 'fundamental human rights' (*Grundrechte*) indicates those human rights that are posited in law or church order, while the term 'human rights' has a philosophical, ethical or moral inclination.

### *Object of fundamental human rights in state and church*

German Protestantism reflects a fluctuating discussion on the question whether fundamental human rights should be adopted by the church. On the one hand it is clear that fundamental human rights are viewed as a category of state law. Fundamental human rights are not directed to the church, but directed against the state (see Smend 1953, 113). In 1953, Rudolf Smend, probably the doyen of Protestant German state church law (*Staatskirchenrecht*) scholars of his era, argued that to accord fundamental human rights within the church would be to contradict the essence of the church and evangelical church polity (see Smend 1953, 125). These rights guard the church against the abuse of state power and according to its nature cannot be applied in the church (see Smend 1953, 113). In German Protestantism it is generally accepted that religious freedom, probably the most important fundamental human right, cannot be realized in the church (see Robbers 2004A, 409f.; Von Campenhausen 1983, 91), i.e., the church cannot be religiously neutral like the state (see Robbers 2001, 654). The principle at stake is that the separation of church and state does not allow the state to enforce its secularly-founded fundamental human rights in the church. It also accentuates the incompatibility of a religious governance system and state law. The neutral state does not have the competence to endorse its (secularly-founded) human rights legislation in churches or to express it on the internal matters of a religious body. The church and not the state have full responsibility for the internal organization of the church.

The same principle applies to the position of churches in Germany. Churches function independently of the state and receive the status of corporations under public law (see Robbers 2001, 649). These churches and religious organizations in the public sphere are not incorporated into the state hierarchy. The church's position in Germany is a position *sui generis* (in a class of its own). Fundamental human rights create the space for the church to function independently of the state.

On the other hand the realization that fundamental human rights became an inevitable part of contemporary rule of law gives rise to the question whether the rights of church members can be protected in and against the church according the example of relevant state legislation. The objective is not to surrender the church to a heteronymous standard, but to position it (as any juridical community should) against possible threats of stronger powers or coercion (see Pirson 1972, 365). Scriptural and confessional pronouncements indicative of subjective rights are therefore developed into internal church fundamental human rights catalogues to safeguard members against abuses of the church (see Stoltz 1989, 249–253). These catalogues distinguish between internal fundamental rights in the church and the rights of Christians (cf. Robbers 2004A, 409f.). These catalogues do not bring church or state into conflict with the Constitution's provision for the separation of church and state. Smend's thesis that to accord fundamental human rights within the church would be to contradict the essence of evangelical church polity is, according to advocates of the opposite thesis, not applicable to the development of internal church fundamental human rights catalogues. It is not about state interference in internal church matters (not an *ius in sacra*) but an expansion of church polity by the church (*ius circa sacra*) providing for the protection of subjective rights of church members.

*Possibility of fundamental human rights in the church*

Against this background I want to emphasize some aspects that made it possible to raise the question whether fundamental human rights founded in and confined by Scripture and theology may be applicable in the church, and at the same time to reflect on some of the presuppositions tabled for the adoption of these rights in the church.

First, a main impetus for internal church fundamental human rights catalogues is developments in juridical concept. The important insight is that religious communities do not necessarily ascribe subjective rights to members in the same way that rights are supposed by liberal democratic thought. The question is whether the church's juridical concept allows for subjective rights of church members in and against the church. Against this background three main trends in the development of juridical concept can be distinguished. A *positivistic* juridical like that of Rudolf Sohm basically rejects the adoption of human rights in a church order (see Robbers 2004A, 409f.). A *dualistic* notion on the other hand views human rights exclusively as a legal discipline. A *monistic* juridical notion maintains that the concept 'juridical' as such is undivided, and that accordingly church polity is part of the juridical whole (*Größe*) established in church and society. Church polity shares historical limitations and social deficiencies (see Robbers 2004B, 217). Subjective rights are inherently part of such a juridical concept. The latter makes it possible to pose the questions *whether* and *how* fundamental human rights should be adopted in a church order (see Robbers 2004A, 409). It should therefore be established whether the applicable juridical theory of evangelical church polity allows for fundamental human rights in the church.

Second, the question is whether human rights are necessarily part of any juridical order other than that of the state (see Pirson 1972, 364). Are fundamental human rights based on universal, timeless principles, or is it an arbitrary, historically-determined system that constitutes a specific kind of state governance (see Pirson 1972, 364)? Pirson comes to the conclusion that from its historical premises fundamental human rights are a product of a juridical-political confrontation in a specific historical context. But he adds that it is also possible to argue that former juridical orders based on justness (in the juridical-political context of the day) were supported by fundamental human rights thought or at least respected it (see Pirson 1972, 363). It became clear that fundamental human rights are not founded on a subjective justification against the execution of power by sovereign authority-bearers. These rights give general obligatory criteria for the state government which result in however controversial consequences (see Pirson 1972, 364). This perspective makes it possible to view fundamental human rights as substantive rule of law. Then it is possible that the actions of authority-bearers other than the state are also inherently part of and confined by fundamental human rights principles (see Pirson 1972, 364). It is therefore possible and appropriate to speak of fundamental human rights in the church.

Third, from the viewpoint of evangelical church polity the development of juridical concept makes it possible to pose the question whether a church member's participation in the community (of believers) constitutes a complex of subjective rights in and against the church (see Pirson 1967, 347). The question may be stated as follows: can the applicable juridical concept be understood to entail a complex of subjective rights of church members? This question emphasizes the difference between the church's and the state's approaches towards fundamental human rights. The state's juridical order focuses on the interests of the individual. In the church however the focus is not on the balancing of individual and community interests. The church focuses on the objective of church and this object should be accounted for when the rights of church members are considered (see Pirson 1967, 352). But the difference in approach between church and state does not exclude that church membership inseparably implies a complex of subjective rights of members (see Pirson 1972, 352). Stolz indicates that the first article of the *Church Order of Emden 1571*'s rejection of the domination of churches and office bearers over each other already introduced a subjective right into evangelical church polity (see Stolz 1987, 96–103). These rights should be viewed in light of the inseparable link that exists between the rights and obligations of church members.

Fourth, the incorporation of fundamental human rights in the church is founded on an expression of the democratic nature of church and church polity (see Huber and Tödt 1978, 204ff.). It is fundamentally directed against any form of hierarchical church regimen. According to Huber and Tödt, Paul characterized the church as the body of Christ (see Huber and Tödt 1978, 170–171, 207f.). In the body all Christians are equal through baptism. The subjacent view is the priesthood of all believers inherited from the Martin Luther and endorsed by scriptural passages like 1 Peter 2:5–9 that emphasize the mutual responsibility of all Christians in the life of the congregation. There is no possibility of distinguishing between a priesthood and laity; all church authority comes from the community of baptized Christians. The unique office of a minister of religion is also bound by the election and consent of the congregation. According to these authors the presbyterial and synodical ways of mutual collaboration in the church came into existence in interaction with the development and realization of the democratic structures of the state. The contemporary concept of the *Volkskirche* (people's church) for example entails that the *Volk* (the people) participates in the building up of the church and take part in decisions concerning the future of the church. In that sense the right of the church members to participate in the decision making of the church is representative of the democratic structure of the order of the church (see Huber and Tödt 1978, 208).

Fifth, the adoption of fundamental human rights in the church initiates the possibility of a new hermeneutic of church orders. The hermeneutical key that should be applied to realize fundamental human rights in the church is that all fundamental human rights in the church are to be interpreted from the double command to love. The fundamental aspects of secularly-founded fundamental human rights (freedom, equality and participation) make "the double commandment of love to a common reference point, from him they win their precise meaning for the coexistence within the Christian community" (Huber and Tödt 1978, 208). Irrespective of the fact that the state's legality is vested in a certain morality, it is impossible for the state to make the same claim as the church on the double command to love. This command constitutes the fundamental difference between the church's and the state's implementations of fundamental human rights. In light of the command to love it is also possible to view freedom, equality and participation as the regulative principles for the execution of a church order (see Huber and Tödt 1978, 204). The realization of fundamental human rights in the church is therefore a point of orientation "in which complex life contexts it comes to matters of the experience and the realization of God and love of neighbor" (Huber and Tödt 1978, 201).

*Theological foundation*

Different sources for the theological foundation of fundamental human rights in evangelical church polity can be distinguished. I will mention a few examples.

From Matthew 25:23ff.: the latter is indicated as the basis for a human rights formulation of human dignity *ex iure divino*; Matthew 28:18–20 a human right of participation *ex iure divino*; Matthew 23:8ff. in relationship with Galatians 3:28 a fundamental human right of equal administration *ex iure divino* and a fundamental human right of the individual or minority to be heard in service of the unity of the church; and with reference to 1 Corinthians 12:12ff. and Matthew 18:21 an administrative authority of the church (also in service of church unity) (see Stolz 1989, 249ff.).

From Martin Luther's thesis of Christian brotherly love: Christian equality and Christian freedom — the God-given fundamental human rights of Christians in society — are indicated and used as the basis for fundamental human rights in the church (see Stolz 1989, 249ff.). Following Luther, John Calvin also rejected any human domination in the church and secured equal rights for all ministers of the Word.

From Martin Luther's thesis of the priesthood of all believers: Luther did have an eye for the offices as ordained by God, but he also viewed the offices as generative from the congregation. The priesthood of all believers became an impetus to give expression to the democratic principle of the church (see Stolz 1989).

From Karl Barth's use of the term 'fundamental human rights' in different contexts, but always with reference to the relationship between Jesus Christ and the church: for Barth Jesus Christ is the Head of the community (see Barth 1958, 680–691). Christ is the primary subject and the acting *communio sanctorum* the secondary. To say 'community' is at once to say 'law and order'. This constitutes a form, a law to which the community is always subjected. In the community it is always about the ordering, commanding and controlling of Jesus Christ. And for the sanctified it is about their obedient subordination to him. For Barth this relationship constitutes the Christian community: "This relationship constitutes the Christian community. It is its principle of order, its basic law" (Barth 1958, 680).

From the fifteenth and sixteenth centuries' Protestant church orders: which rejected — nowhere more prominently than in article 1 of the *Church Order of Emden 1571* — the domination of churches and office bearers over each another. It indicated the way for the development of the *Barmen Theological Declaration* (BTD, *Barmen Theologische Erklärung*, 1934), and, in the secular world, the

American rights of freedom. The Emden formulation should therefore be viewed as a fundamental human right in its original context as well as in contemporary society.

From the BTD where the 'community of brothers' (*Gemeinschaft von Brüdern*) is used to formulate seven fundamental human rights in the church (see BTD, art. 3). These rights are the right of admission to faith, the right of unity, the right of Christian brotherly love, the right of liberty of conscience and opinion, the right of the integrity of the person, the right of equality, and the right to take part in church decisions (see Huber and Tödt 1978, 204).

From the *Belhar Confession* (which developed in South Africa during the apartheid era): from which came a possibility to formulate an internal fundamental human right for the church that rejects discrimination against persons on the grounds of complexion. The *Belhar Confession* declares that different ethnic groups confessing the same biblical truths cannot be denied the right of full church membership or be forced into a separate church because of their descent (see Huber and Tödt 1978, 248ff.).

### *Practical embodiment*

The Evangelical-Reformed Church (*Evangelisch-reformierte Kirche*; previously with the addition: *Synode evangelisch-reformierter Kirchen in Bayern und Nordwestdeutschland*) was one of the first (if not only) churches in Germany to adopt such a catalogue in a church order. This catalogue states:

> "(1) The message of the Holy Scriptures of the Old and New Testaments applies to all people. Therefore everyone has the right to participate in the worship and life of the whole church. Everyone has the right to be member of the church community. No one may be compelled against his conscience to membership.
> (2) As a community of brothers and sisters the Evangelical Reformed Church (Synod of Evangelical Reformed Churches in Bavaria and Northwestern Germany) witnesses to Jesus Christ as the Head of the Church. In it, all the differences people have lose their decisive significance. Therefore, no one may be discriminated against because of his origin or his race.
> (3) In its order and in its actions the Evangelical Reformed Church (Synod of Evangelical Reformed Churches in Bavaria and Northwestern Germany) has to pay attention to the dignity of every individual and advocate for it" (EK 2005).

According to advocates of fundamental human rights in the church, such a catalogue gives the church opportunity to fulfill its mandate with internal peace while at the same time orienting its internal matters according to fundamental human rights principles accepted by the state and enjoying the security the state provides (see Van't Spijker 1974; Van't Spijker 1990, 309–332).

*Perspective*
It seems clear that the development of fundamental human rights in the church in Germany is at this point in time an isolated development in the German Protestant context. Most Protestant German church polity scholars still view fundamental human rights as a category of state law and not as a category of church polity. But what can this discussion contribute to the wider Calvinist church polity discussion?

In the broader framework of church polity, different concepts of church developed since the Reformation. For centuries conciliarity exercised a dominant influence on the broader Calvinist tradition. In later years a reaction against the conciliar church, with its synodical structures, manifested in a move to a Congregationalist concept of church. Both conciliarity and congregationalism emphasize the contribution of human agency in the establishment of the church. Both have the tendency to orient the internal order of the church according to the form of state government, and in recent times especially also to forms of corporate business and the management sciences. Both have a rationalist approach to church influenced by the development of rationalism shortly after the sixteenth-century Reformation.

It is, however, clear that the concept of church underlying the discussion is fundamental to determine whether fundamental human rights should be accommodated by the church. In fact, the operative concept of church determines to a large extent the direction of the discussion. Underlying the church's concept of justice is, after all, a specific concept of church. For example, if the church were considered to be (in a typical rationalist way) a mere human society, we would expect to see a growing insistence upon accommodation of fundamental human rights in the church. Reformed church polity, however, developed in line with the views of John Calvin who held that the spiritual government of the kingdom of God and the civil government are things 'widely separated' from another. For Calvin, church liberty is spiritual; it is placed in the soul or inward man and it relates to eternal life. For Calvin it does not matter what a Christian's condition is among men nor under what laws a person lives, because the kingdom of Christ does not at all consist in human laws. For Calvin the natures of spiritual and civil government are altogether different from each other. These views of Calvin vastly contributed the formulation of the Belgic *Confession*, articles 29–32. Therefore it is important, it seems to me, for Reformed church polity to consider the question of analogy: is there an analogy between church government and state government? It is a centuries-old question, but it seems that a re-evaluation of the concept of church may guide Reformed church polity in this inquiry.

### *Abbreviations and bibliography*

BTD: Barmen Theological Declaration. Accessed July 25, 2011. http://de.wikipedia.org/wiki/Barmer_Theologische_Erklärung.

EK 2005: Evangelische Kirchenverfassungen in Deutschland. Aktualisierung/ Ergänzung zu: Dieter Kraus (Hg.). 2011. Evangelische Kirchenverfassungen in Deutschland: Textsammlung mit einer Einführung. Berlin: Duncker und Humblot. Accessed July 1, 2011. http://www.kirchenrecht.net/de/evkir.

Barth, Karl. 1958. Church Dogmatics. Volume IV. The Doctrine of Reconciliation. Part 2. Translated by G.W. Bromiley and T.F. Torrance. Edinburgh: T & T Clark.

Huber, Wolfgang, and Heinz E. Tödt. 1978. Menschenrechte: Perspektiven einer menschlichen Welt. Stuttgart: Kreuz Verlag. 2nd edition.

Huber, Wolfgang. 1983. Folgen christlicher Freiheit: Ethik und Theorie der Kirche im Horizont der Barmen Theologischen Erklärung. Neukirchen-Vluyn: Neukirchener Verlag.

Koffeman, Leo J. 2007. For external use only? Some thoughts on Human Rights and Church Law. In: Scriptura 95(2007), 269–277.

Papier, Merten (ed.). 2004. Handbuch der Grundrechte in Deutschland und Europa, Band I. C.F. Müller Verlag.

Pirson, Dietrich. 1967. Die Mitgliedschaft in den deutschen evangelischen Landeskirchen als Rechtsverhältnis. In: Zeitschrift für evangelisches Kirchenrecht 13(1967), 337–358.

Pirson, Dietrich. 1972. Grundrechte in der Kirche. In: Zeitschrift für evangelisches Kirchenrecht. 17(1972), 358–386.

Provost, James, and Kurt Walf. 1992. The Tabu of Democracy within the Church. Concilium (1992)/5, vii–viii.

Robbers, Gerhard. 2001. Religious Freedom in Germany. In: Brigham Young University Law Review. Vol. 2001/2, 643–668.

Robbers, Gerhard. 2004A. Menschenrechte aus Sicht des Protestantismus. In: Papier 2004, 409–410.

Robbers, Gerhard. 2004B. Warum Kirchenrecht? In: Zeitschrift für evangelisches Kirchenrecht, 49(2004), 215–220.

Smend, Rudolf. 1953. Glaubensfreiheit als innerkirchliches Grundrecht. In: Zeitschrift für evangelisches Kirchenrecht. 3(1953), 113–125.

Stoltz, Winfried. 1989. Menschenrechte und Grundrechte im evangelischen Kirchenrecht. In: Zeitschrift für evangelisches Kirchenrecht 34(1989), 249–253.

Van 't Spijker, Willem. 1974. Democratisering van de kerk anno 1562. Apeldoornse Studies 8. Kampen: Kok.

Van 't Spijker, Willem. 1990. Aspecten van gemeenteopbouw in de Reformatie – voornamelijk bij Luther, Bucer en Calvijn. Theologia Reformata 33(1990)/4, 309–332.

Von Campenhausen, Axel Frhr. 1983. Juristische Kurz-Lehrbücher. Staatskirchenrecht. München: Beck Verlag. 2nd edition.

Witte, John. 2007. The Reformation of Rights: Law, Religion and Rights in early Calvinism. Cambridge: University Press.

# RE-UNDERSTANDING THE DORDT CHURCH ORDER IN ITS DUTCH POLITICAL, ECCLESIASTICAL AND CULTURAL CONTEXT

(1559–1816)

Fred van Lieburg

## 1. *Two weeks in May 1619*

This essay deals with the history of the Reformed church order that was established by the Synod of Dordrecht of 1618–1619. Known as the *Dordtse Kerkorde (Kerkenordening)* in the Netherlands, it has received international renown as the *Dor(d)t Church Order* (abbreviated here as the DCO). Basically, its story is not simply a matter of church history but of general political history as well. A dramatic illustration of this is the coincidence that the drafting of the DCO started on the very same day on which the great statesman Johan van Oldenbarnevelt was beheaded. He had been the political leader of the Dutch Republic for almost thirty-three years. A conflict with Prince Maurice over the self-governance of the public church during the Twelve Year's Truce of the war against Spain became fatal after eight months' imprisonment. He died on the scaffold before the eyes of the people who had gathered at the Binnenhof in The Hague (see Van Eijnatten and Van Lieburg 2011).

A couple of hours later on that Monday morning, 13 May 1619, the Dutch National Synod was re-opened by its president, Johannes Bogerman, in the Great Church of Dordrecht. A large number of visitors were present. The assembly had been gathering already for half a year in the *Kloveniersdoelen*, elsewhere in the town. Ministers and elders from the Dutch provinces, professors of theological faculties, representatives of the States-General, as well as theologians from abroad, had been talking about the major point at issue: the proposal of the so-called Remonstrants for a revision of the *Belgic Confession*. Debates over the doctrine of predestination had threatened the unity of the church, peace among the people and the stability of the state. Ample discussion resulted in a negative judgment of the synod on the five articles of the Remonstrants, nowadays known as the *Canons of Dordt* (see Goudriaan and Van Lieburg 2011).

Having decided on doctrine and having said farewell to the foreign visitors, the synod continued its sessions in the *Kloveniersdoelen*. The so-called *Post acta* were concerned with the revision of the church order, which had most recently been established by the former national synod of The Hague in 1586. During the afternoon, the 79 articles of the revised church order were read out. All members promptly agreed with the substance of this set of rules. Some members had to enter a reservation because of the particular church orders established by their provincial States. The synod intended to request the States-General to approve and authorize the articles as public laws in order to restore peace and piety in church and society (see Kuyper 1899).

Apparently, the church order also contained non-substantial elements, on which further agreements were to be made among the deputies from the provincial churches and between the clergymen and the politicians as well. Moreover, the provincial synods had proposed a lot of amendments. It took two weeks before the final text, consisting of 86 articles, was signed by the five members of the moderamen on 28 May, 1619 (see Groot placaet-boeck 1683, 464). On the next day, Saturday, 29 May, the synod was solemnly closed with a thanksgiving service in the Great Church. The great event that immortalized the city of Dordrecht in national and ecclesiastical history was over.

## 2. *Two flash-backs: May 1559*

Thus far the origins of the 1619 document which has become known as the DCO. In order to place its previous and later history in the right perspective, we go back to the middle of the sixteenth century (see also Benedict 2002). At that time a political unity of Seventeen Netherlands under a shared sovereign, Philip II of Habsburg, also the king of Spain, still remained. Then as well an ecclesiastical unity under the Church of Rome, represented by several bishops and a lot of pastors in the local parishes, continued. Formally, the Netherlands were still part of the Holy Roman Empire. However, this empire had lost its religious unity in the meantime, since some town councils and regional princes had given their fiat to church reforms in accord with the ideas of Martin Luther and others. With the Peace of Augsburg, the German Empire accepted the coexistence of Catholic and Protestant areas.

Now I want to make two flashbacks, both to May 1559, sixty years prior to the closure of the Dordt Synod. The first one brings us back to the palace of the Pope in Rome, where Franciscus Sonnius was received as a deputy of Philip II. Pope Paul IV signed the bull *Super Universas*, which was meant to reform ecclesiastical life in the Netherlands to conform with the decisions of the Council of Trent. The former geography of dioceses was adapted to the current political structure. New bishops, to be appointed both by the Pope and the ruler, were to create better training of priests and reinforcement of pastoral care. Intensive church visitation and inquisition were to help prevent or fight against abuses and heresies more effectively. One thing that remained intact was the control of local rulers over the election of pastors.

The other scene occurred two weeks later, this time in Paris and certainly not in a palace. From 25 to 29 May 1559, a clandestine meeting was held by Calvinists or Huguenots, known as the first French Reformed synod. They followed John Calvin, who had developed a full alternative to the Church of Rome, including a theology, a confession and a church order, the *Ordonnances Ecclésiastiques*. His church model was characterized by local congregations that were administrated by consistories consisting of ministers, elders and deacons elected by the church members themselves. In the city of Geneva, this model was being practiced with success. However, it was impossible to do the same in France, since the Protestants were persecuted heavily by the Roman Catholic king. Nevertheless, the Calvinist gathering in Paris organized an underground church by designing its own confession and church order following to the Genevan example.

Calvinism, which was also strengthened by the establishment of an international minister's training in Geneva, was a serious threat to European rulers on the Catholic side. Hence, still in 1559, even the political arch-enemies France and Spain made a treaty to drive back growing Protestantism. The Netherlands, ruled by the Spanish king, were included in this program. At that moment, there were already consistories, especially in the Walloon provinces, but also in Flanders, Brabant and Zeeland. In the service of these Calvinists, Guido de Brès, secret minister of the Word in the city of Doornik, adapted and translated the *French Confession* into the *Belgic Confession* in 1561, which was printed in both the French and Dutch languages. From 1563 onwards, clandestine congregations in Wallonia, Flanders, Brabant, Limburg and Zeeland gathered in synods and made decisions on church life, thus laying the basis for a Dutch Calvinist church order (see Knetsch 1982).

### 3. *Twofold confessionalization*

During those years of political suppression in the Spanish Netherlands, two groups opposed each other. Both professed the Christian faith, the one in line with tradition, the other in the spirit of renewal. Both expressed their conviction in confessions, the one in that of Trent, the other in those of Geneva, Paris or Doornik. And the principles of their confessions were elaborated in church orders. The firm fundament of a *corpus doctrinae* was always combined with a more flexible *corpus disciplinae* for the building up of the churches. In opposition to the episcopal model of the Catholics, the Calvinists developed their Presbyterian model with permanent consistories and occasional gatherings of supra-local synods (see Thysius 1615).

Additionally, a *corpus morum* was required in the field of manners or social life. This field was touched by the church but controlled by the state. In line with the tradition of Western Christianity, two options were open. A government supported either the one or the other variant of the true faith of the former centuries. In accordance with modern historical language, were can speak of 'confessionalization', the process whereby a government supports the religion within its territory and organizes it according to a confession of faith in the narrow sense of the word. In a broader sense, the confession concerns the whole of public religion: how to set standards for legislation and the law, how to use church buildings, train the clergy, confirm marriages, educate children, and so forth. In that context, the church order was an organic part of a broader political and social-religious order. It was not a separate phenomenon belonging to a free minority (see Schilling 1995).

In the Netherlands, the highest authorities had in 1559 unambiguously opted for Catholic confessionalization. However, a small group of subjects was absorbed by the ideal of Calvinist confessionalization as worked out by Dutch church councils and synods following foreign examples. This process had to be limited since the Calvinists lacked political power and had to operate in secret. Some Calvinists escaped the cross and chose exile. In and around free towns in England and Germany Dutch refugee communities came into existence. They all shared the hope that the political situation would someday change in such a way that the Catholic confessionalization could be exchanged for a Calvinist one. This hope made a number of representatives of these refugee congregations head for the town of Emden in 1571 in order to hold a national synod. The hoped-for religious revolution was prepared by the drafting of a church order which could be introduced at a local, regional, provincial and national level when new rulers would take power (see Lomberg 1973).

That political as well as religious revolution in fact took place. How and when this occurred is a complicated story which I cannot go into here. In every case it is essential to recognize the primacy of politics in the Dutch Revolt. Local and regional rulers wanted to get rid of their sovereign because he did not respect their privileges and aimed for absolutist control over the provinces, which differed so much from each other. Certainly, they were quite annoyed at the cruel persecution of heretics, who were often simple and well-meaning people who were sentenced to pay fines, suffer corporal punishment or were even sentenced to death. But they did not really intend to exchange the Roman Catholic religion for the Calvinist one, not even for the Lutheran one. They rather aimed for a *modus vivendi* for subjects who had turned away from the Roman Catholic Church, such as the Anabaptists among others. Nearly all Dutchmen were simply still Roman Catholics. They were not interested in a public church according to the Calvinist model, such as in the Emden church order (see Duke 1990).

### 4. *Confessional revolution*

Forced by the armed struggle against Roman Catholic Spain, Roman Catholic worship was eventually prohibited in the Dutch provinces that declared themselves independent. But what would replace it? Which type of confessionalization would receive political support? William of Orange, the leader of the Revolt, during a brief period opted for Lutheranism. Invoking the Augsburg peace of religion, he hoped to receive military help from German princes in the struggle against Spain. This was his explicit wish in 1571 when the Emden synod was being planned. But the Dutch Calvinists remained true to their adopted confession and church order. And however small and powerless they were, they felt that they were ready and able to supervise public doctrine, law and order, and morality, in cooperation with a rival government of the Dutch Provinces (see Nauta et al. 1971).

The Prince of Orange, along with the local and regional rulers, could not avoid taking the Calvinists seriously. They formed the nucleus of resistance. From 1572, the Dutch Calvinists indeed acquired influence over public religion, although the state retained absolute control. At a local level Reformed consistories were established to take care of worship, pastoral work and charity. At a regional level they introduced classes in order to guarantee the self-discipline of ministers and uniformity in church government. Provincial synods had the same aims. And a few times, depending on whether the political situation allowed it, the Calvinists met in synods at even higher geographical levels in 1574, 1578, 1581 and 1586 (see Bremmer 1976; Nauta and Van Dooren 1978; Van Dooren et al. 1981; Bremmer 1988). In the latter case, six provinces were represented. Those provinces (Gelderland, Holland, Zeeland, Utrecht, Friesland and Overijssel) formed the Dutch Republic in 1588, or the Seven United Provinces after the connection with Groningen in 1594.

The familiar series of national synods of the Dutch Reformed churches reflects the Calvinists' increasing self-confidence. Although the direct adherence of confessing members was very limited at the time, practical participation in the church services would increase to more than half of the population during the seventeenth century. The partnership of the church with the secular government had entered the picture. The church leaders would have liked, of course, to see the provincial governments, or even better the States-General, officially authorize their guidelines for church and social life. The national synod of Middelburg was the first to compose a compact church order in 1581. What had only been 'synodal decisions' until that time, from then on became a *corpus disciplinae* in four chapters (secondary topics were removed to the category of 'particular questions'). The States-General, however, were not willing to meet the churches' request for authorization.

A second opportunity for ratification followed in 1586. Searching for a powerful sovereign, the States cast their eyes to the English Queen Elizabeth, who appointed a governor-general for the Netherlands. He was Robert Dudley, the Earl of Leicester, and a Calvinist. He gave his Dutch fellow-believers permission to organize a national synod in the interests of peace and unity in the commonwealth. Church deputies and a number of political delegates met at the *Binnenhof* in The Hague during the summer. On 1 August 1586 the members of the synod offered Leicester a revised church order, which was approved by him on 6 August, anticipating authorization by the States-General. Leicester wanted to have the church order printed together with the *Belgic Confession* and liturgical formularies, but nothing came of this. The Dutch regents felt that Leicester showed a lack of understanding of the Dutch situation in church as well as political matters. He returned to England.

### 5. *Modi vivendi*

Why was it so difficult for the new governments in the Northern Netherlands to adopt the church order offered by the Calvinists? Why was not the Roman Catholic confessionalization unambiguously replaced by a Calvinist one? From a legal point of view the problem was how to accommodate Calvinist pretentions: to free self-government, including the election of ministers by the members of the congregation; to the strong autonomy of towns in general religious policy; and to the existing right of patronage of political rulers as far as the election of the clergy was concerned. The episcopal system may have been rejected at the time of the Revolt, but the parochial system had been maintained. Both town magistrates and rural lords felt that it was quite a concession to have ministers examined in the future by the new ecclesiastical bodies. They absolutely wanted to hold on to their right to elect ministers (see Van Deursen 1974).

The provincial States refused to adapt this system to the wishes of the church party and to infringe upon the rights and freedoms of the political establishment. The Calvinists at their subsequent national synods eagerly sought compromises. In 1578 they came up with the idea that the church councils would 'register' the ministers appointed by them with the 'Reformed authorities', thus only by non-Roman Catholic magistrates. Three years later they tried to stake out their domain by stipulating that 'as civil affairs are the field of politicians, so church affairs must be dealt with by the clergy'. In 1586 there was a more concrete concession by the Calvinists in the form of a recognition of a right of political approval. The church council would elect a minister, but the actual appointment could only take place after the approval of the candidate by the local government.

On the basis of their conviction of the primacy of politics in the affairs of the church, the provincial governments followed their own course as opposed to the national synods. The States of Holland drew up ecclesiastical rules in 1576, 1583 and 1591, cooperating with ministers who favored such policies. The so-called Hague Church Laws of 1591 went furthest: they required that both ministers and elders be appointed by the magistrate. The background of this requirement was the politicians' distrust of Calvinists of radical leanings who had come from the Southern Netherlands and were being elected into the Reformed consistories. The draft of the States' church order met with so much opposition among the ministers that the States did not dare to introduce it. Governments in provinces where Calvinism had not yet struck any roots among the population found themselves in an easier position. The States of Utrecht introduced a church order in 1590 and those of Zeeland in 1591. In Gelderland, Friesland and Overijssel this did not seem necessary. A church order was introduced without any difficulty in Groningen and Drenthe from 1594 onwards under the direction of the Calvinist stadholder (see Hooijer 1865).

The establishment of a provincial church order in Zeeland, including a special solution for the election of ministers, was most notable. Calvinism in these islands was still characterized by the spirit of cross and exile as a result of the huge immigration from Flanders and Brabant. Trust in the government was at such level that the church itself asked for strong political protection and support. One occasion for this was the quarrel of a minister who ventured his doubts on the doctrine of predestination. He was sentenced by the 1591 synod of Zeeland for his deviation from the *Belgic Confession*. The same synod designed a church order, which provided for *collegia qualificata*, consisting of magistrate's and consistories' delegates in order to elect or dismiss ministers. The States of Zeeland established this church order, promoting orthodoxy and homogeneity among the clergy for many decades (see Goudriaan and Van Lieburg 2011, 1–22).

### *6. The Ultimate Test Case*

Around 1600 a *modus vivendi* between the state and the church had in fact been reached in every province of the Dutch Republic. The Reformed religion had a monopoly on public church services on the basis of confession and catechism. Consistories, classes and synods cooperated as much as possible with magistrates and the various provincial States. Ministers of the public church were allowed to confirm marriages and were obliged to baptize every child of Christian parents. Participation in the Lord's Supper was the privilege of confessing church members, but consequently only they were subject to church discipline. Congregations in a strict sense remained small. But governments hoped that there would be a steady growth and that a broad Protestant church would develop. One precondition for this was that the standards in both doctrine and morals were not to be enforced too severely by ministers and the various church bodies.

This prospect was however cruelly disrupted by the theological controversy on predestination. Beginning in 1602, it spread from Leiden University to the local pulpits and congregations. For the governments, especially the States of Holland, the same problem arose as the one experienced by their predecessors in the sixteenth century, but at a lower level of Christian unity. The question then was: how do you maintain peace between Roman Catholics and Protestants? Now the question was: how do you maintain peace between radical and moderate Protestants? That was a political problem which politicians wanted to solve by the promotion of a church without a strict commitment to a particular confession or church order, and without devolving ultimate authority to ministers or ecclesiastical bodies. Provincial synods would not be allowed to determine which doctrine was orthodox or heterodox: all Christians had to be able to find their own place in the church. National synods had not been held since 1586. In political practice, religious matters were considered to fall under the sovereignty of the various individual provinces.

A politician who prototypically thought this way was Oldenbarnevelt, the most powerful man in the Province of Holland. As a student in Heidelberg he had heartily adopted Calvinism. Even the doctrine of predestination was dear to him. But in accordance with his political creed he consistently strove for toleration of dissenting views concerning the *Belgic Confession*. He stood in the way of the organization of a national synod. He wanted to implement the state church order of 1591 in Holland. His political friends in Utrecht had in fact introduced a state church order there in 1612. Holland and Utrecht ultimately even gave permission to cities to use soldiers to enforce law and order in the church. This proved to be the limit for Prince Maurice, the commander of the national army. He disarmed the soldiers and captured his opponents, Oldenbarnevelt included.

The coup of 1618 freed the way for the national synod, the rejection of Remonstrant doctrine and the removal of Remonstrant ministers. The synod also offered a great opportunity for the churches to review the national church order after thirty-three years and to have it authorized. According to one of the delegates, the members of the synod seemed to be "almost burning with desire to finally see the church order vested with public authority by the States-General" (Kuyper 1899, 301). They were already grateful for the official confirmation of doctrinal points which were to be maintained, in the cases of ministers, professors, schoolmasters and comforters of the sick, by obligatory subscription. Gratitude and hope made them receptive to the political authorities, who in the church order held on to the right of patronage of magistrates in the appointment of ministers. The Reformed clergy did not accept a *ius in sacra* but they did accept a *ius circa sacra*. They preferred an authorized semi-Calvinist church order to a non-authorized but fully Calvinist church order.

### 7. *Failing authorization*

This brings us back to the end of the Dordt Synod on 29 May 1619. As soon as the next day, a delegation reported to the States-General in The Hague in Prince Maurice's presence. Printed copies of the revised church order — or perhaps with the revisions as marginalia in the 1586 copy — were sent to the States of seven provinces in the beginning of June in view of the annual conventions which were usually held in summer (see Smit and Roelevink 1981, 142). An interesting aftermath took place in the Chapter of the Utrecht Dom in August 1619. Five important members of the National Synod, among them President Bogerman, attended the Utrecht Synod and there explained some of the articles of the church order, partly at the request of the State's deputies. There was a general satisfaction and that same month the Utrecht States approved of this result of the national synod (see Reitsma and Van Veen 1892–1899, vol. 6, 421–424).

Two of the seven provinces, however, had explicit objections, starting with Friesland in July 1619. The eleven cities were content with the church order, but in the thirty rural areas the local landowners opposed them. The parish members had always had a collective right to call and appoint ministers. They certainly did not want to lose that right, irrespective of whether they themselves were members of the Reformed church or not. But the States of Zeeland also hesitated in September 1619, and were inclined to reject the church order after hearing the Frisian objections. In February 1620 the States of Zeeland declared that they would stick to their church order of 1591. When the case was an item on the agenda of the States-General again on 30 March 1620, five provinces had accepted the church order, whether explicitly or not. A delegation was sent to

Leeuwarden to talk to the Frisians, but strangely enough no delegation was sent to Middelburg to finally try and persuade the States of Zeeland. Perhaps it was thought that Zeeland would follow once the Frisian States changed their mind, but that did not occur (see Rutgers 1890).

In July 1620, it was clear that there would not be a nationwide ratification of the DCO. Gelderland did not want to wait any longer. At the convention in Arnhem, held in May 1620, the church order had been approved with a few small amendments. This version was published, just as the Utrecht version, with an explanation of some articles. The issue did not appear again as an item on the agenda of the States-General. In Friesland in 1622 the power struggle between the cities and rural areas erupted to such a degree that the States took rather aggressive measures. Proponents of the DCO were prosecuted for disturbing the peace. In Holland there was a struggle between the States and the South-Holland synod over amendments to the text. The synod gave way in 1624 (see Rutgers 1890). In 1625, the Overijssel States published an edition of the church order as approved by them. In 1633, the Synod of Drenthe made its own version of the church order which was ratified and published by the States five years later (see Hooijer 1865).

All in all, the national authorization of the revised church order by the States-General was a hopeless failure. We go too far to say that if it had succeeded the DCO could have been regarded as an appendix to the 'fundamental laws' of the Dutch Republic. The fundamental laws were the documents from the Eighty Years' War which had never been meant as the constitution of a state, but in practice they operated as a joint frame of reference for the governmental institutions, among which were the Union of Utrecht, the Placard of Abjuration and the Münster Peace Treaty (see Groenveld 2009). However, we can easily count the DCO as one of the so-called 'public writings', to which as early as the sixteenth century belonged the confessions, the rhymed version of the psalms and the liturgical formularies. In the seventeenth century the acts of the Dordt Synod and the Authorized Translation (*Statenbijbel*) of the Bible were added to this group of writings.

### *8. Nationalization of church administration*

By coincidence, the town of Dordrecht repeatedly provided candidates for the office of Grand Pensionary of Holland, both of them consequently being indirect successors of Oldenbarnevelt. In 1650, Jacob Cats went to The Hague, where he became the chairman of a special gathering of the States-General one year later. At this Great Meeting of 1651, Reformed doctrine as established at Dordt in 1618-1619 was mentioned as one of the pillars of the Republic. Some years later Johan de Witt entered the stage as a political leader, who wrote some memorable words about the national awareness of the citizens of the United Netherlands. Family and commercial relationships created unity, just as joint state institutions did. "And are not their hearts and souls united and joined above all by the spiritual and divine tie of one and same religion?" (Ter Braake 2009, 51).

These mystical words could not refer to the limited membership of the public church in the Republic, but they did refer to the supra-regional unity constituted by the *Belgic Confession* and church order, the interregional mobility of ministers, and the cooperation among the provincial synods, the highest church bodies. Cooperation was made possible by article 48 of the DCO, added in 1619, concerning the maintenance of correspondence among the synods. Sending observers to and fro somewhat compensated for the lack of a national synod, which was not allowed after 1619. A special form of these interprovincial contacts among delegates was the so-called Hague Coetus, which gathered every three years starting in 1641 to inspect the original minutes of the Dordt Synod and the autographs of the States Bible. The documents were deposited in a chest in The Hague and were taken to the *Trèvesroom* every time for this purpose.

The Dutch church remained a conglomerate of provincial churches that shared a number of fundamental documents. The States were the political sovereigns and their approval was needed for a synod to be held. Zeeland traditionally is seen as an example of political intransigence in this field. No synods were allowed here after 1620 — there was only one in 1638 when the church order of 1591 was revised and authorized afresh. But there were informal opportunities for the four Zeeland classes to consult regularly. This makes Zeeland less of an exception to the general rule. The rule in all provinces was that synods could gather every year, although political observers were to be present in all cases. This *modus operandi* simply continued throughout the seventeenth and eighteenth centuries, usually in good harmony (see Van Lieburg 2011).

Thanks to the renowned article 49 of the DCO, church affairs could easily be managed on a daily basis in all provinces. At every provincial synod, delegates were appointed who took care of current affairs until the next synod was held. These delegates also remained in touch with the classes falling under the synod and were involved in examining future ministers. In brief, the Dutch churches had all sorts of politically authorized opportunities to operate as if they had a national church order. The provincial synods could even rely on the States-General to enforce article 66 of the DCO on the keeping of public fasts and days of prayer. The States-General announced such a national day of penance every year for the whole population and thereby in a supremely Christian fashion gave substance to the 'spiritual and divine tie' of which De Witt had spoken as the deepest form of unity in the Dutch Republic (see Van Rooden 2004).

*9. National tradition of church order*

On the juridical level there were only provincial church orders, but they shared the essentials of Reformed church polity. In accordance with their geographical scope, printed editions of church orders were restricted to those of the provinces. Later on, they were also inserted in the provincial collections of placards. Not earlier than 1686, a book seller published an edition of the DCO as an independent general document, although it used the Gelderland version and in a defective way. This edition received seven printings, the final one in 1758. Owing to this series, the book market promoted a national awareness of a common church order, with the 1619 version of the DCO as the standard. In this way, regular church members could gain knowledge of the ecclesiastical system, including procedures and possibilities of appeal in cases of discipline.

In addition to the static editions of the DCO, several collections of successive church orders were brought onto the book market. They aimed at giving a dynamic view of the tradition on these matters. The need for this information first arose from quarrels during the Twelve Years Truce. In 1612, the former minister Reynier Donteclock, a veteran of Flemish Calvinism living in the town of Delft, published a collection of decisions of four national synods, adding several provincial church orders as well as the political regulations of 1583 and 1590 (for reasons of impartiality). He provided an extensive preface on the history of Christian gatherings since New Testament times and the early middle ages. Emphasizing that the Reformed churches, during the period of bloody persecution, were compelled to organize classis and synod meetings, he claimed this was the only means of protection against division and heresy: they did not intend to set up an alternative political structure or ecclesiastical hierarchy (see De kercken-ordeninghen 1612).

The Contra-Remonstrants were induced to demonstrate that their view of confession as well as church order had good historical testimonials. In 1618, just before the National Synod, the Leiden professor Festus Hommius published an inventory of controversies on the *Belgic Confession* and added a Harmony of Dutch Synods, composed by Simeon Ruytinck, Dutch Reformed minister in London (see Hommius 1618). Ruytinck possessed the copy of the church order drafted by a private meeting in Wesel in 1568. Ruytinck introduced the idea of a Convent of Wesel as the first on the list of Dutch synods, thereby initiating a peculiar history of an archival error in Dutch historiography.

After the Dordt Synod, no collection of church orders has experienced more influence than the anonymous edition by Donteclock from 1612. Remarkably, the revised editions still contained four church orders — the DCO was not added as the fifth one, but was only seen as the revised version of 1586. This is all the more remarkable because the same publisher in Delft had printed the original text of the DCO by charge of the States-General in 1619. The edition of 1612 was eventually the basis for the so-called *Church Handbook*, of which five editions were published between 1732 and 1795. This book contained the 1619 version *in extenso*, as well as the *Post-Acta* underlying the DCO which had been circulating in print since 1666. The old preface of Donteclock was maintained through the last edition. Moreover, the *Handbook* contained the decisions of magisterial and ecclesiastical bodies concerning swearing, marriage and other issues concerning the social relation between church and state.

### *10. Dynamics of the church polity*

Having outlined the origins and rise of the DCO, the final sections will be devoted to its decline as the religious framework of the Dutch Republic. As I mentioned, the last *Church Handbook* was published in 1795, while the last independent edition of the DCO had been printed as early as 1758. If these years suggest something about the decline of the church order as the backbone of the confessional state during the eighteenth century, then something must have changed in the functioning of ecclesiastical rules in politics, culture and society as a whole. We have seen that that function ultimately had its roots in medieval Christianity with its belief in the coherence of doctrine, order and morals. At an even deeper level it found its basis in the belief in the rule of God over the world in accordance with the *do ut des* principle: purity is rewarded, sin is punished. We also find the dynamics of divine favor and wrath in the late medieval tradition of fasting and prayer days, which continued to be held in the early modern Republic until its demise (see Van Lieburg 2013).

The Acts of the national synod of Middelburg in 1581 give an early and clear example of the natural embedment of ecclesiastical ordinances into a larger domain of religious and moral law under Protestant rule in the Netherlands. Someone there asked the question "whether it would not be a good thing to insist with the government, that the desecration of the Sunday, luxurious brothels and all other sorts of public excess and sin, contrary to the first and second tables of the law of God, should be stopped and suppressed?" The answer was that it would be necessary to submit requests to both the States-General and the States of each province. In Zeeland itself some ministers indeed went to the States to recommend the 'reforms' that were meant here. Two years later an edition of a police placard followed, not accidentally on the same day as the issue of a school order which dealt with primary education in Zeeland in accordance with the Confession and the Catechism (see Van Dooren et al. 1981, 140–143).

The Zeeland police placard of 1583 — which regulated all sorts of issues having to do with the celebration of Sunday and the affirmation at the conclusion of marriages — was largely based on a similar placard issued earlier by Holland in 1580. Both, moreover, had their foundation in legislation regarding matters of public life that had been codified in the Netherlands as early as the reign of Charles v. A comprehensive survey of all Northern Dutch ordinances in matters of public law and order, marriage, education and the church could be made on the assumption of their common Christian origin. A nice specimen of the contextuality of early modern church orders is an Overijssel edition which comprised both the *Belgic Confession* and DCO and a provincial marriage ordinance (*Nederlantsche Belydenisse*). This survey would also apply to the territories overseas in which the Republic had a say and to the foreign territories of the House of Orange, such as the County of Lingen which received a Calvinist church order in 1678 at the command of Prince William III.

I would like to mention the 'Draft for a further reformation of the doctrine, law and order, and morals' as a final example of the integral significance of the confessional state (see Concept van nader reformatie 1682). It was drawn up in 1682 by the classis of Zuid-Beveland. It was occasioned by a case of heavy flooding — a sign of God's wrath — which in turn seemed to have been provoked by the surge of new theological and philosophical views and the decline in the moral exemplariness of politicians, ministers, elders and families. The perceived threats to Reformed doctrine provoked the Classis of Walcheren in 1692 to draw up new doctrinal articles as an addition to the confessional writings (see Van Lieburg 2013). As unique as this example of a dynamic way of dealing with doctrinal identity is, so too are the multiple laws and regulations to improve church organization introduced by a number of classes and synods in the course of two centuries. The DCO was in practice a legislative framework that was able to accommodate continuous additional decisions in concrete situations in day-to-day church life.

### *11. Transformation of the confessional state*

In the course of the eighteenth century the relationship between the confessional state and the public church became weaker. The ministers' obligatory signing of the old doctrinal formularies became a mere formality. Church discipline of offending members had long lost its intensity. Academic theology increasingly focused on human reason and love as pillars of a Christian society that transcended the boundaries between churches. The annual prayer days issued by the general government were increasingly inspired by the idea of national unity with religious tolerance and without a ruling church. Confessional Christianity, many felt, turned into a civil religion based on inner civilization, moral education and spiritual enlightenment. The church increasingly became an outward organization around an internal faith, just as a society, association or club gave shape to personal and individual ideals of free citizens (see Van Eijnatten 2003).

In the Batavian-French era of 1795–1813 these shifts in dominant thought were gradually expressed in a transformation of the confessional state into a civil nation-state. The National Assembly took away the public church's monopoly and financial security. As a consequence, the church would spend years securing its material interests rather than trying to realize its moral ideals. Ministers focused their remaining positive energy on new societies for Christian mission, the distribution of Bibles and religious literature rather than on replacing the particularistic church system by a national church order. It was the government itself which, after a new, generally Christian school law had been introduced in 1806, took the initiative with this purpose in mind in 1809. A commission received the pragmatic assignment "to retain everything of the earlier church orders which did not contradict the present circumstances in which people found themselves, and to add to this whatever could then be seen as necessary" (Hooijer 1865, 490).

It was not until 1813 that the necessary peace came about as a result of the newly-won independence, which in turn made it possible to give shape to the new nation-state with a central government and uniform legislation. In the field of church polity this resulted in the drawing up, still by a political commission, of the *General Regulation* of 1816. This resulted in the Presbyterian hierarchy being turned upside down to the effect that a general synod, directly under the auspices of King William I, was given authority over a governmental civil service in which an obliging elite of ministers made decisions at the provincial and regional levels. The involvement of the government was regarded as a matter of purely external church administration, with religion itself being left entirely free. What in fact happened was that the formal commitment of ministers to the Confession was ended. The proponents' formula enabled every enlightened theologian to follow his own views, but equally it did not prevent orthodox ministers from preaching the old truths (see De Groot 1992).

The introduction of this *General Regulation* put a legal end to the eight provincial church orders and numerous synodal and classical regulations which only reminded people of the Ancien Régime's fragmented administrative system. The Reformed ministers were happy with the new unity, stability, and their own secure existence. The inherent elements of discontinuity therefore were outweighed by those of continuity, however much subsequent generations have seen in the *General Regulation* an anti-Calvinist and revolutionary reversal of the DCO as an ideal type. What remained and was even strengthened was the joint responsibility of government and church for the religious and moral education of the people in terms of general Christian and societal virtues and the cultivation of love for King and Fatherland.

## *12. Conclusion*

Coming to conclusions, I repeat my statement at the beginning: The story of the DCO is not just an ecclesiastical story, but a political story as well. My historical explanation should have made clear that the DCO was an integral part of a social order, in which the government took responsibility for shaping Christianity for all the people on its territory. The view of this essential 'theocratic' function of Calvinist church order must not be obscured by the peculiar political culture and the decentralized structure of the Dutch Republic. In addition, my contribution should have clarified the dynamic character of Reformed polity, distinguished by the *semper reformanda* that goes back to the fourth volume of Calvin's *Institutes* (see Van Lieburg 2013). Precisely because it was embedded in a living community, the DCO was the result of as well as the starting point for successive adaptations. If the church could have gathered in synods regularly, the church order at the end of the eighteenth century would certainly have been different from the one composed in 1619.

The hidden dynamics of Dutch Reformed church policy in the early modern period account for the seemingly subversive, but actually conservative, revision of the church order in the decades between 1795 and 1815. Looking back, we can now continue the timeline into modern times and conclude that the most decisive turning-point was 1848. Indeed, in the first half of the nineteenth century the government still maintained a close connection to the former public church, while only privileging religious groups that already existed in 1815, not those that presented themselves as new denominations. The question whether the seceded churches after 1834 could trace their existence to the past was precisely the cause of a juridical debate that was settled in favor of the secessionists. It was the 1848 constitution which created a radical separation of church and state or, in other words, opened up a free religious market. The genius of Abraham Kuyper has made the most of it by using a revised Reformed theology for the purpose of free organization in the political, ecclesiastical, social and cultural fields.

Kuyper also made the old Dutch confessions as well as the church order part of his modern Calvinist reform program in his own creative way. First, he elevated the *Canons of Dordt*, which until then had been just a clarification of the *Belgic Confession*, to the status of a confessional standard. Consequently, we speak of the Three Formularies of Unity from 1878 onwards (see Vree 2007). Next, he provided for editions of the DCO with textual marking of the political passages that had no longer any function in the neutral democratic state (see Kuyper 1886). In that way, the DCO was transformed from a fundamental law into the private rules of a free association, with the old confession serving as its legal articles. At the same time, the way was opened for the introduction of all necessary corrections and additions, without loss of the symbolic value of the historical document. Several Reformed denominations followed this track in the course of time, creating all sorts of discrepancies between church polity as it was confessed and church policy as it was practiced.

However, the mechanisms of ecclesiastical sanctification and cultural recycling of the DCO are the topic of another story, to be reserved for a future opportunity. Let me give just one conclusion from history, remembering the dramatic birth pangs of 1618–1619. Dutch Reformed church orders were developed in times of crisis every time. The synod of Emden was a result of the Revolt, that of Dordrecht of a civil war. The *General Regulation* of 1816 was born during a European war, the *Hervormde Kerkorde* of 1951 originated from World War II. The Protestant Church in the Netherlands, however, did not evolve from a political crisis. Yet, recent synodical documents regarding the profession of Jesus Christ and the church in a democratic society closely approximate ideas of general social responsibility that formed the basis of earlier Dutch church orders (see PCN 2009). In our present age, however, no single church can still bear an urgent reformation. Perhaps such a task may be undertaken by the quasi-official and quasi-historical, but also very informal and very postmodern, project of the New National Synods of Dordrecht (2010–2019).

## *Abbreviations and bibliography*

PCN 2009: De kerk en de democratische rechtsstaat — een positiebepaling: bijdrage aan het gesprek in gemeente en kerk. 2009. Utrecht: Protestant Church in the Netherlands (Protestantse Kerk in Nederland).

Baier, Helmut (ed.). 1992. Kirche in Staat und Gesellschaft im 19. Jahrhundert. Neustadt an der Aisch: Degener.

Benedict, Philip. 2002. Christ's Churches Purely Reformed: A Social History of Calvinism. New Haven: Yale University Press.

Brady Jr., Thomas A., et al. (eds). Handbook of European History 1400–1600. Late Middle Ages, Renaissance and Reformation. Vol. 2. Leiden: Brill.

Bremmer, Rolf H. 1976. De 'nationale' Synode van Dordrecht (1574). In: Nederlands Theologisch Tijdschrift 30(1976), 184–206.

Bremmer, Rolf H. 1988. De nationale synode van 's-Gravenhage (1586) in haar politieke en kerkelijke contekst. In: Kerk en Theologie 39(1988), 181–204.

Concept van nader reformatie, in de leer, ordre, en zeden, opgestelt door gedeputeerden des classis van Zuyd-Beverlant. 1682. Utrecht: Willem Clerck.

Cooper, Kate, and Jeremy Gregory (eds). 2004. Retribution, Reconciliation and Repentance. Woodbridge: The Boydell Press.

De Groot, Aart. 1992. Reformierte Tradition im Umbruch der Zeit. In: Baier 1992, 147–160.

Donner, Johannes H., and Simon A. Van den Hoorn (eds). 1885. Acta of Handelingen der Nationale Synode, in den naam onzes Heeren Jezus Christus, gehouden door autoriteit der hoogmogende heeren Staten-Generaal der Vereenigde Nederlanden te Dordrecht, ten jare 1618 en 1619. Leiden: Donner.

Duke, Alastair. 1990. Reformation and Revolt in the Low Countries. London: The Hambledon Press.

Johanna C.M. Fabius et al. 1982. Kerkhistorische studiën: feestbundel, uitgegeven ter gelegenheid van het 80-jarig bestaan van het Kerkhistorisch gezelschap S.S.S., s.n., Leiden.

Goudriaan, Aza, and Fred Van Lieburg. 2011. Revisiting the Synod of Dordt (1618–1619). Leiden: Brill.

Groenveld, Simon. 2009. Unie, Bestand, Vrede: drie fundamentele wetten van de Republiek der Verenigde Nederlanden. Hilversum: Verloren.

Groot placaet-boeck, vervattende de placaten, ordonnantien ende edicten van de ... Staten Generael der Vereenighde Nederlanden (...), Vol. 3. 1683. 's-Gravenhage: Jacobus Scheltus.

Hommius, Festus. 1618. Monster van de Nederlantsche verschillen ofte Belydenisse der Ghereformeerde Kercken in Nederlant (...). Leiden: David Jansz. van Ilpendam.

Hooijer, Cornelis. 1865. Oude kerkenordeningen der Nederlandsche Hervormden Gemeenten (1563–1638) en het concept-reglement op de organisatie van het Hervormd Kerkgenootschap in het Koningrijk Holland (1809). Zaltbommel: Noman.

De kercken-ordeninghen der ghereformeerder Nederlandtscher kercken, in de vier Nationale Synoden ghemaeckt ende ghearresteert. 1612. Delft: Jan Andriesz.

Knetsch, Frederik R.J. 1982. Kerkordelijke bepalingen van de Nederlandse synodes onder het Kruis 1563/4. In: Fabius et al. 1982.

Kuyper, Abraham. 1886. Kerken-ordening gesteld in de Nationale Synode der Gereformeerde Kerken, te zamen beroepen en gehouden binnen Dordrecht in de jaren 1618 en 1619. Amsterdam: Kruyt.

Kuyper, Herman H. 1899. De post-acta of nabehandelingen van de nationale Synode van Dordrecht in 1618 en 1619 gehouden (...). Amsterdam: Höveker and Wormser.

Lomberg, Elwin (ed.). 1973. Emder Synode, 1571–1971: Beiträge zur Geschichte und zum 400jährigen Jubiläum. Neukirchen-Vluyn: Neukirchener Verlag.

Nauta, Doede, and Johannes P. van Dooren (eds). 1978. De Nationale Synode van Dordrecht 1578: Gereformeerden in de Noordelijke en Zuidelijke Nederlanden bijeen. Amsterdam: Buijten and Schipperheijn, and Ton Bolland.

Nauta, Doede, Johannes P. van Dooren, and Otto J. de Jong. 1971. De Synode van Emden, oktober 1571: een bundel opstellen ter gelegenheid van de vierhonderdjarige herdenking. Kampen: Kok.

Nederlantsche Belydenisse des Geloofs, Canones des Synodi van Dordrecht, Nederlantsche Kerken-ordre en Houwlyckx-ordre der kercken van Overisel. 1636. Zwolle: Frans Jorrians en Jan Gerritsen.

Reitsma, Johannes, and Sietze D. van Veen. 1892–1899. Acta der provinciale en particuliere synoden, gehouden in de Noordelijke Nederlanden gedurende de jaren 1572–1620. 8 vols. Groningen: Wolters.

Rutgers, Frederik L. 1890. De geldigheid van de oude Kerkenordening der Nederlandsche Gereformeerde Kerken. Amsterdam: Wormser.

Schilling, Heinz. 1995. Confessional Europe. In: Brady 1995, 641–675.

Smit, Johannes G., and Johanna Roelevink (eds). 1981. Resolutiën der Staten-Generaal: Nieuwe reeks, 1610–1670. Vol. 4: 1619–1620. 's-Gravenhage: Nijhoff.

Ter Braake, Serge (ed.). 2009. De Deductie van Johan de Witt: manifest van de ware vrijheid uit 1654. Arnhem: Sonsbeek Publishers.

Thysius, Anthonius. 1615. Leere ende order der Nederlansche, soo Duytsche als Walsche, ghereformeerder kercken/in twee deelen...; waer van het eerste begrijpt, Corpus doctrinae, dat is, de publijcke, of openlijcke ende alghemeyne Schriften de suyvere Leere aengaende, van den beghinne der Reformatie. Amsterdam: Pieter Pietersz.

Van den Brink, Gijsbert, and Harro M. Höpfl (eds). 2014. Calvinism and the Making of the European Mind. Leiden: Brill.

Van Deursen, Arie Th. 1974. Bavianen en slijkgeuzen: Kerk en kerkvolk ten tijde van Maurits en Oldenbarnevelt. Assen: Van Gorcum.

Van Dooren, Johannes P., et al. 1981. De Nationale Synode te Middelburg in 1581: Calvinisme in opbouw in de Noordelijke en zuidelijke Nederlanden. Middelburg: Koninklijk Zeeuwsch Genootschap der Wetenschappen.

Van Eijnatten, Joris. 2003. Liberty and Concord in the United Provinces: Religious Toleration and the Public in the eighteenth-century Netherlands. Leiden: Brill.

Van Eijnatten, Joris, and Fred Van Lieburg. 2011. Niederländische Religionsgeschichte. Göttingen: Vandenhoeck and Ruprecht.

Van Lieburg, Fred. 2011. Een eiland na de Reformatie: Schouwen-Duiveland 1572–1700. Amsterdam: Bert Bakker.

Van Lieburg, Fred. 2014. Dynamics of Dutch Calvinism: Early Modern Programs for Further Reformation. In: Van den Brink and Höpfl 2014, Ch. 2.

Van Rooden, Peter. 2004. Public Orders into Moral Communities: Eighteenth-Century Fast and Thanksgiving Day Sermons in the Dutch Republic and New England. In: Cooper and Gregory 2004, 218–239.

Vree, Jasper. 2007. De drie formulieren van enigheid: een vondst van Abraham Kuyper. In: Historisch tijdschrift GKN 13(2007), 3–17.

# DORDT AND SOUTH AFRICA

## Church and State Relations in the Netherlands and in South Africa

Pieter Coertzen

### *1. The Church Order of Dordt (1619) in context and meaning.*

#### *1.1 The context of Church and State Relations*

The fourth national synod in the Netherlands was held in 1586 in the Hague under difficult military and political conditions. The war against Spain was not going very well and in 1584 Prince William of Orange was assassinated. It became clear that the States General could not contain the situation. They consulted first with Henry III of France and then with Queen Elizabeth I of England to take over the sovereignty in the Netherlands. Both refused but Elizabeth sent Robert Dudley, the Earl of Leicester, together with 5, 000 troops to the Netherlands. According to Williston Walker his rule was a failure and he returned to England in 1587 (see Walker 1970, 386).

Leicester however did support the Reformed Church in its quest for greater independence from the authorities (see De Jong 1972, 168) and he clearly realized that a well-ordered church was necessary to cope with the variety of viewpoints which threatened to tear the church apart. It was on his instruction that a national synod met in the Hague from 20 June to 1 August 1586 after putting pressure on various provincial states to support the calling of a national synod (see Pont 1981, 158–159).

After the departure of the Earl of Leicester from the Netherlands in 1587 the relationship between state and church in the Netherlands got worse. In the Province of Holland the rulers were viewed as wanting to rule over the church while the rulers were wary that the church wanted too much say in political matters. By the end of 1589 the rulers in the Province of Utrecht for instance removed all Reformed ministers and decided that in the future they would call only 'peace loving ministers'. In the rural areas of Utrecht the owner of a church had the right to take to the authorities the name of a minister of his choice for approval, while in the cities it was seen as the right of the magistrate to appoint a minister.

No classes were established and no provincial synod could be held (see De Jong 1972, 171f.), and the authorities were bent on keeping church discipline in their hands (see Bakhuizen van den Brink and Dankbaar 1967, 276). What in fact was happening was that the system of church-state relations dating from the time of Constantine was being re-established in the Netherlands: the state protected the church but also controlled the church.

Between 1586 and 1619, society in the Netherlands became ever more divided between on the on hand the strict Calvinists (*preciezen*, also called *kerkelijken*) who stood for a strict interpretation of the confession and were against interference by the state in matters of the church, and on the other hand the more tolerant *rekkelijken* (also called the *politieken*) who were afraid of confessional coercion by the church and desired the protection of the authorities against such a possibility (see Bakhuizen van den Brink and Dankbaar 1967, 276). Casper Coolhaes (1534–1615) was a supporter of the latter. He was removed as minister in Leiden for siding with the authorities and because of his heterodox views. In society itself various humanistic traditions dating from Erasmus of Rotterdam could be found and Anabaptism was wide-spread. These expressed themselves in an emphasis on the more practical aspects of religion, in a disinclination towards sharp creedal definitions and a more tolerant attitude such as could be found for example in the ideas of Dirck Coornhert (1522–1590). These ideas came to their fullest expression in the work of Jacobus Arminius (1560–1609) and his followers. Regarding predestination Arminius accentuated the responsibility and free will of humans according to which God chooses a person out of grace for the sake of Christ but in this He takes into account the faith of the person which He foresaw (see Bakhuizen van den Brink 1960, 277–280).

A conflict sprang up between Arminius and Franz Gomarus, his Calvinist colleague at the university of Leyden, over the doctrine of predestination (see Walker 1970, 399). Gomarus maintained that God had decided from eternity whom to elect and whom to reject according to His will. He taught that even the faith through which a person is saved is a free gift of God's grace for the elect (see Bakhuizen van den Brink 1960, 287–288). Soon the two colleagues were in a bitter conflict that affected not only the country but also the international Reformed world. At this time both parties insisted on a general/national synod to resolve the matter. Gomarus and his followers wanted from a synod a decision in their favor while the followers of Arminius saw a synod as a place where a conference could be held about the confession which could lead to a revision of the *Belgic Confession (Confessio Belgica,* CB*)*.

After the death of Arminius in 1609, Johannes Uytenbogaert (1557–1644) and Simon Episcopius (1583–1643) became the leaders of the Arminians. The 'Arminian' views were systematized, opposing the emphasis on minutiae of doctrine and viewing Christianity primarily as a force for moral transformation.

In 1610 at the insistence of the eminent Dutch statesman from the states of Holland and a supporter of religious tolerance, Johan van Oldenbarneveldt (1547–1619), Uytenbogaert, Episcopius and forty-one of their sympathizers drew up a statement of their faith called the *Remonstrance* (Declaration), from which the party gained the name 'Remonstrants'. Van Oldenbarneveldt did not deem a national synod necessary and was of the opinion that the matter could be settled in the Province of Holland. The Remonstrance was directed to the states of Holland (see Nauta 1949, 52). The document was a summary of Arminius's views, a plea for a revision of the *Belgic Confession* and the catechism and an expression of their view that the states had the highest authority over ecclesiastical matters (see Bakhuizen van den Brink 1960, 290–293). In a separate publication Uytenbogaert also stated his opinion that the government stood higher than all ecclesiastical gatherings and as such should have the final say in ecclesiastical matters (see Blei 2006, 30).

The Calvinistic opposition under the leadership of people like Petrus Plancius in Amsterdam, Festus Hommius in Leiden and Sybrandus Lubbertus, a professor in Franeker, issued a Contra-Remonstrance on 11 March 1611 in which they opposed the views of the Remonstrants, rejected talk of a review of the confession and advocated the independence of the church to decide for itself on matters of dogma and doctrine. They recognized the authority of the government regarding matters external to the church but denied that it had the authority to express itself in ecclesiastical differences regarding doctrine (see Bakhuizen van den Brink 1960, 293–300; Bakhuizen van den Brink and Dankbaar 1967, 277; Nauta 1949, 53).

In more than one city the authorities favored the Remonstrants and made it very difficult for the Contra-Remonstrants. In the Province of Holland provincial synods had been prohibited since 1608 (see Nauta 1949, 53–54). On 23 July 1617 Prince Maurits openly attended a worship service of the Contra-Remonstrants in the Hague thereby showing his support for them (see Nauta 1949, 54). The conflict soon affected the whole of the Netherlands as it took on political dimensions, with sharp differences between Prince Maurits of Orange who sided with the Calvinists and Johan van Oldenbarneveldt and Hugo Grotius who sided with the Arminians. In political terms Prince Maurits sided with the so called 'national party' while Oldenbarneveldt and Grotius were the leaders of the 'states rights' party which also included wealthy merchants. At that point in time the 'national party' still desired a national synod to decide the controversy while Oldenbarneveldt and the provinces of Holland (excluding Amsterdam) and Utrecht held that each province should decide its own religious affairs. In 1617 the states of Holland declared themselves against a national synod through the so-called *Scherpe Resolutie* and took steps to maintain order in the cities through the deployment of city troops (see Bakhuizen van den Brink and Dankbaar 1967, 278). Realizing the danger of this event for the Union, Prince Maurits obtained the support of the States General and through a *coup d'etat* in July 1618 overthrew the 'states rights' party. Oldenbarneveldt was beheaded on 13 May 1619 and Grotius was condemned to life imprisonment in Loevestein. He escaped in 1621. The way was now open for the States-General to call the National Synod of Dordt of 1618–1619. The Contra-Remonstrants were assured of victory at the synod, but in the end it meant that future meetings of a national synod would also be subject to permission from the authorities; permission which was not to be granted for nearly 200 years, severely hampering the development of the Reformed Church in the Netherlands. In July 1619 the States-General approved the Canons of Dordt. The government then also cooperated in the execution of disciplinary measures against preachers of the Remonstant party who refused to resign as ministers. Those to whom the measures applied were banished from the country (see Blei 2006, 33). After the death of Prince Maurits in 1625 they returned and in 1634 established themselves in Amsterdam in a theological seminary with Episcopius as professor (see Nauta 1949, 56). They did not receive official recognition until 1795 (see Walker 1970, 400; Bakhuizen van den Brink and Dankbaar 1967, 278).

### 1.2 *The Ecclesiastical Context of the Church Order of Dordt*

To bring the various dispersed Dutch churches together in the sixteenth century, the Convent of Wezel was organized in 1568. This meeting is best understood as a discussion forum between refugee Dutch ministers and elders from various places in Europe and England. At this meeting they formulated, in accord with the *Ordonnaces Ecclésiastiques* of Geneva, certain stipulations for a Calvinistic church order (see Bakhuizen van den Brink and Dankbaar 1967, 273). The Convent of Wezel was followed by the first national synod of the Netherlands in the northern German city of Emden (1571). The church order of Emden founded the Dutch Reformed Church, ready to enter the Netherlands as soon as that country was free from Spanish oppression. The character of that church is seen by some as clearly Calvinistic. Others characterize it as presbyterian/anti-hierarchical (see Bakhuizen van den Brink and Dankbaar 1967, 273). Leo Koffeman sees it as presbyterial-synodical (see Koffeman 2009, 71), meaning that the responsibility for leadership in the church rests with the church councils: the local churches are the *presbyterium* while the broader meetings are the expression of the synodical character of this form of church government. The theology behind this form of church government is, according to Koffeman, the collegial exercise of authority by the offices in the church (see Koffeman 2009, 72). The very first article of Emden is extremely important if we want to understand the Reformed character of Reformed church government and eventually the nature of the Dordt church order (DCO). The way it is put in the church order of Emden reads: "No church shall lord over another church; no minister of the word over another minister, no elder over another elder, neither any deacon over another and everyone will be on guard for any suspicion and longing to lord". On the face of it this article forbids any lording of churches or offices over each other, but behind this wording lies the most fundamental principle of the reformation; namely, that Jesus Christ is the only Lord and Head of the church and none other. It is the insight of John Calvin and the wording of the *Belgic Confession* — "We believe that true church ought to governed according to the spiritual order that our Lord taught us in his Word" (CB, art. 30) — that lie behind Emden's wording (see Bakhuizen van den Brink 1960, 192; Calvin 1559, I, 317; CB, art. 30; Jonker 1965, 12; Pont 1981, 110). The church order of Emden also required that ministers subscribe to either the Dutch or the French confession of faith while either the *Genevan* or *Heidelberg Catechism* could be used for teaching purposes.

The National Synod of Dordrecht took place in the Kloveniersdoelen (see De Jong 1972, 189) in two phases. The first phase was from 13 November 1618 until 5/9 May 1619 (see Walker 1970, 400) while the second phase started on 13 May 1619 and ended on 29 May of the same year. In total the synod consisted of 180 sessions (see Pont 1981, 168). For the first phase the states invited twenty-three theologians as representatives from England, Scotland, Nassau, Wetterau, the Palatine, Hesse, Bremen, Geneva and Switzerland (see Berkhof 1975, 205). Representatives from the French church were also invited to attend but were refused permission by the French authorities. The government was represented by no less than eighteen political commissioners. Also present at the synod were five Dutch theologians, thirty-seven ministers and nineteen elders. Among those ministers and elders were three Remonstrants. The chairperson of the synod was Johannes Bogerman and the scribe was Festus Hommius (see ibid.). On 6 December a group of Remonstrant theologians was summoned to appear before the synod. They were joined by the three representatives who were already at the synod. When the Remonstrants questioned the procedure and legitimacy of the synod they were dismissed by Bogerman on 14 January 1619. A few days later the procedure was approved by governmental decree. The three Remonstrants representatives at the synod also left in solidarity with their fellow party members (see Blei 2006, 31; Bakhuizen van den Brink and Dankbaar 1967, 278; Berkhof 1975, 203). On 6 May 1619 the Canons (Doctrinal Rules) of Dordt were announced. They became the third confessional formula of the Reformed Church in the

Netherlands alongside the *Belgic Confession* (1561) and the *Heidelberg Catechism* (1563). In five chapters the Canons consider 'divine election and rejection', 'the death of Christ and salvation through Him', 'human depravity', 'conversion to God', and 'the perseverance of the saints' (cf. Blei 2006, 32).

In the second phase of the synod attention was given to matters like the church order and also the translation of the Bible. The church order was a revision of the church order of Middelburgh (1586). In broad lines the church order remained unchanged and the typical Reformed characteristics which were already present at the Synod of Emden remained: the offices in the church; the tasks and authority of ecclesiastical assemblies at the various levels; confessional matters; the administration of the sacraments and Sunday worship; and oversight and discipline in doctrine and way of life of church members and office bearers. The DCO concludes with the prescription with which the church order of Emden had begun: "No church shall have any authority over other churches, no minister over other ministers, no elder or deacon over other elders or deacons" (DCO, art. 84). Article 30, on the functions of the various levels of assemblies, had already been formulated by the Synod of Dordt of 1578 (see Blei 2006, 33).

Nauta remarks that at Dordrecht the Contra-Remonstrants gained a convincing victory over the Remonstrants but on one point they could not score and that was on the authority of the state over church matters (see Nauta 1949, 57). In the calling of a minister it was determined that a consultation with the local Christian government would be required. And after the choice had been made, subsequent approval had to be obtained not only from the members of the congregation but first from the same government (see art. 4). The government also obtained the right to have one or two of its representatives on church councils "to listen and to share in the deliberations of matters on the agenda" (art. 37). The governmental representatives of course had to be members of the congregation. A new article in the DCO was article 28 which dealt with the relation of the church to the government. The first part of article 28 stated that it was the office of a Christian government to advance and protect the ministry of the church. The second part of the article introduced a new emphasis into a Reformed church order whereby the vocation of the church in relation to the government was described as consisting of two matters: first, it was the duty of all ministers, elders and deacons to zealously and faithfully inculcate in the entire congregation obedience, love and honor owed to the magistrates (rulers); second, with becoming respect (and correspondence) the ministers, elders and deacons had to seek to waken and maintain the favor of the government toward the churches so that all second-guessing and mistrust could be avoided and concord be maintained for the well-being of the churches (see Blei 2006, 33–36).

### 1.3 *Preliminary Conclusion*

In regard to both the political and the ecclesiastical situations in the Netherlands we find that the relationship between church and state played an exceptional role. During the first part of the Synod of Dordt of 1618–1619—when doctrinal matters were on the table—it was the political situation that made it possible for the synod to be called. The States-General invited the international representatives, they ratified the decisions of synod, and they took disciplinary measures against the Remonstrants. We have also seen the extent to which the church was willing to write measures into the DCO giving the state very strong control over the church. It was in fact so strong that after Dordt 1618–1619 it was not possible for the Reformed Church to meet again in a national synod.

## 2. *The DCO in South Africa*

### 2.1 *Under the DEIC, 1652–1795*

On 22 August 1650 the Dutch East Indian Company (DEIC; *Verenigde Oostindische Compagnie*, VOC), i.e., the, decided that for the sake of greater security and refreshment for their ships they would start a settlement at the Cape of Good Hope (see Vorster 1956, 11).

In 1652, Jan van Riebeeck, an official of the Dutch East Company, together with about two hundred Company employees, landed at the Cape to start a refreshment post for the fleets of the Company that passed the Cape on their way to and back from the East (see Hanekom 1965, 290). Van Riebeeck was a member of the Reformed Church in the Netherlands and the Company which he served had, as a condition in its second charter of 1622, that it was Company policy to advance the Reformed religion among the peoples of the countries where they did business.

In fact, from 1652 to 1795 the responsibilities for religion and spiritual care of the people of the Cape resided with the Political Council under the leadership of the Commander (see Vorster 1956, 38). The DEIC appointed comforters of the sick and ministers in the various places. The ministers appointed by the DEIC were not in the first place ministers of the Reformed Church but officials of the Company who had a rank equal to that of a vice-merchant. The churches in the Netherlands could claim no rights with regard to comforters of the sick and ministers in the service of the DEIC (see Van Boetzelaar van Dubbeldam 1906, 119); they were subject to Company officials of higher rank than they. The commanders assumed the right to give comforters of the sick authority to administer baptism; they appointed and also dismissed ministers; comforters of the sick and ministers could receive no instruction from classes in the Netherlands other than those approved by the Lords XVII (see below); in any civil case they were subject to the authorities of the Company both on sea and on land; at any time the Lords XVII could recall them without giving reasons; they were allowed to correspond with a classis if the classis were involved in a matter, but the classis served only an advisory role.

The charter awarded to the DEIC on 22 December 1622 by the States-General gave the DEIC Board — consisting of seventeen administrators and therefore known as the 'Lords XVII' — full sovereignty with regard to navigation, trade and warfare in the areas to which they expanded but also obliged them to conserve the "public faith" (Vorster 1956, 11). In practice this meant that the DEIC or the Lords XVII also had full control over church matters in the places where they traded. Before describing what this meant in practice the question about which church order had authority at the Cape needs our attention.

The church order of Van Diemen had been accepted in 1643 for the East Indies. It was done by Van Diemen without any consultation with the fatherland. This church order determined that permission of the government was necessary for nearly any action by the churches, including the election of elders. The church in East India was completely controlled by the government (see Van Boetzelaar van Dubbeldam 1906, 139) and thereby effectively lost its freedom. Vorster makes a very strong case that the church order of Van Diemen was never used at the Cape of Good Hope and that it was rather the DCO 1619 that guided the life of the church at the Cape. In 1710, J. Martens, a visiting minister, suggested in a meeting with the Governor and the Rev. d'Ailly that the church order of Batavia (Van Diemen) might be used at the Cape since Batavia was geographically much nearer to the Cape, at least until further clarity was obtained (see Spoelstra 1907, 610). To this consideration the Rev. d'Ailly responded, "The Church Order can easily be found in the Acts and Post-acts of the Synod of Dordt — in exceptional cases they could however consult with the foreign brothers" (Spoelstra 1907, 612). Upon this the Political Council at the Cape decided on 10 March 1710 to ask the Lords XVII which church order must be used at the Cape — the one of the fatherland or the one of Batavia. On 30 March 1710 a letter was written to the Lords XVII; on 8 October 1710 they recognized receipt of the letter. The Lords XVII postponed their answer and eventually never responded. From the questions asked and the information given it is clear that the church at the Cape was satisfied to observe the DCO and that they did not really need anything else (see Vorster 1956, 83). It must however be clearly understood that the DCO was never officially accepted as a church order for the church at the Cape. The position was very similar to the situation in the Netherlands where the DCO was also not officially accepted by all the states of the union and also not by all the provincial synods. We know that the Classis of Amsterdam, which was responsible for all the overseas churches, did follow the DCO. Apart from the above-mentioned request there are also other indications in the life of the church at the Cape that they followed the DCO even though that church order was accepted neither by the States-General and all the provinces in the Netherlands nor was it applicable in all the synodical areas (see Bakhuizen van den Brink and Dankbaar 1967, 278). It is clear that the articles of Dordt were followed at the Cape with regard to preaching from the *Catechism*, house visitation before Holy Communion, and the subscription of teachers to the Confessions of Faith. When in 1743 there was the attempt to introduce a combined meeting of the different church councils at the Cape it was the DCO that guided the meetings from 1745 to 1759 (see Van der Watt 1976, 43f.).

However, in spite of all of these indications that the church at the Cape took the DCO into account, the facts remain that it was never officially accepted at the Cape and that the church was subjected to the rule of the DEIC in and through the Political Council. The DEIC protected the Reformed religion in the areas where they worked but they also clearly controlled the Reformed Church, just as the authorities in the Netherlands both protected and controlled the Reformed Church.

In 1689 the Political Council refused the request of the French refugees to install their own church council in Drakenstein (*Resolutie Pol. Raad,* 28 November, 1689). When the local churches constituted a combined meeting between them they had in mind a structure equal to a classis. When they informed the Classis of Amsterdam of their achievement they received praise and blessings. The Classis of Amsterdam did however advise them not to call the combined meeting a classis but rather a 'coetus' or a 'convention'—the reason being that they could not perform all the duties of a classis, such as the examination of candidates and ministers for the ministry or the appointment and installation of ministers. In answer to this the churches at the Cape decided to call their meeting a 'combined meeting'. In practice it performed the duties of a classis. In constituting the meeting they followed the prescriptions of the DCO and on their agenda they treated all the matters usually found on an agenda of a classis meeting. The combined meeting also decided to draw up bylaws for church visitation. In 1759 the combined meeting was suddenly prohibited by the Political Council at the Cape. The reasons they gave were that the costs for the meeting were too high and that the meeting did not restrict itself to its purpose (see Van der Watt 1976, 38). It was clearly an attempt by the Political Council to keep the church in a state of subordination. This decision had a serious impact on the development of the church in South Africa.

About the situation in the eighteenth century McCall Theal, as quoted by Vorster, writes: "The Church was in one sense merely an engine of the State, and was always and in every sense subordinate to the Council of Polity" (Vorster 1956, 39). Many more examples of the Political Council controlling ecclesiastical matters could be cited in addition to the matters mentioned above (see Vorster 1956, 39–43).

All of this attests to the fact that between the years 1652 and 1795 the Political Council at the Cape had a typically Constantinian approach towards the church in South Africa: one of not merely protecting the church but also controlling it, just as was the case in the Netherlands.

### 2.2 *After 1795*

After 1795 the rule of the DEIC at the Cape came to an end. It was followed by the first British occupation from 1795 to 1803. That was followed by the Batavian rule under Governor de Mist and, from 1806 on, English colonial rule. Under all these rulers the same approach with regard to the church was followed: they protected the church but they also controlled the church.

### 2.3 *The Synod of 1824*

The decision of the Political Council in 1759 to stop the meetings of the 'combined meeting' of churches clearly hampered the normal development of the church at the Cape because it was only in 1824 that the church received permission from the then- English authorities to hold a synod. In 1822 the three ministers of the church in Cape Town — Abraham Faure, Jan Christoffel Berrange and Johann Heinrich von Manger — wrote a letter to the Governor asking his permission to call a meeting of a synod or a general meeting according to the terms of the church order drawn up by De Mist (1804), article 46. Among the reasons they noted were that church councils and synods are the ways by which Presbyterian Churches are governed; further, it would help to overcome differences, advance religious education, and promote unity among the different ministers. Following the loss of support from the classes and synods in the Netherlands, it was argued, the ministers were more or less left to themselves and church councils had no 'higher' body to join. Also, the numbers of the Dutch Reformed Church were growing and an increasing number of previously-unknown religious bodies were making their appearance, which could disrupt the existing order. Permission was granted and the first synod of the Dutch Reformed Church met on 2 November 1824. In drawing up articles for the management of the church, the meeting took as its basis the *Algemene Reglement* (General Regulations) of the Reformed Church in the Netherlands, but when the Praeses and Scribe wrote to the Governor after the meeting they requested that the *General Church Order* of the National Synod of Dordrecht also be printed by the government press, "being a fundamental piece of all our regulations to which each of us is held" (Moorrees 1937, 554). Thus it is clear that in 1824 the DCO still played an important role in the mind of those gathered at the Synod of 1824.

### 2.4 *Ordinance 7 of 1843*

In 1843, the Church Ordinance of De Mist was replaced by the Ordinance Number Seven of 1843. This ordinance apparently made the church more free from control by the government in that political commissioners no longer took seats in church meetings and the church received the power to regulate its own internal affairs. The Ordinance was presented under the heading of 'The Separation of Church and State Petition'. Yet in practice the church remained subject to government in so far as the government controlled the church through the so-called 'power of the purse' and the privilege of presenting ministers to congregations. Furthermore the Ordinance restricted the church with regard to the character of its faith, its organization, its competence, and its geographical limits (see Kleynhans 1973, 80–84). It was generally accepted that Ordinance Number Seven of 1843 severely restricted the freedom of the church (see Van der Watt 1980, 44–46).

The Dutch Reformed Church in South Africa (The Cape Province) eventually decided on 21 October 1957 to ask the government to revoke Ordinance Number Seven of 1843: "The Dutch Reformed Church in South Africa declares and confirms its historical view that this church as an organized body had an independent existence in its own competence even though always subjected to the articles of law applicable to the church. Since the existence of the church is not dependent on the articles of law, Synod, given the legal advice which was obtained, mandates the Moderature to approach the authorities to revoke Ordinance Number Seven of 1843" (Kleynhans 1973, 95).

### 2.5 *11 February 1859*

One of the results of the Great Trek to the northern parts of South Africa during the third decade of the nineteenth century, and of providing pastoral care to the people there, was the eventual establishment of two other Reformed churches in South Africa: the Netherdutch Reformed Church (*Nederduitsche Hervormde Kerk*) on 1 November 1853, and the Reformed Churches in South Africa on 11 February 1859. On 12 January 1859 twelve persons signed a declaration of secession which they handed to the meeting of the General Council of the Church in the Transvaal. In the declaration they indicated that they wished to withdraw from the existing church community and to exist in the future as a Free Reformed Church according to the teaching, discipline and ministry of the fathers as revealed at Dordt in 1618. They also indicated that they would apply the DCO in accordance with the circumstances in which they lived (see Van der Watt 1977, 67, 84). Today this church is known as the Reformed Churches in South Africa. To this day its confessional base is still the three Formulae of Unity and its accepted church order is still the DCO — as amended for South African conditions (see Vorster 2008, 383; Vorster 2003, 2–9).

2.6 *1948*

In 1948 the Nationalist Party came into power and very soon after started to enforce its policy of apartheid on the whole of the country, including the churches. Of that time it cannot be said there was no tolerance of different faith convictions in the country or that churches did not have the freedom, for instance, to determine their own church orders, but all the while the government was controlling the churches through its policies. Sadly it must be said that in many cases Afrikaans-speaking churches not only subscribed to the policies of the government but also encouraged them. Even if there were certain freedoms for churches, the Constantinian approach of protect-and-control remained the main characteristic of church-state relations until 1994.

2.7 *Nov–Dec 1959*

In May 1959 the Council of Dutch Reformed Churches meeting in Bloemfontein accepted a concept church order for the government of the Dutch Reformed Church. Willie Jonker comments that this concept church order would not only serve as a basis for the organic unification of the Dutch Reformed churches in the different provinces of the country but that it would also serve to strengthen and establish the Reformed character of the church (see Jonker 1959, 795), enabling the church to be governed by the Word of God through its church order. He then points out that it was the explicit intention of the drafting commission that the new church order be linked as closely as possible to the DCO. He writes: "The church order of Dordt is without doubt the best and purest historical formulation and summary of the scriptural principles on which Reformed Church government rests in spite of a few articles which could be formulated in another way, due to the changes in time" (Jonker 1959, 796). He continues by saying that the Dutch Reformed Church, in spite of not having the DCO as a document, never lost the spirit and main principles of the DCO (see Ibid.). The new concept church order that was approved tried to stay as closely as possible to Dordt in its different chapters and sometimes even in the way in which articles were formulated (see Ibid.). It must of course also be kept in mind that the new church order of the Reformed Churches in the Netherlands (1957–1959) also had a big influence on the new church order of the Dutch Reformed Church. Nevertheless it can be said that the DCO, with its Reformed principles, formed and still forms the foundation of the church order of the Dutch Reformed Church. Jonker mentions a few points where he thought the church order of the Dutch Reformed Church could still be brought closer to the principles Dordt—for example, there should not be a permanent moderature following the meeting of synod (see Jonker 1959, 835). It is interesting that at the meeting of the General Synod in October 2011 exactly this change was approved in the church order, showing that the Dutch Reformed Church is continuously looking at its church order to bring it in line with Reformed principles of church government.

### 3. *New developments in South Africa*

In 1994/1996 a new *Constitution* for South Africa was approved. With the new *Constitution* a new era for church-state relations in South Africa started. Actually, not only new church-state relations started, but so did new relations between the state and religions as well as between religion and religion. In the *Constitution*, religion (churches) is dealt with in article 9(3) where it is stated there can be no discrimination against a person on grounds of religion. Article 31 says that persons belonging to a religious community have the right to enjoy and practice their religion, form, join and maintain religious associations and other organs of society. Article 185 provides for a 'Commission for the Promotion and Protection of the Rights of Cultural, Religious and Linguistic Communities'. Very important for religions in South Africa is article 15 of the *Constitution* which states: (first part) "Everyone has the right to freedom of conscience, religion, thought, belief and opinion;" (second part) "religious observances may be conducted at state-aided institutions, provided that (a) those observances follow the rules made by the appropriate public authorities; (b) they are conducted on an equitable basis and (c) attendance is free and voluntary". The third part of article 15 allows for marriages in South Africa to be concluded under any tradition or system of religious, personal or family law. Also important for religions is the fact that article 7(2) of the *Constitution* reads that "The state must respect, protect, promote and fulfill the rights in the Bill of Rights" (Constitution 1996). All of these are very strong securities and opportunities for religions in South Africa since 1994/1996. Added to all of this there is also article 234 of the *Constitution* which, in order to deepen the culture of democracy, allows for Parliament to adopt Charters of Rights consistent with the provisions of the *Constitution*. Religions in South Africa have taken up this challenge and in the past few years have developed a *South African Charter of Religious Rights and Freedoms* which they endorsed and are now are in the process of taking to Parliament. The Dutch Reformed Church has already decided to make the *Charter* part of its official documentation through inclusion in the *Church Order Book* of the church (see DRC 2011, 286).

Freedom of religion implies the right of religions to the free exercise of the religion, the right for a plurality of religions to exist in one country, the equality of all religions under the *Constitution* and before the laws of the land, the separation of religion and the state, and the disestablishment of religion by the state (see Witte 2000, 37). For a religion as such — be it a church or whatever other religion — freedom of religion entails institutionally that it has a right to: (i) a creed/creeds, which defines the accepted cadre of beliefs and values concerning the ultimate origin, meaning, and purpose of life; (ii) a cult, which defines the appropriate rituals, liturgies and patterns of worship and devotion that give expression to the beliefs; (iii) a code of conduct (one can call it a church order in the case of churches which defines the appropriate individual and social habits of those who profess the creed and practice the cult; and (iv) the right to be a confessional community, which defines the group/individuals who embrace and live out the creed, the cult, and the code of conduct, both on their own and with fellow believers (see Witte 1996, xxv).

### *4. In conclusion*

From 1652 to 1994 the state authorities in South Africa always had, to a greater or lesser degree, a say in the affairs first of the Dutch Reformed Church and later in the affairs of all churches in South Africa. It was a typical Constantinian situation whereby the state protected churches but at the same time also controlled them. Understanding this relationship between state and church in South Africa sheds a completely new light on the accusation, often made, that it was the church(es) through a theocratic relationship with the state that were responsible for the ideology and practice of apartheid. It was not theocracy — where the policies of the church indeed control society — but rather the Constantinian relationship between church and state that was largely responsible for the state ideology of apartheid. It must however also be recognized that the churches often asked the government for apartheid measures to be taken.

The new situation in South Africa for religions (since 1994/1996) brings about most definite freedoms not only for Christian churches but for all religions. At the same time it also brings certain obligations. It is of little avail for religions to have constitutional guarantees of freedom of religion and a *Charter of Religious Rights and Freedoms* spelling out the religious rights religions can claim if religions themselves do nothing to appropriate those rights. If religions do not claim and use the religious space provided for them in the *Constitution* and the *Charter of Religious Rights and Freedoms*, the consequence will be that any right that they claim will be adjudicated in terms of the laws of the land. A religion, for instance, cannot limit the rights of employees in labor relations if its own order gives proof that freedom of religion in labor relations has not been appropriated in its own rules. A religion also cannot claim special rights with regard to disciplinary hearings and, for instance, limit the rights of the accused with regard to legal representation if it does not show proof that it has used the right to freedom of religion in making sure its disciplinary hearings are done in accordance with its faith identity. All of this makes it very important for churches and religions to ensure that their church orders or rules of order conform to their faith identities. That is what the DCO intended to do with regard to the life of Reformed churches. Unfortunately the relationship between state and church did not always allow for that. Freedom of religion in a constitutional state creates the opportunity for a church or a religion to create its own order, as long as it can be shown that the order is based in the faith identity of the church or religion and that limitations on rights among its members are also in conformity with the church's faith identity. Also, for the Dutch Reformed Church there is now the guaranteed freedom to lay down its own rules for matters such as church unification, labor relations, disciplinary actions, theological training, etc. as matters of fact for the whole life of the church.

## *Abbreviations and bibliography*

CB: The Belgic Confession. In: This We Believe, Thus We Confess. The Doctrinal Standards of the Dutch Reformed Church. 2000. Harare: DRC Synod of Central Africa.

DCO: Dordt Church Order (1619)

DEIC: Dutch East Indian Company (Verenigde Oostindische Compagnie)

DRC 2011: Agenda vir die veertiende vergadering van die Algemene Sinode van die Nederduitse Gereformeerde Kerk. Birchwood Konferensiesentrum, Boksburg. Maandag 10 tot Vrydag 14 Oktober 2011.

Bakhuizen van den Brink, Jan N. (ed.). 1960. Documenta Reformatoria Dl 1. Teksten uit de Geschiedenis van Kerk en Theologie in de Nederlanden sedert de Hervorming. Kampen: Kok.

Bakhuizen van den Brink, Jan N., and Willem F. Dankbaar. 1967. Handboek der Kerkgeschiedenis, Deel III: Reformatie en Contra-reformatie. Den Haag: Bert Bakker — Daamen NV.

Berkhof, Hendrikus, and Otto J. de Jong. 1975. Geschiedenis der Kerk. Nijkerk: Callenbach. 9th edition.

Blei, Karel. 2006. The Netherlands Reformed Church 1571-2005. Translation Allan J. Janssen. Grand Rapids Mi — Cambridge: Eerdmans.

Calvin, John. 1559. Institusie van die Christelike Godsdiens. Translation H.W. Simpson,1991. Potchefstroom: Nasionale Media.

Constitution of the Republic of South Africa 1996. Act 108 of 1996.

De Jong, Otto J. 1972. Nederlandse Kerkgeschiedenis. Nijkerk: Callenbach.

Gaum, Frits, et al. (eds). 2008. Christelike Kern-Ensiklopedie. Wellington: Lux Verbi. BM — Bybelkor.

Hanekom, Tobias N. 1965. Afrika van Suid tot Noord. In: Wegener 1965, 281-301.

Jonker, Willem D. 1959. Die Nuwe Kerkorde, dl I, II and III. In: Die Kerkbode 18 November 1959, 759-796 and 800; Die Kerkbode 25 November 1959, 835-837; Die Kerkbode, 2 Desember 1959, 870-871 and 883.

Jonker, Willem D. 1965. Om die regering van Christus en sy kerk. Pretoria: Unisa.

Kleynhans, Ewert P.J. 1973. Die Kerkregtelike Ontwikkeling van die Nederduitse Gereformeerde Kerk in Suid-Afrika 1795 — 1962: 'n Kerkhistories-Kerkregtelike Studie. PhD diss., Universiteit van Stellenbosch.

Koffeman, Leo J. 2009. Het goed recht van de kerk: Een theologische inleiding op het kerkrecht. Kampen: Kok.

Moorrees, Adriaan. 1937. Die Nederduitse Gereformeerde Kerk in Suid-Afrika 1652-1873. Kaapstad: S.A. Bybelvereniging.

Nauta, Doede. 1949. Het Calvinisme in Nederland. Franeker: Wever.

Pont, Adrianus D. 1981. Die Historiese Agtergronde van ons Kerklike Reg. Deel 1. Pretoria — Kaapstad: HAUM.

Spoelstra, Cornelis. 1907. Bouwstoffen voor de Geschiedenis der Nederduitsche-Gereformeerde Kerken in Zuid-Afrika. Deel II. Amsterdam: Hollansch-Afrikaansche Uitgevers-Maatschappij.

Van Boetzelaar van Dubbeldam, Carel W. Th. Baron. 1906. De Gereformeerde Kerken in Nederland en de Zending in de dagen der Oost-Indische Compagnie. Utrecht: P. den Boer.

Van der Watt, Philip B. 1976. Die Nederduitse Gereformeerde Kerk 1652-1824. Pretoria: NG Kerkboekhandel.

Van der Watt, Philip B. 1977. Die Nederduitse Gereformeerde Kerk 1834-1866. Pretoria: NG Kerkboekhandel.

Van der Watt, Philip B. 1980. Die Nederduitse Gereformeerde Kerk 1824 — 1905. Pretoria: NG Kerkboekhandel.

Vorster, J.M. (Koos). 1956. Die Kerkregtelike Ontwikkeling van die Kaapse Kerk onder die Kompanjie 1652 — 1792. Potchefstroom: Pro Rege-Pers. Beperk.

Vorster, J.M. (Koos). 2003. An Introduction to Reformed Church Polity. Potchefstroom: Potchefstroom Theological Publications.

Vorster, J.M. (Koos). 2008. Gereformeerde Kerke in Suid-Afrika (GKSA). In: Gaum et al. 2008, 383.

Walker, Williston. 1970. A History of the Christian Church. Edinburgh: T.& T. Clark.

Wegener, Günther S. 1965. Die Lewende Kerk. Afrikaanse Uitgawe geredigeer en aangevul deur T.N. Hanekom. Kaapstad — Pretoria: Human and Rousseau.

Witte, John. 1996. Introduction. In: Witte and Van der Vyver 1996, XVII–XXXV.

Witte, John. 2000. Religion and the American Constitutional Experiment. Boulder: Westview.

Witte, John, and Johan D van der Vyver (eds). 1996. Religious Human Rights in Global Perspective: Religious Perspectives. The Hague: Martinus Nijhoff Publishers.

# DORDT IN THE USA AND CANADA

## Church Polity Challenges for North American Reformed Churches

Henry DeMoor

As one might expect, members of Dutch Reformed Churches who emigrated to North America carried the *Church Order of Dordt* (DCO) with them like they carried their family heirlooms—without question and without fanfare. The adoption of this document—Dordt's rules for the life of the church—seemed to them a perfectly natural and undisputed event necessitated by their assent to the creeds of the sixteenth century: the *Belgic Confession*, the *Canons of Dordt*, and the *Heidelberg Catechism*. The Reformed Church in America (hereafter: RCA), known at the time as the Reformed Protestant Dutch Church, translated the rules of church government of 1619 into English in 1792, adding 'explanatory articles' for purposes of 'adapting the rules to American conditions'. In 1833 the rules and explanatory articles were formed into a single document (imprecisely) called the 'Constitution'. From 1968 on they were taken up into the RCA's Book of Church Order (see CO-RCA, 6). History repeated itself in the latter half of the 19th Century when a new wave of immigrants found their way to Iowa and Michigan. These folks, after all, were followers of the *Afscheiding* or Secession of 1834 whose leaders had deliberately chosen to defy the 1816 state-imposed revisions and to return to the original DCO. The Christian Reformed Church in North America (hereafter: CRCNA), formed when several congregations became leery of an initial union with the RCA, adopted the DCO at its first 'classical assembly' (Dutch: "*classicale vergadering*") held in May of 1857. Certain 'general regulations' were subsequently adopted at the Synod of 1881 (in the Dutch language), also—as in the RCA—for purposes of adapting the order where necessary to the new homeland (CRCNA 1881, art.4).

The adoption of 'explanatory articles' and 'general regulations' already signals the fact that Dordt's provisions for church life were not viewed as laws of the Medes and Persians. There was an immediate contextual awareness. North American church leaders knew of John Calvin's distinction between particular practices and rules, on the one hand, and more 'general rules' on the other, where only the latter are clearly "drawn from Scripture" and, therefore, "wholly divine" (Calvin 1559, IV, 10, 30–32). Among these would be the basic pattern of church offices, assemblies, sacramental practices, Reformed worship and the exercise of church discipline. More specific regulations in each area were not legalistically followed in every jot and tittle but, instead, were viewed as flexible concretizations of principle in a particular context. Major revisions of the RCA 's *Constitution* were drawn up and adopted in 1874, 1910–1916, 1958–1959, and 1965–1968. Equally major revisions of the CRCNA 's *Church Order* were drawn up and adopted in 1914 (the first English edition), 1920, 1957–1965, and 1987–1991. Beyond these major revisions, lesser amendment of the order "is an almost annual process" (CO–RCA, 6) in both denominations.

Not surprisingly, the prevailing culture of the 'New World' immediately began to pose various challenges to this constitutional basis of the church. For the sake of brevity, I will limit myself to developments in the CRCNA, the denomination to which I belong, and mention just four areas of challenge that happen to correspond with the traditional subdivisions of the DCO: the Offices, the Assemblies, the Task and Activities, and the Discipline of the Church.

*The Offices*

It is an irony of CRCNA history that the denomination has sometimes viewed what is required by Scripture and creed as optional while at the very same time elevating the optional to the level of creedal necessity. An example of the former is the practice by some of infant dedication as an alternative to infant baptism. A good example of the latter occurred as the church took on the huge task of missionary outreach and church planting in the North American expanse. While everyone agreed this ought to be done, few agreed on how lay evangelists might be acknowledged as properly authorized organs of Christ's ministry. It had come to be a matter of principle that the church could have only three offices: minister, elder, and deacon. This ecclesiological extension of the *munus triplex* construct — first suggested by Kuyper and Bavinck — had become so engrained as an increasingly rigid theological presupposition, that the CRCNA found itself embroiled in bitter controversies over the status of lay evangelists for more than a half a century, beginning in 1910 (DeMoor 1986, 142–155). Should they be elders with a special task? Should they simply be believers with a special commission, not office? Should they be associate ministers? Heaven forbid they should be ministers of the Word if they haven't been educated enough! It was not until 1978 that synod officially put an end to these 'obstacles' by boldly creating a fourth office of evangelist (CRCNA 1978, 74–78, 534–555), later to be named 'ministry associate' (CRCNA

2003, 611), an umbrella office for missionaries, chaplains, church planters, and the like. So it is only in the last three decades that lay evangelists have finally and increasingly received the 'dignity and honor' (CO-CRCNA, art.2) their significant service deserves (DeMoor 1986, 205–224). The challenge for the denomination is to uphold the principle of the *Belgic Confession* (art. 30 and 31) that the ordained are organs of Christ's ministry, yet also remain flexible on the precise office structure that is most useful and relevant within an increasingly secularizing culture.

### *The Assemblies*

In early 17th Century Netherlands, a person was 'born into' a church and a church was 'born into' denominational ties with other churches. In 21st Century North America, persons and groups are sovereign consumers who voluntarily choose their relationships with others. People even use language that suggests they *choose* their nuclear family and must also *choose* their own religious affiliation (see Bellah et al. 1985, Bibby 1987). When I served the then *Gereformeerde Kerk* of Doornspijk in The Netherlands, in the 1980's, I noticed that believers in Oostendorp had to have obtained permission from the classis to continue worshiping in Doornspijk once a church was established in Elburg. In Grand Rapids, Michigan, where I currently live, folks don't ask permission. They just choose to pass by five or six congregations — in the same denomination or in another — in order to attend where they believe their needs will be better met. Membership papers follow in due time — if they are thought about at all. In the same way, congregations increasingly choose not to be designated as CRCNA, calling themselves the such-and-such Community church instead. So now the denomination has been forced to codify what would have been unthinkable in the culture of Dordt: that a congregation might just wish to disaffiliate and go independent; or, as an alternative, disband, or merge with another, revert to unorganized status, or join another denomination (CO-CRCNA, art. 38). Church ties are very fragile and no longer assumed. They are even tested in the courts of our lands when schism occurs and property and assets are at stake. So if our creedal position remains the same — that by God's sovereign grace we have been placed in a community of Christ, locally, regionally, and nationally, and unity is a given in Christ and thus assumed, not created, as the *Belgic Confession* teaches in articles 27 and 28, then the challenge will be to ensure that this unity be experienced, that there will be accountability to one another, as persons, as congregations and as groups of congregations.

### *The Task and Activities*

True to Dordt's article LVI, the Church Order of the CRCNA provides in its article 56 that "the covenant of God shall be sealed to children of believers by holy baptism". It is not an option on a menu of churchly rites. It is an insistence on a certain practice because it is called for in the creeds of the Reformation, most notably the *Heidelberg Catechism*, Lord's Day 27. This is not appreciated in many Christian quarters in North America. Such an insistence is considered 'narrow-minded' and exclusivist. The advertised position of the Peoples Church in Willowdale, Ontario, Canada says it well: "We dedicate children, baptize believers, and observe the Lord's Supper, but we do not make baptism a door to communion or church membership". The congregation does not even maintain an official, congregational membership roster. Any person can simply 'consider' Peoples Church his or her spiritual home and choose from among the smorgasbord of available worship rites and educational programs (see Patterson 1991). This is true in many generically evangelical churches in Canada and the USA. The problem, of course, is that infant dedication only speaks of what parents will do for God, not what God has done and is doing for us. Nothing speaks of God's grace quite as profoundly as the water of baptism administered in the sacrament to an uncomprehending child. Those who substitute dedication for baptism rob the entire congregation of an opportunity to celebrate the sacrament, to confess with amazement the mysteries of God's sovereign grace symbolically conveyed in cleansing water (see DeMoor 1994, 168–179). The challenge for the CRCNA is to withstand cultural pressures towards consumerism, manifest in evangelical circles, and insist on the historically Christian and Reformed practice of infant baptism (see DeMoor 2010, 307–315).

### *The Discipline of the Church*

There is one practice bequeathed to the CRCNA by the DCO that simply had to be abandoned. Dordt insisted on the 'three-step method' of disciplining the unrepentant: an initial 'silent censure', a first step of announcement and call for prayer *without* the name, a second step of announcement and call for prayer *with* the name, and a third step of publicly announcing the date of excommunication. For as long as immigrant congregations retained their exclusively Dutch traditions, this practice seems to have been followed in church life with some good effect. But as soon as the denomination began to diversify, drawing into itself a host of other people groups and cultures, it soon became obvious that discipline of members required a significant overhaul. In Native American, First Nation as well as numerous Asian subcultures, a public announcement revealing the name of an unrepentant sinner has the exact opposite effect than what discipline is supposed to accomplish: thoroughly shamed, the person in question will never see the inside of that church again. Dordt's method now guaranteed that reconciliation would not occur. After studying the matter at the synodical level, the CRCNA adopted an entirely new series of provisions for the ministry of discipline (CRCNA 1991, 715–723). While the mandate for it remains, the precise method of discipline is left to the local consistory. Above all, it is to be carried out in "a spirit of love and openness within the fellowship so that erring members may be led to repentance and reconciliation" (CO–CRCNA, art. 79). The challenge for the CRCNA is not to give up on discipline but to insist on mutual accountability in 'doctrine and life'. Only that will satisfy the creeds' requirement we do still share with the Synod of Dordt: the faithful exercise of the 'keys of the kingdom', namely, the "preaching of the holy gospel and Christian discipline toward repentance" (*Heidelberg Catechism*, Lord's Day 31).

In short, Reformed churches in North America, having assented to the three ecumenical creeds and the three sixteenth-century confessions will, in the midst of change aplenty, have to be vigilant about maintaining four principles that flow from those confessions: a high view of office, mutual accountability in ministry, faithful worship practice, and appropriate measures to uphold the holiness of the body of Christ.

As noted earlier, I have limited myself to developments in the CRCNA for the sake of brevity. It would be satisfying if similar processes of needed adaptations of church order in the Reformed Church in America or the Canadian Reformed Churches or, for that matter, any number of other 'transplanted' denominations or groups of congregations could be documented in further research and writing. We might learn from one another.

### *Abbreviations and bibliography*

CO–CRCNA: Christian Reformed Church in North America. 2012. Church order and its supplements. Grand Rapids MI: Christian Reformed Church in North America.

CO–RCA: The book of Church Order of the Reformed Church in America. 2012. New York: Reformed Church Press.

CRCNA 1881: Christian Reformed Church in North America. 1881. General regulations. Grand Rapids MI: CRCNA.

CRCNA 1978: Christian Reformed Church in North America. 1978. Acts of Synod. Grand Rapids MI: CRCNA.

CRCNA 1991: Christian Reformed Church in North America. 1991. Acts of Synod. Grand Rapids MI: CRCNA.

CRCNA 2003: Christian Reformed Church in North America. 2003. Acts of Synod. Grand Rapids Mi: CRCNA.
DCO: Dordt Church Order.

Bellah, Robert N. et al. (eds). 1985. Habits of the Heart. New York: Harper and Row.

Bibby, Reginald W. 1987. Fragmented Gods. Toronto: Irwin Publishing.

Calvin, John. 1559. Institutes of the Christian Religion. Two volumes. Edited by John T. McNeill. Translation Ford Lewis Battles 1960. Philadelphia: The Westminster Press — London: SCM.

DeMoor, Henry. 1986. Equipping the Saints. Kampen: privately published.

DeMoor, Henry. 1994. Erosion at the Font. In: Calvin Theological Journal 29(1994),168–179.

DeMoor, Henry. 2010. Christian Reformed Church Order Commentary. Grand Rapids Mi: Faith Alive.

Patterson, R.W. 1991. In search of the visible church. In: Christianity Today, 11 March 1991, 36.

# THE CHURCH ORDER OF DORDT (1619)

## and Church Polity/Church Order Contextualization Challenges in Reformed Churches in Indonesia

Lazarus H. Purwanto

### *A sketch of Protestant churches in Indonesia*

First of all, I would like to present in brief some general information about Indonesia, a country that is commonly called the 'Emerald of the Equator' (Shadily et al. 1982). Situated in South-East Asia with a width (5,150 km.) that stretches between the Pacific and Indian Oceans, bridging two continents (Asia and Australia), equal to the distance from Ireland to the Caspian Sea in Europe, Indonesia is the world's largest archipelago, with a total number of 17,508 islands. Indonesia has around 230 million citizens spread over more than 3,000 inhabited islands, making it the third most populated country in Asia and the fourth in the world. More than 60 percent of the population lives on the island of Java alone, which covers only 6 percent of the entire area of Indonesia. Another important point worth noting is Indonesia's extensive ethnic diversity: there are no less than 250 ethnic groups; at least twenty-five of them are the major ethnicities. It is also true with regard to culture and language: there are about 250 different languages and dialects spoken and written. Indonesia is enormously rich in culture and art: these are intertwined with religions and age-old traditions dating from the time of early migrants on the one hand to Western thoughts and cultural values initially brought by Dutch colonialists on the other. Finally, there is diversity in terms of its religion. There are five world religions – Islam, Catholicism, Protestantism, Hinduism and Buddhism—officially recognized in Indonesia. But, along with the variety of ethnic groups, there are different religions which have also been accepted and are called "traditional faiths" (*aliran kepercayaan*). Among all these religions and traditional faiths, Islam, having more than 80 percent of the Indonesian population as its followers, is the largest.

I will now introduce a general sketch of the Protestant church in Indonesia. In view of the wide-ranging variety of Protestant churches in Indonesia, I will follow the historical denominational grouping proposed by Dr. Th. van den End (Van den End 1995; cf. De Jonge 1998, 22–44, and Purwanto 1997, 11–15). Based on the historical background, Van den End divides the Protestant church in Indonesia in general into two major sections: a group of denominations which came from Europe and denominations that were historically rooted in the United States. Included in the second group of churches are Methodist, Baptist, "Faith Mission, " Pentecostal, Adventist, and the Salvation Army. The group of denominations from Europe is again divided into three groups. First is the group of Reformed/Calvinist churches with a Dutch Christian background. This group consists of two subgroups: churches that were set up by the Dutch colonial establishment (state church in character) and churches that were founded by various Dutch missions (either *hervormd* or *gereformeerd*). The second group consists of the Lutheran churches, comprising churches that were the fruits of the missionary works carried out by the Rheinische Missions-Gesellschaft from Germany and the Baseler Mission from Switzerland. These are, in fact, not purely Lutheran since Lutherans and Calvinists worked closely together in the two missionary societies. Thirdly, there are the Mennonite churches.

*Traces of the Church Order of Dordt in Reformed churches in Indonesia*

In this part the focus will be given to this question: what were the position and the role of the *Church Order of Dordt* (DCO) in Reformed churches — as part of Protestant churches — in Indonesia in terms of dealing with the churches' church polity/church order matters when they were established? In this regard, fortunately in Indonesia there is a good, complete Indonesian translation of the DCO available (Van den End 2000, 381–395).

To answer this question, I will sketch some observations about the church orders of several Protestant churches with European backgrounds. I have selected the following churches solely on the basis of data availability (i.e. the church orders concerned). I will briefly compare the first church orders of the churches (i.e. the church orders at the time the churches were established) to the DCO.

*A. Churches with gereformeerd Dutch missions background*

1. The Javanese Christian Church (*Gereja Kristen Jawa*; GKJ)

The first church order of the GKJ, adopted in 1932, was *The Order of the Christian Church in Southern Part of Java Island* (*Pranatan Pasamuwan Kristen in Tanah Djawi Tengah sisih Kidul*) (Purwanto 1997, 54–59). This church order, written in the Javanese language, was divided into four parts:

a. Concerning Offices in the Christian Church (*Bab Kaloenggoehan sadjroning Pasamoewan Kristen*)
b. Concerning Church Meetings (*Bab Parepatane Pasamuwan*)
c. Concerning Implementation of the Lord's Work in the Church (*Bab Tumindake Ajahane Gusti sadjroning Pasamuwan*)
d. Concerning Discipline in the Christian Way (*Bab Pamardi tjara Kristen*)

If we thoroughly read all of these parts, we can easily observe that *Pranatan Pasamuwan Kristen in Tanah Djawi Tengah sisih Kidul* comprehensively followed the DCO.

2. The Central Java Indonesian Christian Church (*Gereja Kristen Indonesia Jawa Tengah*; GKI JATENG)

The first church order of the GKI JATENG, entitled *The Church Order of the Synod of the Central Java Indonesian Christian Church* (*Peraturan Gereja Synode Gereja Kristen Indonesia Jawa Tengah*), was adopted in 1950 (Purwanto 1990, 3–5). The structure of the church order is as follows:

a. Church Offices (*Jabatan-jabatan Kegerejaan*)
b. Church Meetings (*Persidangan-persidangan Kegerejaan*)
c. Doctrinal Bases, Sacraments and Church Ceremonies (*Azas Pengajaran, Sakramen dan Upacara Kegerejaan*)
d. Church Discipline (*Siasat Kegerejaan*)

If we read the whole *Peraturan Gereja Synode Gereja Kristen Indonesia Jawa Tengah* we can easily conclude that this particular church order was nothing other than an adapted translation of the DCO.

3. The North Sumatra Indonesian Christian Church (*Gereja Kristen Indonesia Sumatra Utara*; GKI SUMUT)

The first church order of GKI SUMUT, adopted in 1969, was *The Polity of the North Sumatra Indonesian Christian Church* (*Hukum Gereja Kristen Indonesia Sumatra Utara*). The arrangement of the church order is as follows:

a. Church Offices (*Jabatan-jabatan Kegerejaan*)
b. Church Meetings (*Persidangan-persidangan Kegerejaan*)
c. Doctrinal Bases, Sacraments and Liturgy (*Azas Pengajaran, Sakramen dan Upacara Kegerejaan*)
d. Church Discipline (*Siasat Kegerejaan*)

If we look at *Hukum Gereja Kristen Indonesia Sumatra Utara* as a whole, we will find that this church order was taken over from the DCO, possibly indirectly.

*B. Churches with state church background*

1. The Protestant Church in West Indonesia (*Gereja Protestan di Indonesia bagian Barat*; GPIB)
The GPIB was established in 1948. The first church order of the GPIB was *The Church Order for the Protestant Church in West Indonesia* (*Kerkorde voor de Protestantse Kerk in Westelijk Indonesië*). This church order was set up not in a vacuum but in reference to the ongoing process in the Netherlands Reformed Church (*De Nederlandsche Hervormde Kerk*; NRC) at that time as it was arranging its new church order (Draft Church Order NRC 1947; *Ontwerp voor een kerkorde der Nederlandsche Hervormde Kerk 1947*). As a result, if we compare the *Kerkorde voor de Protestantse Kerk in Westelijk Indonesië 1948* to the *Ontwerp voor een kerkorde der Nederlandsche Hervormde Kerk 1947*, we see that the two have a lot in common, not only in terms of outline or structure, but also in terms of basic ideas and formulation (Purwanto 1997, 16–25). Thus, there is no direct influence of the DCO on the *Kerkorde voor de Protestantse Kerk in Westelijk Indonesië 1948*.

2. The Evangelical Christian Church in Timor (*Gereja Masehi Injili di Timor*; GMIT)
The first church order of the GMIT, approved in 1949, was The Order of the Evangelical Christian Church in Timor (*Peratoeran Geredja Masehi Indjili di Timor*). If we compare this to the first church order of the GPIB, we can say in general that the latter followed the former in terms of structure and content. This is understandable since both churches, though they were independent churches, belong to the uniting Protestant Church in Indonesia (*de Protestantse Kerk in Indonesia*; GPI) (Purwanto 1997, 18–20). Therefore we can conclude that *Peratoeran Geredja Masehi Indjili di Timor 1949* was indirectly following *Ontwerp voor een kerkorde der Nederlandsche Hervormde Kerk 1947*. Thus, as in the GPIB, here we cannot see any direct influence of the DCO.

*Some remarks on church polity/church order contextualization challenges*
Having the above observations in mind, I will put forward my remarks on the contextualization efforts of church polity/church order in the Protestant churches in Indonesia in general.

*Calvinist traditions*
In general, the Protestant churches in Indonesia inherited and thus have been influenced by the Calvinist church order traditions (De Jonge 1998, 115–145). As we have seen in the above survey, in some churches the inheritance and influence of Calvinist traditions were obtained directly from the DCO by the first church

orders of those churches when they were established. The first challenge that arises is the perspective of traditionalism among the churches, through which certain ecclesiastical traditions — including church order — have been made sacred and used as the main lens through which to view and develop their ecclesial lives and services. Given that each church order essentially has the nature of being "bound by space and time, " every church in Indonesia is thus challenged to develop a contextual and functional church order for the sake of a transformation process (Purwanto 1990, 18–21; Purwanto 1997; Koffeman 2010A, Koffeman 2010B).

*Transformation processes*

Church order issues in Indonesia should be placed precisely within the framework of the churches' presence and missional function in accordance with God's mission and calling in Christ through the power of the Holy Spirit. The main challenge for the church is how to become a church with a strong divine-human identity in order to fulfill its mission in Indonesia. Basically, this involves processes of transformation. Such transformation processes should be the primary concern for the being and the functioning of the church as the church of God in Indonesia in the midst of a rapidly changing situation. A church order in itself does not contribute directly and operationally to the transformation processes. But every church order should be able to provide an adequate constitutional and structural basis for continuity in the transformation processes. In this regard, every church order in Indonesia must also undergo a process of transformation in itself that must be done through contextualization efforts (Purwanto 1990; Purwanto 1997).

*Church order as ordering of the offices*

The DCO, as in the other older Calvinist church orders, focuses mainly on the regulation of ecclesiastical offices in the life of the church (Van 't Spijker 1992, 97–101). This tradition has inevitably been inherited by the Protestant churches in Indonesia in general. This has resulted in the Reformed-Calvinist church orders in Indonesia being dominated by the ecclesiastical position and function of the office-bearers. We cannot leave the church order situation just like this. We are challenged to re-arrange the ecclesiastical offices proportionally and effectively by putting them into the church's overall contextual struggle to find its identity. In short, we can say that the arrangement of ecclesiastical offices should be placed within the framework of an appropriate theology of the people. In this view, the place, function and authority of church offices should be formulated within the framework of the place, function and authority of all believers as God's people (Purwanto 1997).

*Missional church order*

From its historical context we can fully understand that a missional aspect is (nearly) missing in the DCO. Because the DCO was based on and dominated by ecclesiastical office, it goes without saying that the ministerial services were arranged to be performed only by the church's office-bearers, and they were all directed inward to the life and welfare of the church (doctrine, the sacraments and ceremonies). As has been touched on above, one of the fundamental and biggest challenges facing the churches in Indonesia, including the Protestant churches, is how to become God's church in carrying out its mission in the midst of and for the nation or the people of Indonesia. Therefore, it is a challenge for the churches that inherited the DCO (whether directly or indirectly) to reconstruct or renew their church orders so that the church orders can support a functional means of service by the church as a whole (not only that of office-bearers), in order to realize the churches' mission in Indonesia (Purwanto 1990, 30–34; Koffeman 2010A).

*Local church (congregation) as basis*

One of the strengths of the DCO, patterned by the presbyterial-synodical system of church government, is that the local church forms the basis of the system of broader structures. In its development in Indonesia, we can find many variants of the presbyterial-synodical system of church government. For the churches in Indonesia, the system should be viewed only as a way of structuring the church. The system is a means, nothing more and nothing less. It is definitely not a goal. With this perspective, every Calvinist church in Indonesia, taking into account seriously the system as part of the ecclesiastical tradition it has inherited, should manifest itself in a structural and governmental arrangement that is considered most suitable. In this instance, the view that the local churches make up the organizational basis is a strong starting point. The issue then is how a Calvinist Indonesian church can contextually and properly define and formulate a self-manifestation or self-definition and its organization in all of its scopes and/or levels.

*Parity of ecclesiastical offices*

The DCO is anti-hierarchical in character. This is another strength of the DCO. There is in it the principle of parity (equality of position) among all ecclesiastical office-bearers. This particular principle basically gives no room for the concentration of authority in a certain ecclesiastical office-bearer or a particular church institution/board. In Indonesia the churches are faced with a question: if we regard this as a positive principle, how and to what extent should we adhere to it? This question arises not only for the churches that live in societies with a hierarchical world-view, such as the Javanese community, but also for churches with a more or less non-hierarchical community background. In fact, there are churches which are inclined to have and develop their own system that are more hierarchical or synod-centralized. In all likelihood, there are at least two reasons for this development. On the one hand, there is the attitude and practice of the foreign missionaries in the past in assuming their position and the decision-making processes above (beyond?) the local church office-bearers/ leaders. On the other hand, there is the Indonesian cultural background that is characterized by feudalism and paternalism. The bottom line is that this issue should be resolved by the churches in their ecclesiological construction as they self-manifest or self-define. In this respect, the churches should firmly hold the anti-hierarchical character of the DCO.

### *Collegial-collective church leadership*

The leadership functions in the DCO are carried out in the institution of (local) church councils and church meetings/proceedings. We can say that the nature of the leadership institution and the church meetings is collegial-collective. This is also a strength of the DCO. We have to note that the collegial-collective nature of church leadership is correlated with the principle of parity of the ecclesiastical offices. An issue will naturally emerge if the principle of anti-hierarchy and the principle of collegial-collective leadership are abandoned by the Indonesian churches that purposefully set up a hierarchical and/or centralized system of church order: it will lead to serious ecclesiological problems that must be resolved properly. This places even more stress on the importance of contextual struggles of every Calvinist church in Indonesia to seek a relevant and effective church order. The emergence of new variants of the presbyterial-synodical system will enrich the treasures of church order in Indonesia, if the contextualization efforts are mainly directed to the proper functioning of the churches in Indonesia in the processes of continuous transformation.

## *Abbreviations and bibliography*

DCO: Dordt Church Order
NRC: Netherlands Reformed Church

De Jonge, Christiaan. 1998. Apa Itu Calvinisme? Jakarta: BPK Gunung Mulia.
Koffeman, Leo J. 2010A. Requirements for an Academic Approach of Church Law. First Lecture at Sekolah Tinggi Teologi Jakarta on March 17. Unpublished.

Koffeman, Leo J. 2010B. Challenges to Church Law in the 21st Century. Second Lecture at Sekolah Tinggi Teologi Jakarta on March 18. Unpublished.

Purwanto, Lazarus H. 1990. Towards the Church Polity with the Indonesian Perspective. Master Thesis. The Theological University of the Reformed Churches in the Netherlands. Kampen: unpublished.

Purwanto, Lazarus H. 1997. Indonesian Church Orders under Scrutiny: The Relation between the Church Members and the Church Office-bearers: How it is and how it should be. PhD diss., Theologische Universiteit Kampen. Kampen: Van den Berg.

Shadily, Hassan, et al. (eds). 1982. Indonesia. In: Ensiklopedi Indonesia. Vol. 3. Jakarta: Ichtisar Baru-Van Hoeve, 1418-1439.

Van den End, Thomas. 1995. Denominasi-denominasi Protestan di Indonesia. In: Koinonia Buletin PERKI se-Eropa, Easter Edition 1995, 58-74.

Van den End, Thomas. 2000. Tata Gereja Belanda 1619 (Tata Gereja Dordrecht). Enam Belas Dokumen Dasar Calvinisme. Jakarta: BPK Gunung Mulia, 381-395.

Van 't Spijker, Willem. 1992. De opvattingen van de reformatoren. In: Van 't Spijker and Van Drimmelen 1992, 86-103.

Van 't Spijker, Willem, and Leen C. van Drimmelen (eds). Inleiding tot de studie van het kerkrecht. Kampen: Kok. 2nd edition.

# CANON LAW AND COVENANT IN ANGLICANISM

Norman Doe

The church has always had norms of conduct designed to assist its mission and witness to Jesus Christ. Alongside the normative texts of scripture and liturgy the church also has its law-books. Recent years have witnessed a rising tide of interest in these — the study of the internal laws and other regulatory instruments of Christian churches (ecclesionomology) as distinct from study of other traditions of religious law (such as Jewish Law or Islamic law), and religion law (i.e. national State laws and international laws on religion). Today, learned societies, university courses and secondary literature are growing to promote the study of systems of canon law (such as in the Catholic and Orthodox traditions), as well as systems of church order (such as in the Reformed Protestant traditions) — and a similar trend may be discerned within global Anglicanism. This article examines elements of the legal systems of Anglican churches (the so-called provinces of the Anglican Communion), as well as two related developments in the last ten years — the articulation of principles of canon law common to the churches of the Anglican Communion, and the move towards adoption by each church of the Anglican Communion Covenant. The article also sets these three Anglican phenomena in the wider context of other Christian traditions and draws some conclusions about the role of law in the wider ecumenical enterprise.

## *I. The legal systems of Anglican churches*

At international level, the Anglican Communion has no formal body of law applicable globally to its forty-four churches in communion with the See of Canterbury. Whereas each church is autonomous (with its own legal system), the Communion is held together by 'bonds of affection': shared loyalty to scripture, creeds, baptism, Eucharist, historic episcopate, and its institutional instruments of communion — Archbishop of Canterbury, Lambeth Conference, Anglican Consultative Council, and Primates' Meeting; but these cannot make decisions binding on churches. Instead, law operates at the level of each provincial, national or regional church. Within each church, general law, typically provincial, is created by a synod or other assembly representative of bishops, clergy and laity, and laws made at more localised levels (such as diocesan law created by the diocesan synod of bishop, clergy and laity) must be consistent with the general law. Some churches have a code of canons only, but most have a constitution, canons, and other regulatory instruments, including rules, regulations, and liturgical norms found in the service books. Alongside written laws are less formal sources, such as customs, decisions of church courts, or, more rarely, the English Canons Ecclesiastical 1603, or even pre-Reformation Roman canon law. In addition, churches today increasingly use ecclesiastical quasi-legislation — informal administrative rules designed to supplement formal laws; these resemble laws (with prescriptive language) but may not bind in the same way as laws properly so-called.

Typically, *constitutions* deal with faith and doctrine, governmental and institutional organisation (legislative, administrative, judicial), appointment of bishops, discipline, and property; and *canons* address functions of ordained and lay ministers, and liturgical and sacramental matters. However, the law has its limits: it cannot encompass all facets of ecclesial life; and it functions predominantly in the public sphere of church life. In turn, the purposes of law are shaped by how each church sees the church universal (ecclesiology) and itself as an institution (its ecclesiality). Consequently, there is an intimate relationship between church law and theology. Whilst Anglicans have not yet developed a systematic theology *of* canon law, they often recognize theology *in* canon law. Nevertheless, law is the servant of the church with a theological foundation, rationale and end, intended to express these publicly along with the practical policies of a church; and law exists to uphold the integrity of the faith, sacraments, and mission, protect ecclesial order, support communion among the faithful, put into action Christian values, and prevent and resolve conflict. As such, church law should reflect the revealed will of God, and laws often present scripture as the ultimate standard and rule in matters of faith; but there is no clear evidence of a general Anglican practice that divine law vitiates contrary canon law.

At the practical level, laws define the rights and duties of the institutions and members of each church (and as such clarify roles and responsibilities). However, in some churches the laws bind only ordained ministers, but in others they bind both ordained and lay persons. Often church members must undertake to comply with the law, and in all churches canonical obedience requires clergy to obey the lawful and honest directions of their bishops. For the resolution of conflict, courts and tribunals are ordered hierarchically and their jurisdictions carefully prescribed; and failure to comply with law may result in proceedings before these for offences and the imposition of sanctions (typically seen as medicinal and corrective, such as rebuke, suspension and exclusion). Finally, other than the established Church of England, most Anglican churches function in civil law as voluntary associations — their internal rules have the status of terms of a contract entered into by the members (the doctrine of consensual compact) and are enforceable in matters of property in State courts (see Doe 1998a).

### *II. Principles of canon law common to Anglican churches*

Whereas at the global level ecclesial communion has been maintained historically in Anglicanism by non-juridical 'bonds of affection' and the persuasive authority of the instruments of communion (Archbishop of Canterbury, etc), recent tensions in the Communion have stimulated discussion of the ways in which the laws of churches may contribute to more visible international ecclesial unity in Anglicanism. In March 2001, on the basis of a paper discussed at the event (see Doe 2002, cf. Doe 2003), the Primates' Meeting decided to explore whether there is an unwritten common law (or *ius commune*) shared by the churches of the Communion. An Anglican Communion Legal Advisers Consultation meeting in Canterbury in 2002 tested and then accepted the hypothesis. In April 2002, the Primates' Meeting discussed a report on the Consultation and concluded: "The Primates recognized that the unwritten law common to the Churches of the Communion and expressed as shared principles of canon law may be understood to constitute a fifth 'instrument of unity'". Later in 2002 the Anglican Consultative Council (ACC) welcomed the establishment of a Network of Anglican Legal Advisers to produce 'a statement of principles of Canon Law common within the Communion' and in October 2003, the Primates' Meeting urged completion of the work as did the Lambeth Commission in 2004. A Network drafting group met in 2005 and 2006, and after extensive consultation *The Principles of Canon Law Common to the Churches of the Anglican Communion* (Rees 2008) was launched at the Lambeth Conference in 2008. In 2009, the ACC expressed its gratitude to the Network for its work, commended the Principles for study in every province, invited the provinces to submit comments on the document, requested a report on these, and encouraged provinces to use the Network as a resource in dealing with legal issues in those provinces.

The Legal Advisers Consultation, at Canterbury 2002, formulated six conclusions which became fundamental to the project (cf. www.acclawnet.co.uk).

First, "there are principles of canon law common to the churches within the Anglican Communion". In point of fact, the category 'the principles of canon law' had previously been formally recognised by at least four Anglican churches (West Indies, Const. art. 6.2(1); Southern Africa, Can. 50; Central Africa, Can. 32.1; Nigeria, Const., art. XIX.v) as well as by other churches (cf. CIC, c. 9; CCEO, c.

1501). Moreover, many churches in the Communion explicitly appeal to principles in their own laws, as the foundation for more detailed rules, giving the latter shape, coherence, meaning and purpose. Principles of canon law tend to be in the nature of general propositions or maxims, expressing fundamental ecclesial or theological values, and rooted in the inherited canonical tradition. Principles differ from *rules* (particular norms), enjoy a dimension of weight, and may be shared with secular legal systems.

Secondly, "the existence of the principles can be factually established". The principles of canon law are induced from the profound factual similarities between the actual laws of each church. Their recognition is a scientific task—an exercise in careful observation and comparison of legal texts. Often legal similarities are generated by the churches using a common historical source, such as a Lambeth Conference resolution, rubrics of the *Book of Common Prayer 1662*, or even the *Canons Ecclesiastical 1603*.

Thirdly, "each church contributes through its own legal system to the principles of canon law common within the Communion". The Anglican *ius commune*, as the collective effect of similarities between legal systems, is not imposed from above. The immanence of common principles in actual legal similarities means that each church is the legislator of the *ius commune*. Whenever a church legislates, it contributes to the store of principles and its law may function as a precedent for other churches. Whilst churches are autonomous, as a matter of practice they often adopt or adapt provisions in the legal systems of fellow churches; and unilateral legislative adoption from another church may augment the authority of the principle.

Fourthly, "the principles have a strong persuasive authority and are fundamental to the self-understanding of each church in the Communion". Whilst most principles may derive from similarities between written laws, some are based on unwritten assumptions implicit in written laws, and frequently churches portray a legal principle as having a deeper authority, beyond that of the formal law in which it appears. For instance, the former Church of India, Pakistan, Burma and Ceylon, under the heading 'Of the authority of the principles and customs set out in the preceding Declarations' says that the church has received these 'from the Holy Catholic Church of ages past' and 'believes that is was by the guidance of the Holy Spirit that those principles came to be recognised and those customs adopted' (Constitution [1930], Declaration 11). Accordingly, the principles have the appearance of laws (they may be perceptive, prohibitive, or permissive), but they are not themselves laws: they are principles of law.

Fifthly, "the principles have a living force, and contain in themselves the possibility of further development". The idea here is that each church through its own legislative activity may contribute to or subtract from the store of principles, particularly when such developments are replicated around the Communion. For example: churches are increasingly legislating to forbid racial discrimination in church membership and government; also, churches are developing rules on the admission of the unconfirmed to Holy Communion, particularly children. Such examples may indicate the evolutionary character of the *ius commune* of the Anglican Communion.

Finally, "the existence of the principles both demonstrates unity and promotes unity within the Anglican Communion". The principles might be perceived by some as a threat to the autonomy of the member churches, or as a stimulus for global divisions (cf. Jones 2005, 117). However, the principles are themselves a product of the exercise of the autonomy of churches and of their promotion of communion through their contributions to the statement in which they are articulated. Provincial autonomy is unaffected: as we have seen, churches remain free legally to depart from or to add to them. Indeed, that legal systems converge in shared principles of canon law is a concrete expression of the very character of Anglicanism, its commitment to the values presented in them, and, in so far as each church contributes to them, the individual responsibility of each church for the shape and maintenance of Anglican identity. Indeed, first principles may be a useful resource for churches seeking to reform their own legal systems (cf. *Bentley v Anglican Synod of the Diocese of New Westminster* [2009], Supreme Court of British Columbia, 1608).

The Legal Advisers Consultation 2002 agreed broadly (but was not overly exercised by the issue) that a number of tests may be formulated to establish whether a principle is one common to the churches, like: unanimity, majority, face validity, reversal, common source, canonical tradition; fundamental ecclesial value; theological dimension; perception; consensus (cf. Rees 2008, 101). *The Principles of Canon Law Common to the Churches of the Anglican Communion* provides that: "A 'principle of canon law' is a foundational proposition or maxim of general applicability which has a strong dimension of weight, is induced from the similarities of the legal systems of churches, derives from the canonical tradition or other practices of the church, expresses a basic theological truth or ethical value, and is about, is implicit in, or underlies canon law" (Rees 2008, 95). The hundred principles in the document are arranged under eight Parts; together, the hundred macro-principles consist of over six hundred micro-principles. Part I, 'Church Order', deals with the necessity for law in ecclesial society, law as the servant of the church, the conditional nature of church law, the sources, subjects and forms of church law, the rule of law in the church, the requirement of authority, and the effect, application, and interpretation of law. Part II concerns 'The Anglican

Communion' and includes principles relating to the nature of the Communion, the instruments of communion, provincial autonomy, mutual respect, juridical presumptions, and the mutual availability of ministrations. Principles of 'Ecclesiastical Government' are in Part III on: polity, leadership and authority, administration, delegation, representative government, legislative competence, lay participation in church government, visitations, and judicial process in courts and tribunals. Part IV carries principles of 'Ministry': the threefold ordained ministry of bishops, priests and deacons; primates, archbishops, admission to the episcopate, the ministry of diocesan and assistant bishops, ordination, authority to minister in a diocese, ministry of priests and deacons, termination of ordained ministry; and the laity, church membership rolls, rights and duties of the faithful, lay ministers and officers and professional and personal relationships in ministry. 'Doctrine and Liturgy', Part V, includes principles on profession of the faith, sources and development of doctrine, preaching, teaching and outreach, doctrinal discipline; and public worship and liturgy — making and authorising forms of service, the administration of public worship, and liturgical discipline. Principles on baptism, confirmation, Holy Communion, marriage, confession and burial are in Part VI, 'Ecclesiastical Rites'. Part VII contains principles about 'Church Property' including ownership and administration, places of worship, clergy residences, registers and records, the distribution and control of funds, sources of income, investments, insurance, and clergy stipends and pensions. The final section, Part VIII on 'Ecumenical Relations', features principles relating to ecumenical responsibilities, freedom, recognition, agreements, collaboration, admission and reception as well as the admission of non-Anglicans to Holy Communion.

Other than the sections on church order, and the Anglican Communion, the grouping of principles into these Parts is conditioned by the systematisation of laws employed by the churches of the Communion, treating as they do governance, ministry, doctrine and liturgy, rites, property and, increasingly, ecumenical relations. The principles are derived from various sources. Most are from constitutions and canons, and many from the liturgical norms of service books (which themselves enjoy canonical authority), like Principle 69, on the nature of marriage. Others are derived from:

› historical sources (the authority of which may be canonically recognised by the churches), such as the *Book of Common Prayer 1662*; e.g. Principle 64.6, on baptism and confirmation of mature persons;
› the canonical tradition; e.g. Principle 25.6: *nemo iudex in sua causa* (an aspect of judicial impartiality);
› divine law; e.g. Principle 47.2, on the duty to proclaim the Gospel; or

› the practice of the church universal; e.g. Principle 60.1, on that baptism effects incorporation into the church of Christ.

Others are rooted in

› a theological idea expressed in laws, like Principle 53, on worship as a fundamental action of the church; or
› from guidance issued by ecclesiastical authorities to supplement church law, like Principle 43, on the professional ethic of public ministry.

Whilst the vast majority derive from similarities between the written laws of churches, some are based on unwritten assumptions, general propositions implicit in church laws. The juridical values of clarity, conciseness and consistency govern the form of the principles which themselves are cast in a variety of juridical formulae: most are permissions ('may'), many are precepts ('shall', 'must'), some are prohibitions ('shall not', 'no-one shall'); many are exhortations ('should': aspirational), and some maxims ('is').

The document *The Principles of Canon Law Common to the Churches of the Anglican Communion* has appeared at a time of great tension in the worldwide Anglican Communion. However, this project might have been undertaken, with the exactly the same results, at any time. The underlying idea is not revolutionary. For the most part, the document is simply a statement or description of facts derived from the convergences of Anglican legal systems. The *ius commune* is not a 'top-down' binding global legal system imposed by a central Anglican authority (none is competent to create such a system) but a 'grass-roots' development growing from the exercise by each church of its own autonomy through its legal system. The statement clearly shows how much Anglicans share in common, using law as the medium. The principles also provide an accessible resource for ecumenical partners in developing their own understanding of Anglicanism from a global perspective. As such, the *ius commune* enriches rather than undermines traditional Anglican ecclesiology (cf. Cameron 2008, 69).

### *III. The Anglican Communion covenant*

The Primates' Meeting in 2001 considered a paper which (along with the principles of canon law project) proposed adoption of 'a concordat for incorporation by individual churches in their own canonical systems' (cf. Doe 2002, 241, 262). The Lambeth Commission on Communion was established in 2003 to address 'the legal and theological implications' of the decisions of the Episcopal Church (USA) to select a priest in a committed same sex relationship as one of its bishops, and of the Diocese of New Westminster (Canada) as to services for use in connection with same sex unions; its mandate was also to make "practical recommendations for maintaining the highest degree of communion possible in the circumstances resulting from these decisions" (TWR, 13, Mandate 1 and 2). Amongst other things, its *Windsor Report* (2004) proposed the adoption by the churches of the Anglican Communion of a covenant, in order to increase the profile of communion, to define their inter-church relations, and for the resolution of inter-Anglican conflict (cf. Doe 2002). The report included a draft covenant (WDAC, cf. TWR, Appendix Two, 81; cf. Doe 2004, 147). *Towards an Anglican Covenant*, published in 2006 to take the proposal forward, was endorsed later that year by the Joint Standing Committee of the ACC and Primates' Meeting. A Covenant Design Group was set up, offered its first draft covenant in 2007 (the Nassau Draft Covenant), and following a provincial consultation in 2007 revised this in its St Andrews draft covenant in 2008 (see Doe 2008). The latter was discussed at the Lambeth Conference in the summer of 2008. The Covenant Design Group met in September 2008 to consider the reflections of the Lambeth Conference and produced its Ridley-Cambridge draft in 2009. Section 4 of this draft was revised after discussion of it by the ACC in May 2009. Once the Standing Committee of the Anglican Communion agreed the final text in December 2009, the Anglican Communion Covenant was circulated to the churches of the Communion for ratification or rejection in accordance with their own particular formal processes (cf. TACC:ASG, TACC:QAA).

Whilst the Windsor Report did not define 'covenant' for the purposes of its proposal, the idea emerged from subsequent consultations that a covenant is a solemn agreement based on a voluntary relationship responsive to God involving an exchange of promises which generate commitments. This is, essentially, the understanding adopted by the Communion in its guidance on the Anglican Communion Covenant, which itself consists of affirmations and commitments. A formal covenant at global level between Anglican churches may be novel, but the Communion stresses that the Covenant itself simply articulates the relationship of covenantal affection already operative in the Communion. Indeed, historically the non-binding informal norms of inter-Anglican relations are covenantal in the sense that they are mutual commitments agreed globally (principally by the Lambeth Conference); the Lambeth Quadrilateral is seen as typical. Anglicans are nonetheless also familiar with formal juridical covenants internationally, nationally (each church has its own consensual compact: see above), and ecumenically. The Windsor reception process stimulated a broad consensus that the strategic purposes of a covenant should be, variously: unity; reconciliation, and recommitment; clarity about Anglican identity; order and stability (including mutual accountability); and mission and witness. However, many justifiably questioned the operational capacity of a covenant to achieve these goals. Nevertheless, today the Covenant is seen to reflect the call of Anglicans to be in communion in witness and mission so as to enrich the common life of the Communion; enabling "the Churches to live together in mutual care and affection as one Communion ... to witness ... to the biblical commands of charity and unity" (TACC:QAA, sect. 3, cf. sect. 4; cf. Doe 2008).

The Anglican Communion Covenant consists of a Preamble, four Sections and a Declaration. The Preamble sets out the reasons for covenanting: to proclaim the grace of God revealed in the gospel, to respond to the needs of the world, to maintain unity, and to attain the full stature of Christ. The first three Sections, on faith, mission and unity, consist of affirmations followed by commitments arising from those affirmations; it is each church of the Communion that makes the affirmation and the commitment. The first section is entitled "Our Inheritance of Faith". Each church affirms its communion in the one, holy, catholic and apostolic church, the catholic and apostolic faith revealed in scripture and set out in the catholic creeds and historic formularies of the Church of England (where acknowledged provincially), the Chicago–Lambeth Quadrilateral (on scripture, creeds, sacraments and historic episcopate), shared patterns of worship, and its participation in the mission of the people of God (TACC, 1.1). The covenantal commitments address a common approach to the contextual application of the shared inherited faith. In living out the inheritance together in their varying contexts, each church commits itself, *inter alia*, to teach and act in continuity and consonance with scripture and the catholic and apostolic faith, order and tradition, as received by the churches, to faithful, coherent and respectful interpretation of scripture, and to nurture and sustain Eucharistic communion (see TACC, 1.2.1–8; cf. TACC:ASG, p. 6).

The second section on "The Life We Share with Others: Our Anglican Vocation" deals with mission. Each church affirms that communion is not an end in itself but seeks to proclaim and witness to God and that God has been at work in Anglican history in shaping its worldwide mission; each church also confesses its failure to live up to that calling and undertakes to cooperate with other Anglicans in mission and with other Christians ecumenically. In turn, each church commits itself: to share its resources to evangelize, heal and reconcile the broken world; to engage in mission; to be humble and open to conversion; to renew structures for mission; and to root mission in the worship of God, particularly in Eucharistic communion (see TACC, 2.2.1–5).

The third section, "Our Unity and Common Life", deals with the exercise of provincial autonomy in the context of ecclesial communion (cf. TWR, para. 76). Each church affirms its call to live in peace and build up the common life of the Communion, its resolve to live in a communion of churches, its autonomy (its own system of government and law), the absence of a central global authority in Anglicanism, the role of bishops and the threefold ministry, and the importance of the instruments of communion in global Anglicanism (Archbishop of Canterbury, Lambeth Conference, Anglican Consultative Council, and Primates' Meeting) (see TACC, 3.1.1–4). The covenant provides that: "It is the responsibility of each Instrument to consult with, respond to, and support each other Instrument and the Churches of the Communion. Each Instrument may initiate and commend a process of discernment and a direction for the Communion of Churches" (Ibid.). In other words, the covenant provides for a persuasive authority (or jurisdiction) for the instruments (even though they are not themselves signatories to it). Next, each church commits itself to have regard for the common good of the Communion in the exercise of its autonomy, to support the work of the instruments of communion and to receive their work with a readiness to reflect on their counsels and endeavour to accommodate their recommendations. Moreover, each church must respect the constitutional autonomy of all the churches of the Communion, uphold mutual responsibility and interdependence, seek to discern the will of God through listening, prayer, study and debate, and seek a shared mind (consistent with canon law) in matters of common concern through consultation. Each church must also act with diligence, care and caution in matters which may provoke controversy "which by its intensity, substance or extent threaten the unity of the Communion and the effectiveness of its mission". In conflicts, a church must participate in mediated conversations and bear in mind that the bonds of affection and love of Christ require maintenance of "the highest degree of communion possible" (TACC, 3.2.1–7).

Section four is entitled "Our Covenanted Life Together". This sets out the procedures for adopting the covenant and living together by it, and includes rudimentary procedures for conflict-resolution. Each church affirms a set of principles and procedures and, reliant on the Holy Spirit, commits itself to their implementation. By adopting the covenant a church freely offers a commitment to other churches "to live more fully into the ecclesial communion and interdependence which is foundational to the Churches of the Anglican Communion" (TACC, 4.1.1). The Anglican Communion is seen as "a fellowship, within the One, Holy, Catholic and Apostolic Church, of national or regional Churches, in which each recognises in the others the bonds of a common loyalty to Christ expressed through a common faith and order, a shared inheritance in worship, life and mission, and a readiness to live an interdependent life" (Ibid.). Adoption means that a church recognises that the covenantal statement of faith, mission and interdependence of life is consistent with its own life, but such mutual commitment does not represent submission to any external ecclesiastical jurisdiction. Every church of the Communion, as recognised under the ACC Constitution (i.e. those churches listed on the schedule of membership of the ACC), is invited to enter the covenant according to its own constitutional procedures. However, if a church does not adopt the Covenant, this does not mean that it is no longer a part of the Anglican Communion; it still retains its Anglican identity (see TACC:QAA, sect. 6; cf. Doe 2008, Ch. 8). The Covenant is active for a church when it adopts the Covenant through the procedures contained in its own constitution and canons (see TACC, 4.1.6; cf. TWR, para. 118).

The next set of provisions deals with maintenance of the covenant and resolution of disputes. The covenanted position may be summed up in the maxim: the Communion guides; each church decides, thus protecting provincial autonomy and giving no coercive jurisdiction to the central instruments of communion. Each church has a duty of 'fidelity' to the Covenant. The Standing Committee of the Anglican Communion (responsible to the ACC and Primates' Meeting) must monitor "the functioning of the Covenant in the life of the Anglican Communion on behalf of the Instruments [of Communion]". When questions arise about "the meaning of the Covenant, or about the compatibility of an action by a covenanting Church with the Covenant, it is the duty of each covenanting Church to seek to live out the commitments [of mutual accountability and interdependence]". When a shared mind has not been reached, the Standing Committee must make every effort to facilitate agreement. The Covenant does not provide a system of sanctions in the event of breach of covenant by a signatory church. The Committee may request a church to defer a controversial action; if the church declines to do so, the Committee may recommend to any Instrument of Communion 'relational consequences' which may specify a provisional limitation of participation in or suspension from that Instrument until completion of the following process. The Committee may also (on the advice of the ACC and the Primates' Meeting) make a declaration that an action or decision is 'incompatible with the Covenant'. On the advice received, the Committee must make recommendations to the churches and Instruments as to relational consequences which flow from such incompatibility—namely, the extent which the decision of the covenanting church in question impairs or limits the communion between that church and other churches of the Communion and the practical consequences of this. Each church or Instrument then determines whether or not to accept the recommendations. Each church must also have its own structures to oversee the maintenance of the Covenant in the life of that church and to relate to the Instruments of Communion on matters pertinent to the Covenant (see TACC, 4.2.9; cf. WDAC, art. 25). Finally, any covenanting church may decide to withdraw from the Covenant, the Covenant may be amended with the consent of three quarters of the covenanting churches (see TACC, 4.4.2; cf. ACC Const., Articles of

Association, art. 7.2). and the signatories declare their churches "to be partakers in this Anglican Communion Covenant" (TACC, "Our Declaration"). That the Covenant binds a church is in line with the canonical principle (with its long historical and theological pedigree) *pacta sunt servanda*: agreements must be kept (see Doe 2008, Ch. 9).

The Covenant represents a major historical development for worldwide Anglicanism. It raises a host of both theological and legal issues, ranging from the theological nature of communion, through the legal character of provincial autonomy, to the theological and juridical implications of covenanting. The initial Windsor proposal and draft covenant were not universally welcomed: some accepted the covenant principle and the draft; others, the principle but not the draft; and some rejected both (cf. Adams 2004; Adams 2005, 70). Following publication of the Nassau, St Andrews and Ridley-Cambridge drafts, responses indicated a greater general sympathy for a covenant and voices rejecting the principle became fewer. Respondents generally agreed about the voluntary and relational character of a covenant with commitments (cf. Goddard 2008, 47; cf. Williams 2006), though several attacked analogies between a covenant and a contract as too juridical and likely to undermine the consensual character of Anglicanism (see Lewis 2005, 601). Many respondents felt that a covenant accords with the notion of the Communion as a consensual family of churches (see Radner 2005, 609; see also Gladwin 2008, 3), but for the critics a covenant is at odds with the spirit of Anglicanism, crisis-driven, a 'quick fix' which would translate the bonds of affection into a formal (juridical) commitment (see Chapman 2008a, 33; see also Bolt a.o. 2005). Some say that there are too many practical obstacles in the process of adoption in each church (see Tong 2005, 58), that it will make divisions within the Communion even more visible, and that it makes new demands on the Instruments of Communion (see e.g. TACC:QAA, sect. 10; cf. CT 2011). However, much depends on how it will be received in the life of the Communion (see TACC:QAA, sect. 10).

The Covenant project should not be seen in isolation. It may usefully be measured against covenant models in scripture, sacramental theology, ecumenism, and comparable global ecclesial communities (see Doe 2008, 47–51). First, prior to circulation of the Covenant, much was made of the idea that existing covenantal relationships in Anglicanism have biblical foundations, and it was often proposed that scriptural covenants may provide an inspiration for development of an ecclesial covenant (cf. Seitz 2008, 81). Indeed, covenantal theology (particularly in Protestant tradition) maintains that scriptural covenants may legitimately function as models for ecclesiastical polity: covenants associate an ecclesial community. Secondly, in the sacramental covenants of baptism, marriage and ordination, the parties are called to covenant, exchange promises, undertake commitments, and limit their autonomy by the duty to have regard for others; the sacramental covenants are entered solemnly, bind the parties and are regulated by canon law (with consequences for non-compliance with their commitments). Thirdly, ecumenical covenants and other agreements are today normal vehicles by which Anglican churches enter and regulate their relationships of communion or inter-communion with other churches, often after negotiation following a call to covenant; they are voluntarily entered, involve affirmations of common identity, and prescribe commitments through pledges and other solemn undertakings. They enable shared ministry, worship and mission, and represent a witness to the unity for which Christ prayed. Often provision is made in them for their own development, for tiered membership and differentiated commitments. They may be unilateral, bilateral or multilateral, but generally recognise and protect the autonomy of the partner churches as compatible with being in communion. Finally, as well as parallels which may be drawn with historical and contemporary covenants entered between Anglicans, the Anglican covenant shares many similarities with the instruments of comparable international ecclesial communities in the Orthodox, Lutheran, Methodist, Reformed and Baptist traditions (cf. Thomas 2004, 9; Hind 2008, 112; Doe 2008, Ch. 3). To these we now turn.

### *IV. Anglican juridical instruments in context*

Anglicans should be reassured that there is little that is extraordinary in the Anglican Communion Covenant, the Principles of Canon Law document, and the legal systems of each church in the Communion. As to the Covenant, agreements are widely used by other international ecclesial communities to co-ordinate community activities, to regulate its affairs, and even to establish the community itself. In contrast to the Roman Catholic Church worldwide, governed not by a covenant but by a Code of Canon Law (1983) promulgated unilaterally by the Pope, the Orthodox Church, like the Anglican Communion, is understood a 'a family of self-governing Churches', held together 'not by a centralized organization', but 'by the double bond of unity in the faith and communion in the sacraments'. Each local Orthodox Church is 'autocephalous' or 'autonomous' yet in full communion with its 'sister Churches'. It is covenantal in that it is 'gathered in one Eucharistic community' around the bishop. Orthodox churches also have inter-church agreements. Orthodox hierarchs, of several different churches, have associated together in the Standing Conference of Canonical Orthodox Bishops in the Americas (SCOBA). Their constitution contains a 'theological foundation for the agreement', which expresses their 'common testimony' and enables them 'to actualize this unity in all those fields in which a common effort is required'.

The Conference exists for 'the consideration and resolution of common problems, the coordination of effort in matters of common concern, and the strengthening of that unity which is the essence of Christianity'. However, the constitution preserves the jurisdictional autonomy of the member churches (cf. SCOBA, Const., art. II).

The statute of the International Old Catholic Bishops Conference in the Union of Utrecht (2000) "describes the kind of communion we are committed to and the obligations of the bishops in order to promote and to realize it"; the Conference unites the bishops as members of "the same church-family": the statute "can be seen as our 'covenant' in which the ecclesiological identity of the Old Catholic churches is phrased", but each church remains "autonomous and interdependent within the same communion" (Vercammen 2005). Similarly, the Lutheran World Federation is 'organized under' its constitution, as "a communion of churches which confess the triune God, agree in the proclamation of the Word of God and are united in pulpit and altar fellowship"; the Federation is an "instrument of its autonomous member churches" helping them "to act jointly in common tasks" (LWF, Constitution, articles I–IV). In similar vein, the World Communion of Reformed Churches is "a communion of churches", that "does not limit the autonomy of member churches" (WCRC, Const. art. III, VI.F), the Baptist World Alliance exists "as an expression of the essential oneness of Baptist people in the Lord Jesus Christ … [and] recognizes the traditional autonomy and interdependence of Baptist churches and member bodies" (BWA, Const., Preamble), and the 'fellowship' of the World Methodist Council has no legislative authority (see Wilson 2008, 175). Covenants and other agreements are also commonplace in church-state relations (cf. Puza and Doe 2006; Doe 2011, Ch. 1).

Secondly, that each church of the Anglican Communion has its own legal system is not exceptional in the context of the wider ecclesial environment of other Christian traditions. Every institutional church has its own regulatory system which deals with governance, ministry and matters of ritual and worship. In the Roman Catholic (Latin) Church, 'particular laws' apply to a specific territory (a particular church, such as a diocese) or a group of people (such as a religious community). The Code of canon Law (1983) itself "facilitates … an orderly development in the life of both the ecclesial society and of the individual persons who belong to it" (SDL 1983); laws do not replace faith, grace, and charity, and the supreme law is the salvation of souls (CIC, c. 1752). Each Eastern Catholic church is *sui juris* (not a concession of the Latin Church) with its own juridical system operative within the common law of the Code of 1990. In Orthodoxy, for example, the Greek Orthodox Archdiocese of America, under the jurisdiction of the Ecumenical Patriarchate of Constantinople, is regulated by a Charter, the

Holy Scriptures, the Holy Canons, and the regulations promulgated by it; and, "as to canonical and ecclesiastical matters not provided therein, by the decisions thereon of the Holy Synod of the Ecumenical Patriarchate" (GOAA 2003, art. 1). Lutheran churches generally employ constitutions and bylaws: the Lutheran Church of Australia (e.g.) has a central constitution, bylaws, rules and regulations (which may be amended by its General Synod representative of congregations and pastors), and it recognises custom. In turn, each district of the church, and each congregation within a district, has its own constitution and bylaws which must be consistent with the central constitution and bylaws (see LCA, Const., Arts. VI–IX; III.(k); Bylaws, art. IV.1). By way of contrast, Presbyterian churches employ systems of 'law' or of 'church order' (cf. Weatherhead 1997; Coertzen 1998). Other churches employ a plethora of regulatory instruments: in Britain, for instance, the Methodist Church has its Constitutional Practice and Discipline expressing 'Methodist Law and Polity'; and the United Reformed Church has its Scheme of Union and Manual. In the Lutheran and Reformed tradition: 'the external juridical order of the church should be at the service of the proclamation of the word' and so 'must be tested ever anew by the confession of faith, and on no level of legal church life can juridical questions be solved without relation to the church's confession'; church law is not a 'constitutive', but a 'consecutive' and 'regulative' element of a church (cf. the Barmen Synod of 1934; see Reuver 2000, 3f.). Comparative study of these legal systems reveals a wealth of substantive similarities (and not surprisingly differences) with Anglicanism in a host of areas (see Doe 2008A, 271). Indeed, a comparative approach to regulatory instruments can be deployed imaginatively in ecumenism, through the induction of common principles, to determine in practical ways (despite differences in doctrine) both the scope for and concrete limits on greater visible unity (cf. Reuver 2000, 5).

Thirdly, the Principles of Canon Law Common to the Churches of the Anglican Communion may be compared with the approaches of other international ecclesial communities to global ecclesiastical order. No other global ecclesial community has engaged in a project similar to this. However, the Anglican *ius commune*, as a collection of principles, is similar to the code of the Roman Catholic Church (which is also comprehensive, covering governance, ministry, sacraments and property), but different insofar as the former emanates from the grass roots by the legislative activity of the churches of the Communion, whereas the latter is derived from a central authority, the papacy, and binds all particular churches worldwide. The Anglican *ius commune* seems to resemble a little more the Code of Canons of the Eastern Catholic Churches promulgated by Pope John Paul II in 1990 which represents their 'common law': it embraces 'the laws and legitimate customs' of the entire Church and those common to all the Eastern Churches (cf. CCEO, cc. 1, 1493). Like the Anglican Communion, the Orthodox Church worldwide has no universal code. The 'law of the church' globally is, rather, 'her canonical tradition', 'an outgrowth of the holy canons' deriving principally from the early Councils and Fathers of the Church; these are contained in several collections of which the most widely-used today in Greek-speaking Orthodox churches is the *Pedalion* ('The Rudder', 1800)—its coverage is also comprehensive (cf. Patsavos 1984, 145). No attempt has been made to articulate what the modern instruments of Orthodox churches share, though whether Orthodox laws should be codified is the subject of debate (cf. Bartholomaios 1973). In any event, Orthodoxy proposes that canon law is at the service of the Church, to guide her members on the way to salvation; its main function is the spiritual growth of the faithful (cf. Patsavos 1984). Unlike the Anglican *ius commune*, the *constitutions* of other global ecclesial communities (outlined above) are not an articulation of principles induced in ascending fashion from similarities between the regulatory instruments of their member churches. They are, rather, instruments *de novo* enabling worldwide collaboration in (an essentially small range of) matters of common concern. A key difference between the Anglican *ius commune* and instruments of other global ecclesial communities concerns enforceability. Whereas the Anglican entity does not bind internationally but is persuasive, the Latin Code binds all the faithful directly in the particular churches, bishops, clergy and laity alike (see CIC, c.1, cf. c.11). The Eastern catholic code is similar (see CCEO, cc.1489–1491). In Orthodoxy there is a lively debate as to whether the canonical tradition binds in the sense of letter or spirit (cf. Erickson 1991, Ch. 1). 'Acceptance' of its constitution is required for membership of the Lutheran World Federation (cf. LWF, Const., art. V). With some instruments the decisions of the central body of the global community bind only that body; they do not bind as to matters within the competence of the autonomous member church (cf. SCOBA, Const. art. II(a)1).

## *Conclusion*

This contribution represents an exploratory examination of a vast field. However, three conclusions may be drawn. First, there would seem to be good reasons to study the individual legal systems of Anglican churches. Such study has until relatively recent years been much neglected. One may speculate on the reasons for this. Perhaps they have to do with the historical antithesis between grace and law, the view that law is essentially coercive (and that it frustrates the spirit in the life of the church), the dominance of theological study over the legal practicalities of ecclesiastical administration (law is for lawyers). Indeed, the theological education recommended in recent years by Theological Education for the

Anglican Communion (TEAC) involves indirectly a host of subjects related to canon law, though canon law itself remains largely un-named (cf. Doe 2009A, 91), and perhaps the assumption that ignorance of law tends to make it more difficult to question authority. On the contrary, law is not an end in itself but the servant of the church, existing to facilitate and order its communion and mission. Canon law is in reality applied ecclesiology and its study tells us much about ecclesial governance, ministry, doctrine, worship and ritual in terms of the rights and duties of all the faithful. That law is a normal function of the church is underscored when Anglican churches are compared with churches of other Christian traditions: all churches have their laws and other regulatory instruments.

Secondly, the study of comparative canon law enables an understanding of what Anglicans share in terms of their respective systems of polity. Articulation of this in *The Principles of Canon Law Common to the Churches of the Anglican Communion* indicates well a collective commitment by the churches of the Communion to a particular way of being part of the church universal. For this reason, the document also represents a major resource for ecumenical dialogue, and perhaps even a model for similar projects between ecumenical partners. So often canon law and other systems of church order can be perceived as obstacles to the advancement of fuller visible communion because of their need for clarity, certainty and stability. But the theological character of canon law (and the opportunities for theological reflection upon it), its susceptibility to comparative study, and its capacity to point up in the form of principles what separated churches actually share normatively, call for a renewed appraisal of its place in ecumenical dialogue and activity (cf. ELJ 2009, 284). Indeed, the recognition by churches of 'the principles of church law and order' suggests that canon law and its equivalents may be perceived as a generic phenomenon, having an existence independent of the legal systems of particular churches and communions (see Doe 1998b, 221).

Thirdly, the Anglican Communion Covenant represents an historical landmark in global Anglicanism. It is generally understood that the absence of such an agreed framework to-date has to a significant degree exacerbated such recent conflicts in the worldwide Anglican Communion as those over human sexuality and same-sex partnerships. But conflicts have consequences. They jeopardise the mission of the church, damage ecumenical relations, and result in claims of impaired communion. They may also lead to laws created in other churches offering facilities for those who abandon Anglicanism and seek to continue their traditions elsewhere. It was this absence of an agreed global mechanism, and its consequences, which led the Lambeth Commission in 2004 to suggest the adoption by each church of an Anglican Communion Covenant. Its critics see it as too strong — that it will restrict the freedom of churches to innovate. Others see it as too weak — that it does not give the Communion and its institutions enough authority to direct churches in controversial matters. Yet, its supporters see it as an adult way of setting out the basic ground rules by which the worldwide Anglican family should achieve its objectives and how it should address making decisions on difficult issues of common concern. Indeed, that is the fundamental principle at the heart of the Covenant in terms of global Anglican polity — the Communion guides, each church decides. It also meets the need for ecumenical partners to have a coherent view of global Anglicanism. Moreover, spiritual, sacramental and structural covenanting it is a well-trodden Christian path not least amongst the ecumenical partners of Anglicans. Importantly, the Covenant does not represent the Communion as the primary manifestation of Anglicanism with authority to limit the freedom (or autonomy) of its member churches (the 'red-light' model). The Covenant does not see the autonomous provincial church as the primary manifestation of Anglicanism under which the province has an unfettered freedom without any restraint possible from the global family (the 'green-light' model). Rather, the Covenant sees partnership between the Communion (the family) and each autonomous church as the primary manifestation of Anglicanism, one which protects the autonomy of the province (its legal freedom) subject to the competence of the Communion (through its instruments) to guide in a limited field of highly contentious matters of common concern (the 'amber-light' model). This is the Anglican canon.

*Abbreviations and bibliography*

CCEO: Codex Canonum Ecclesiarum Orientalium (1990).

CIC: Codex Iuris Canonici (1983).

CT 2011: The Anglican Covenant: A Church Times Guide, Church Times, 18-3-2011.

ELJ 2009: Colloquium of Anglican and Roman Catholic Canon Lawyers, A decade of ecumenical dialogue on canon law. In: Ecclesiastical Law Journal 11(2009), 284-328.

GOAA 2003: Charter of the Greek Orthodox Archdiocese of America (2003).

SDL: John Paul II, Sacrae Disciplinae Leges, Apostolic Constitution (25 Jan. 1983). See: www.vatican.va.

TACC: The Anglican Communion Covenant. Anglican Communion Office.

TACC:ASG: The Anglican Communion Covenant: A Study Guide (2009). Anglican Communion Office.

TACC:QAA: The Anglican Communion Covenant: Questions and Answers (2009). Anglican Communion Office.

TWR: Lambeth Commission, The Windsor Report. Anglican Communion Office (2004).

WDAC: Windsor Draft Covenant 2004.

Adams, Marilyn. 2004. How to quench the spirit. In: Church Times, 29-10-2004.

Adams, Marilyn. 2005. Faithfulness in crisis. In: Linzey and Kirker 2005, 70–80.

Bartholomaios, Metropolitan. 1973. A common code for the Orthodox churches. Kanon I (1973), 45–53.

Bolt, Peter G., Mark D. Thompson and Robert Tong (eds). 2005. The Faith Once For All Delivered. Camperdown, NSw: Australian Church Record.

Cameron, Gregory K. 2008. A tortoise in a Hurry: the Ordering of the Anglican Communion. In: International Journal for the Study of the Christian Church (2008), 69–80.

Chapman, Mark (ed.). 2008. The Anglican Covenant. London: Mowbray.

Chapman, Mark. 2008A. Introduction. In: Chapman 2008, 1–33.

Coertzen, Pieter. 1998. Church and Order: A Reformed Perspective. Leuven: Peeters.

Doe, Norman. 1998. Canon Law in the Anglican Communion: A Worldwide Perspective. Oxford: Clarendon Press

Doe, Norman. 1998A. Ecclesiastical quasi-legislation. In: Doe et al. 1998, 93–103.

Doe, Norman. 1998B. The principles of canon law: a focus of legal unity in Anglican and Roman Catholic relations. In: Ecclesiastical Law Journal 5(1998), 221–240.

Doe, Norman. 2002. Canon law and communion. In: Ecclesiastical Law Journal 6(2002), 241–263.

Doe, Norman. 2003. The common law of the Anglican Communion. In: Ecclesiastical Law Journal 7(2003), 4–16.

Doe, Norman. 2004. The Anglican Covenant proposed by the Lambeth Commission. In: Ecclesiastical Law Journal 8(2004), 147–161.

Doe, Norman. 2008. An Anglican Covenant: Theological and Legal Considerations for a Global Debate. London: Canterbury Press.

Doe, Norman. 2008A. Modern church law. In: Witte and Alexander 2008, 271–291.

Doe, Norman (ed.). 2009. The Formation and Ordination of Clergy in Anglican and Roman Catholic Canon Law. Cardiff: University of Wales Press.

Doe, Norman. 2009A. Theological education in Anglicanism: global policy and its canonical dimensions. In: Doe 2009, 91–102.

Doe, Norman. 2011. Law and Religion in Europe: A Comparative Introduction. Oxford: Oxford University Press.

Doe, Norman, Mark Hill and Robert Ombres (eds). 1998. English Canon Law. Cardiff: University of Wales Press.

Erickson, John H. 1991. The Challenge of Our Past. Crestwood, NY: St. Vladimir's Seminary Press.

Gladwin, John. 2008. The local and the universal and the meaning of Anglicanism: Kenya. In: Stevenson 2008, 3–16.

Goddard, Andrew. 2008. Unity and diversity, communion and covenant: theological, ecclesiological, political and missional challenges for Anglicanism. In: Chapman 2008, 47–80.

Hind, John. 2008.The idea of an Anglican Covenant: a faith and order perspective. International Journal for the Study of the Christian Church 8(2008), 112–123.

Jones, Gareth. 2005. Thy Grace Shall Always Prevent... In: Linzey and Kirker 2005, 116–137.

Lewis, Harold T. 2005. Covenant, contract and communion: reflections on a post-Windsor Anglicanism. In: Anglican Theological Review 87(2005) 601–608.

Linzey, Andrew and Richard Kirker (eds). 2005. Gays and the Future of Anglicanism: Responses to the Windsor Report. Winchester: O Books.

Litsas, Fotios K. (ed.). 1984. A Companion to the Greek Orthodox Church. New York: Greek Orthodox Archdiocese of North and South America.

Patsavos, Lewis. 1984. The canonical tradition of the Orthodox Church. In: Litsas 1984, 137–147.

Puza, R., and N. Doe (eds). 2006: Religion and Law in Dialogue: Covenantal and Non-Covenantal Cooperation between State and Religion in Europe. Leuven: Peeters.

Radner, Ephraim. 2005. Freedom and covenant: the Miltonian analogy transfigured. Anglican Theological Review 87(2005) 609–618.

Rees, Canon John (ed.). 2008. The Principles of Canon Law Common to the Churches of the Anglican Communion. London: Anglican Communion Office.

Reuver, Mark. 2000. Faith and Law: Juridical Perspectives for the Ecumenical Movement. Geneva: WCC.

Seitz, Christopher. 2008. Canon, covenant and rule of faith — the use of scripture. International Journal for the Study of the Christian Church 8(2008), 81–92.

Stevenson, Kenneth (ed.). 2008. A Fallible Church: Lambeth Essays. London: Darton, Longman and Todd.

Thomas, Phillip H.E. 2004. Unity and concord: an early Anglican 'Communion'. In: Journal of Anglican Studies 21(2004), 9–21.

Tong, Robert. 2005. How would the Anglican Church of Australia commit itself to an Anglican Covenant? In: Bolt et al. 2005, 55–59.

Vercammen, Joris A.O.L. 2005. Letter of 25-1-2005 2000.

Weatherhead, James L (ed.). 1997. The Constitution and Laws of the Church of Scotland. Edinburgh: Board of Practice and Procedure.

Williams, Rowan. The Challenge and Hope of Being Anglican Today: A Reflection for the Bishops, Clergy and Faithful of the Anglican Communion (27-6-2006): Anglican Communion News Service 4161.

Wilson, Kenneth. 2008. The Methodist idea of covenant. In: Chapman 2008, 175–191.

Witte, John, and Frank S. Alexander (eds). 2008. Christianity and Law: An Introduction. Cambridge: Cambridge University Press.

# SUPPORTING THE VISION WITH THE HELP OF CANONICAL STRUCTURES

## The Interaction of Doctrine and Canonical Structures in the Roman Catholic Church

Myriam Wijlens

The topic of my lecture has accompanied me for the past 25 years. I remember well how during my studies in theology I attended classes in ecclesiology and ecumenism where I learned about Vatican II and the many insights it had brought to the fore: the participation of all baptized in the threefold ministry of Christ, the insertion of a chapter on the people of God before the chapter on the hierarchy in *Lumen gentium*, the affirmation that the local church is truly and fully church and that the diocesan bishop is not a mere delegate of the pope but is indeed the vicar of Christ for his diocese, the doctrine that all Christians are first and foremost united through their baptism in Christ and therefore the language of heretics and schismatics would no longer apply to them. I learned that the Decree on Ecumenism did not focus so much on individual baptized non-Catholics and their relationship to the Catholic church, but the Decree focused on the ecclesial community or church to which these baptized Christians belong, because in and through their community or church they would receive grace.

I thus found myself confronted with the teaching of Vatican II and asked the rather simple question: what do all these new insights in doctrine mean in real life?

This question got me thinking and wondering what the church would need in order to transfer its doctrine into real life. What would it take for the community, for the church at large, to act in agreement with this council? I wondered what would be the point of holding an ecumenical council in Rome if it was not going to have an impact on the life of the people in my parish and other parishes around the world.

I discovered that the Code of Canon Law promulgated in 1983 was and is intended and considered as a vehicle to assist the community to act in agreement with the doctrine of Vatican II. I realized quickly that the norms could assist, yes even promote the implementation of the doctrine, but by the same token they could also hamper or even impede this process. I decided therefore to study canon law.

During these studies I became aware that this relationship between conciliar doctrine and canonical norms was not simply on the level of legislation where the question is asked: what norms are needed to assist the community in appropriating the doctrine? I discovered that the norms themselves are in need of interpretation and that Vatican II not only cannot be left out, but that in fact it is, so to speak, the hermeneutical lens through which the canonical norms must be interpreted. After all, many conciliar terms and notions found their way into the legislation even though they were never defined — terms such as "church, " "ecclesial community, " "subsistit in, " "communion, " etc. How are these terms to be handled in legal texts, considering that the unfolding of their meaning was consciously and deliberately left to theologians for the time following the council? Are canon lawyers asked to take notice of the discussions and findings of theologians? Could canon lawyers assist the theologians in their search? What kind of dialogue between theologians and canon lawyers is required?

I was, furthermore, struck by the numerous canons that require what could be called the "exercise of discretion' By that term I refer to those norms that contain phrases such as "in case of necessity, " "in the judgment of the bishop, " "if opportune, " or "for grave reasons, " etc. I was touched by the wisdom of the legislator to insert these phrases, because it is an excellent way to provide flexibility in applying the law in different circumstances and at different times. This would provide space that can ultimately contribute to the final purpose of the law, namely the salvation of the souls. Yet, what is necessary to fill these terms responsibly? Does Vatican II have something to do with that? If so, how does it work?

If canon law is to assist the community in appropriating its vision, then it is necessary to attend carefully to the moment where law and life meet, that is, to attend to the application of the law. What is the difference between interpretation and application of the law? In interpretation the focus is on the text of the law itself. Typically, interpretation takes place in commentaries and academic writings.

Application on the other hand is that stage in the life of a law where it is confronted with life itself. In the chaos and turmoil of life, the law itself has to be applied in order to achieve what the legislator with the help of the law wants the community or the person to appropriate. The application of the law takes place when administrators, judges, bishops, pastors or the faithful as such act on it. However, they always do so in a specific context and at a specific time. The application of the law concerns a specific situation, so the first step in the application involves being attentive to the way the situation is verbalized. What theological perspectives and notions are used to describe the case? Are these in line with Vatican II, or do they display former theological thinking? Is it necessary to rephrase the question so that indeed the teaching of the church at Vatican II can be more fully received?

In my reflections so far I have implicitly argued that there is a connection between Vatican II and the post-conciliar legislation. After a short reflection on this thesis, I will speak about the implications of it for their interaction on the three levels of legislation, interpretation and application.

*The Second Vatican Council and the Code of Canon Law*

It has been more than fifty years since Pope John XXIII convoked the Second Vatican Council in 1959. The opening session in October 1962 will be commemorated in October 2012. From the beginning, Vatican II was understood to be different from other councils, as it did not react to specific heresies or other threats to the faith. It was the declared intention of Pope John XXIII to rethink and reflect the faith of the church in light of the situation of the world and in light of new insights. His intention was ultimately a renewal, an updating (*aggiornamento*) and the promotion of Christian unity. He said: "Our sole concern is the *bonum animarum* and Our wish is to see the new Pontificate meet the spiritual demands of the present time accurately and forcefully" (John XXIII 1959, 398). He then said that he would, therefore, convoke a synod for the diocese of Rome and a council for the world church. They together would lead "to the desired and long awaited modernization of the Code of Canon Law, which is expected to accompany and crown these two efforts in the practical application of the rules of ecclesiastical discipline, applications the Spirit of the Lord will surely suggest to Us as we proceed" (John XXIII 1959, 400–401).

In 1917 the Catholic Church had seen the promulgation of its first Code of Canon Law in history (!): a book full of laws which, in its appearance, had to contribute to the self-understanding of the church as being a *societas perfecta*, but which, with regard to its content, was not new at all because it was structured in agreement with the books of Justinian. With regard to its content, the 1917 Code was thus not a set of laws related to or governed by a specific ecclesiology or theology. It is important to keep this in mind when considering the Code of Canon Law of 1983 and other post-conciliar legislation, because the latter were from their inception understood as required to be complementary to the conciliar teaching both in the principles that guided its revision process and in the theology that was the basis for the laws. Not only Pope John XXIII, but also Pope Paul VI and later Pope John Paul II, saw an intrinsic relationship between Vatican

II and the subsequent canon law. Pope Paul VI for example gave permission to the commission that was installed to work on the revision of the Code to await the results of the council before commencing its work. The first major event related to the revision of the Code of 1917 was the 1967 Synod of bishops which reflected on the principles that should govern the Code of Canon Law (see *Communicationes* 1(1969), 77–85; John Paul II 1983B, xxxvi–xxxviii). These principles reveal a deep intrinsic link to the council, in spirit and content.

When promulgating the 1983 Code, Pope John Paul II mentioned that it stood in line with Vatican II. He saw the Code as necessarily chronologically following the council (see John Paul II 1983A), xxviii). He concluded in retrospect that Council and Code derive from the same intention, namely, the renewal of Christian life (see John Paul II 1983A, xxviii). The pope saw the Code as a *translation* (emphasis MW) of the conciliar doctrine into canonical language. He was aware that this might be tricky at times and he gave a guideline on how to handle tensions or uncertainties: "If, however, it is impossible to translate perfectly into canonical language the conciliar image of the Church, nevertheless, in this image there should always be found as far as possible its essential point of reference" (John Paul II 1983A, xxx). Subsequently the pope mentioned the old and new doctrine that the council contains. He said: "Hence it follows that what constitutes the substantial *newness* of the Second Vatican Council, in line with the legislative tradition of the Church, especially in regard to ecclesiology, constitutes likewise the *newness* of the new Code" (John Paul II 1983A, xxx).

Pope John Paul II, while promulgating the 1983 Code of Canon Law spoke about a *translation* of the doctrine of Vatican II, in particular of its ecclesiology, into canonical language. There is a lot to be said about all that the translation implies, but before doing so it is necessary to pause for a moment and ask the questions: Why a translation? Why canonical norms in the first place? The questions must be raised because they will allow for a greater appreciation of the need to discuss the relationship between council and Code.

### *Why canonical norms?*

Every individual person is interested in living in agreement with his or her beliefs and convictions. Persons who do so are considered to be persons of integrity; their actions correspond to their words, or to put it differently: their thoughts and words are followed by corresponding actions. A community of people wants to do the same: it wants to live in agreement with its insights and thoughts. A faith community in this sense is no different from other communities: it prefers harmony which is experienced when words and deeds are in agreement. There are thus two moments: the first one concerns a reflection about the faith: *fides quaerens intellectum*. This is what Vatican II did: it reflected on the faith, and new insights came to the fore or were articulated in a new and fresh way. While promulgating the 1983 Code of Canon Law, Pope John Paul II listed four points that he regarded as particularly new in the council and of relevance for canon law:

1. "The doctrine in which the Church is presented as the People of God (LG, § 2), and authority as a service (LG, § 3);
2. the doctrine in which the Church is seen as a 'communion', and which, therefore, determines the relations which should exist between the particular Churches and the universal Church, and between collegiality and the primacy;
3. the doctrine, moreover, according to which all the members of the People of God, in the way suited to each of them, participate in the threefold office of Christ: priestly, prophetic and kingly. With this teaching there is also linked that which concerns the duties and rights of the faithful, and particularly of the laity; and finally,
4. the Church's commitment to ecumenism" (John Paul II 1983A, XXX).

At Vatican II the Catholic Church articulated these insights as its belief. However, a community not only wants to express its belief, it wants to act accordingly. The church that seeks to understand its faith also wants to act in accordance with the answer found (*fides quaerens actionem*).

Hence, the question must be raised: What is needed so that these insights are indeed becoming a lived reality? What is needed so that the community will receive the conciliar teaching in such a way that the doctrine shapes the lives of people and of the community as such? Canonical norms can assist the community in this process. Canon law aims at assisting the community in its search for living in harmony with its own theological insights. Canonical norms can indeed promote and protect insights: it promotes them when certain actions are required and obligatory for all, even for those who might still be in the process of accepting them.

I am very well aware of the fact that what I am describing here is not as easy as it might sound, but it is worthwhile to reflect on it for a moment, because it has a deep impact on the daily operations of the church.

How does such a process of legislation take place? There are two major steps: first, the legislator has to identify the doctrine that is in need of support and protection by canonical norms. Secondly, the legislator has to determine what might be called a "modality" or a "structure" fitting for the community here and now.

First there is the *identification of the doctrine*. It is clear that in regard to Vatican II this was and is indeed a most delicate task, because as Pope John Paul II stated so clearly, there is old and new in the council. How to deal with this old and new? Here the whole issue of the interpretation of Vatican II — the issue of hermeneutics — comes into play. There is old and new in the council that most probably has a lot to do with the manner in which renewal in and by the council took place. The German fundamental theologian Hermann-Josef Pottmeyer was one of the first who was able to explain what happened and consequently to identify the particular challenge which the Vatican II documents pose for the interpretation: in their method, the council fathers linked two concerns: renewal of the church and preservation of continuity. "The method is essentially that of juxtaposition: alongside a doctrine or thesis in preconciliar language is set a doctrine or thesis that formulates some complementary aspect....The limitation of the council was that it did not succeed, and probably could not have succeeded, in going beyond juxtaposition to a new synthesis" (Pottmeyer 1987, 37–38; cf. Rush 2004, 27–30, 42, 49; Gaillardetz 2006, xvi–xviii; Kasper 1989A, 171).

The renewal did take place in leaving old and new standing side by side, because in this way they would not break with anything of the past and yet by introducing new insights they would move forward. This kind of renewal would be introduced in such a way that a person would say, for example, "we all know that," or "we all agree and believe that," and then the familiar doctrine would be expressed. Subsequently the person would say, "however, this does not exclude the following," and then a new aspect would be introduced. Sometimes this mode of proceeding is explicit; often it is done implicitly. The advantage of such a procedure is of course that virtually all can accept and approve the text — and that is what is highly valued in an ecumenical council. The council is full of such juxtapositions.

In light of this it is clear that the task of the legislator to determine which doctrine of the council was and is in need of protection and promotion by way of legislation is rather delicate. How could the legislator handle the juxtapositions? Of course here the whole issue of the intention of the council comes into play. The decisions must be made with a certain set of lenses on.

Not only had Pope John XXIII spoken about an *aggiornamento*, Pope Paul VI also adopted this term "as aim and object" of his own pontificate (ES, § 50), but he urged canon lawyers to take on a *novus habitus mentis*, a new attitude of mind (Paul VI 1973, 100f.; Paul VI 1977, 111). Although he never explained explicitly what he meant by this, it is clear that it is more than just receiving the letter of the council. It is necessary to enter into that which the council was: a church in conversation and dialogue (see ES). It implies a willingness to look at the familiar in a new way.

Vatican II thus turned out to be a council of reform; however, not a reform just of doctrine but of the style in which the church does theology and reflects on its own faith. Receiving Vatican II thus implies more than receiving the doctrine, whether in a juridical or a spiritual way. It is also and above all receiving the style (Routhier 2006A, 23–44; Routhier 2011). To determine the style implies not just attending to the documents the council produced — because the council was not a publishing house — but considering the experience of what happened after and because of the council (cf. Komonchak 2011).

It would go far beyond this paper to reflect on how the process of determining the old and new actually took place and what results came out of it. Nevertheless, Pope John Paul II was very much aware of the existence of these two (at times) conflicting doctrines and thus while promulgating the 1983 Code he said that the newness of the council was to be the newness of the Code (see John Paul II 1983A, xxx).

He used the words *vetera et nova* and thus explicitly acknowledged the existence of old and new. He went on to explain that the newness of the council can be found in the four points I mentioned above. The Pope said: "If, therefore, the Second Vatican Council has drawn from the treasury of Tradition elements both old (*vetera*) and new (*nova*), and the new consists precisely in the elements which we have enumerated, then it is clear that the Code also should reflect the same note of fidelity in newness and of newness in fidelity, and conform itself to that in its own field and in its particular way of expressing itself" (John Paul II 1983A, xxxi).

Pope John Paul II not only referred to the legislative process, but also made clear that the perspective of the newness over and against the old must also guide the interpretation and application of the law.

The Code was promulgated in 1983. Two years later the Synod of Bishops, while commemorating the twentieth anniversary of the closing of Vatican II, reflected on the hermeneutics of the council (Routhier 2006B, 61–90), a topic that has been very much alive ever since pope Benedict XVI commemorated the fortieth anniversary of the closing of the council in December 2005 (Benedict XVI 2005, 40–55; cf. Routhier and Jobin 2010).

He rejected a hermeneutic of discontinuity and favored a hermeneutic of reform. With the latter term he also rejected a hermeneutic of continuity. Pope Benedict XVI argued in favor of a hermeneutic in which fidelity to the past and dynamism because of the future is required when he wrote: "It is precisely in this combination of continuity and discontinuity at different levels that the very nature of true reform consists" (Benedict XVI 2005, 49; cf. Komonchak 2011). It is unlikely that the debate has ended. In fact, one may expect that it will come to the fore most forcefully when the fiftieth anniversary of the council is being commemorated between 2012 and 2015.

So the legislator has a most difficult task in identifying the doctrine that is in need of promotion or protection. As can be imagined, this task is accomplished with, at most, moderate success. Here is good reason, therefore, for theologians and canon lawyers to be attentive to the underlying theological premises of the canonical norms.

The second step that the legislator has to take is to find *a fitting modality*. In search for such a modality the legislator must take cognizance of civil law, culture, available financial and personnel resources, etc. Here a decision is to be made as well as to what is left to particular law and what in light of the unity of the church needs to be legislated upon for the universal church. Another aspect concerns the question whether something would have to be obligatory or be left to discretion. An example of the latter would be the diocesan pastoral council whereas an example of the former would be the presbyteral council. Of course the decision taken by the legislator reveals a certain theological understanding. Another issue that the legislator has to determine is whether a certain action would be for validity or mere liceity. By way of example: Would the bishop be obliged to hear his presbyteral council before he can close a parish and maybe even completely restructure his diocese, or would a simple hearing of the presbyteral council be sufficient? Would he be obliged to hear his diocesan pastoral council? It is easy to detect behind such simple questions major ecclesiological decisions that in one or the other way either hamper or encourage the reception of Vatican II. Finally, the legislator has to decide on what could be referred to as "the tone" or the perspective of the legislation: in light of Vatican II, which did not speak with condemnations but looked for an affirmative language, the 1983 Code of Canon Law in comparison to its predecessor has a general tone of permission and not of prohibition.

It is important to differentiate between the theological insights governing the structures/norms on the one hand and the modality on the other hand, for several reasons:

› the differentiation allows for preventing canonical norms to be lifted to the level of doctrine.
› it allows for (regular) evaluation of the modality in light of the question whether the modality is still the best one for achieving the theological notion(s);
› it opens the possibility for a more relaxed consideration of the healthy tension between diversity and unity both on a synchronic and diachronic level: the church of all times and of all places can indeed change and adapt to new challenges and circumstances. I would like to refer to two major canonical institutions that are benefitting from this differentiation. The first one concerns the sacrament of reconciliation. In the early Middle Ages the sacrament had the

form of a public penance. Because it was rather difficult to do this penance, the sacrament was usually deferred to the end of life which implied that people received the grace of the sacrament at most once in their lifetime. Over the course of history the modality of the sacrament was therefore changed and has taken on the form as it is known today. The elements of contrition, penance and absolution remained, but because the modality was no longer fitting for the people it was changed. The other example concerns the most remarkable invitation by Pope John Paul II, expressed in his encyclical letter on ecumenism "*Ut Unum sint,* " where he invited other churches and their leaders to reflect with him about the exercise of the petrine ministry. The pope did not propose a reflection about the existence of the petrine ministry as such, but he generated discussion about the way the ministry is exercised and the tasks connected to the office (UUS, § 95–96). Over the past years I have been involved not so much in what is classically called "a dialogue" of Catholics and Lutherans, but some members of the Lutheran Church in particular from Scandinavia invited members of the Roman Catholic Church to explain to them the understanding of the petrine ministry in the Catholic Church. The Catholics did not just repeat the doctrine, but offered a new reflection on the petrine ministry whereby Vatican I was read in light of Vatican II and whereby the canonical norms were interpreted in light of the hermeneutics just offered. The Lutherans in turn then asked themselves how Luther had really seen the papacy. In the process of a mutual listening both sides became acutely aware of the need to learn and the need for healing on specific points (cf. Gruppe von Farfa 2011; Puglisi 2010). These examples on the sacrament of penance and the office of the petrine ministry are very important because they concern institutions that belong to the core of the Catholic faith. If they can be adapted to new circumstances, then others that are of theologically less weight can be adapted as well.

### *Vatican II in the Interpretation of the Law*

With regard to the interpretation of the law, it is necessary to be aware that quite often Vatican II decided consciously and decisively that a specific theological notion would not be further explained and certainly not be defined. The council left many terms and issues for theologians to unravel. One could also say that the council employed notions whose deepest meaning still has to unfold as time goes on. They may be referred to as "seminal locutions": they bear a deep theological notion that has not been brought fully to the fore. This may be likened to the flower that goes by the name amaryllis. An amaryllis is usually acquired in the form of a bulb. After it has been put into soil it needs not too much and not too little moisture, not too much sunlight and not too little, not too much heat and no cold. It needs care and the owner needs patience. With the right care a beautiful flower will appear after about eight weeks. The care and the patience are decisive. Seminal locutions are in need of this as well: care and patience. The Holy Spirit must be given time to unfold the richness of the notions to us. It would be a disaster if the in-between stadium would be seen as the final product. Seminal locutions include, for example, the words *ecclesia* and *communitates ecclesiales*. Both words were never defined and no list exists that identifies which denominations are to be considered in one or the other category. When questions were asked, the council stated that it left this to the theologians to discover. Statements have been made that the Roman Catholic Church always kept referring to the Orthodox as "Church". When asked, the council declined to define the terms or make a list. Related to these terms are of course the terms *subsistit in*, *communio*, *communion plena*, etc. All these words need to be considered together and may not be seen in isolation. Of course Vatican II saw many more terms and notions that were left for further unfolding after the council.

Why is it important for canon lawyers to be aware of this? It should be noted that it was not only the legislator who decided consciously against providing any definitions in the Code of Canon Law arguing that it is not a mere textbook (*Communicationes* 15(1984), 38), but also that the legislator received the aforementioned theologically-not-defined terms and notions into the canonical norms. If canon lawyers were to fix them by attempting to determine what they mean they would risk transferring them from theological notions into canonical ones and they could cause the fossilization their meaning, because the canonical notion might hamper further development in understanding the theological notion. If indeed theology is to govern canon law, then this temptation must be avoided at all costs.

### *Vatican II in the Application of the Law*

After attending to the legislation and interpretation, it is now possible to take a closer look at the application of the law. As pointed out in the introductory part, in the application of the law canonical norms and life itself meet. The application of the law usually involves taking different norms into consideration simultaneously, including norms relating to dispensations and equity. Moreover, consideration must be given to universal and particular law, to statutes, to civil law and maybe even to customs. Applying the law is therefore not an easy task. And yet, it is a very responsible task.

The application of the law begins, however, not with the consultation of the canonical sources, but with the *phrasing of the question*. As pointed out above, it is necessary to reflect on the theology and ecclesiology that governs the question being addressed.

I became acutely aware of this when someone asked a question about Cardinal Ratzinger giving Holy Communion to Frère Roger of Taizé at the Requiem Mass for Pope John Paul II. The person asked: so did Frère Roger convert to Catholicism or not? Is he a member of the Catholic Church or not? While thinking about what to answer, it occurred to me that the question itself had been phrased in line with pre-Vatican II theology which used phrases like "being a member of the Catholic Church" and "conversion" to it. Would not Vatican II stipulate a rephrasing of the question, as the council had decided that the word *membrum* had to be eliminated because it has a connotation of all or nothing and does not leave space for grades of belonging? The council had taken recourse to the words *plene incorporare* (LG, §14; cf. UR, §3) and *coniungere* (LG, §15). It, therefore, no longer spoke about a person who had been baptized in another community or church as "converting" to the Catholic Church, but instead employed the words "entering into full communion" (as the Liturgical Rite does as well). Moreover I had learned that Frère Roger at one point had made a public confession that he shared the faith of the Catholic Church with regard to the sacraments. The question addressed should therefore not be whether Frère Roger was a convert and a member of the Roman Catholic Church, but whether a priest of the Roman Catholic Church may refuse the sacrament to a baptized person who stands in communion with the Catholic Church (albeit not in full communion) and who on another occasion had even declared publicly that he shares the faith of the Catholic Church with regard to the sacraments, and feels the spiritual need at this funeral Mass for his longtime friend (a Mass that cannot be repeated) to share in the Eucharist in which the belief in the death and resurrection of the Lord is celebrated?

Here is another example that involves in a way an ecclesiological subject but that could have far reaching consequences for ecumenism: a parish priest asked whether it was necessary to hear the parish pastoral council when intending to close a parish school. There is no explicit legal provision for this, so he was asked what he thought the parish pastoral council was all about? Was it a mere institution that he would consult only when the law prescribed it, or did he see the parish pastoral council as a group of representatives of all who make up the parish community and who through their baptism and confirmation share in the threefold ministry of Christ? How would he see that participation lived out in his parish? Could he see that there might be charisms present in his parish different from his own and that they may also contribute to parish life? The priest indeed enjoyed and appreciated the new perspective on his work in a parish. The change of perspective is relevant for the ecumenical engagement, as these changes in the way people act display a certain understanding of what baptism enables people to be.

The example reveals also that application of the law with regard to ecumenism does not just concern obvious ecumenical topics such as sharing the Eucharist and so-called mixed marriage. Engagement for the unity of the church must also occur on a much more fundamental level.

### *Concluding remarks*

By way of conclusion I offer a few observations:

1. The Catholic Church has legislation that is not to be equated with doctrine, but that translates doctrine into structures that are to assist the community in appropriating the doctrine. Doctrine and structures are deeply connected, but they are not to be equated. A most delicate point will always remain: how much uniformity is necessary for unity to be preserved while allowing for diversity? Diversity might reveal itself with regard to theological notions that stand side-by-side legitimately, as well as in different modalities that reflect differing contexts (available means, civil law, human and financial resources etc.).
2. This presentation reveals my personal view on the law in the Catholic Church. Reflections on the role of law in relation to doctrine are mainly taking place in the German-speaking world where it most likely received decisive incentives from the Protestant colleagues Rudolph Sohm and Hans Dombois. In other parts of the world, an explicit discussion on method and on the relation between insights and norms is rather minimal.

   The commitment to the restoration of Christian unity as a decisive hermeneutical factor in the legislation, interpretation and application of law has been recognized in canon law, but needs to take hold in the overall operations. The international research group "Peter and Paul Seminar, " which unites theologians and canon lawyers, has focused on this for many years and is committed to the question: how can the Church adapt its structures in such a way that they are conducive to the restoration of the church of Christ? (see Wijlens 2004, 229–241).
3. Canon lawyers have a role to play in the search for unity on two accounts: they are to be such that they facilitate unity, and they must protect what has already been agreed on.

### *Abbreviations and bibliography*

ES: Paul VI. 1964. Encyclical Letter Ecclesiam suam. See: www.vatican.va.

LG: Second Vatican Council. Dogmatic Constitution on the Church Lumen Gentium. See: www.vatican.va.

SDL: John Paul II. Sacrae Disciplinae Leges, Apostolic Constitution (25 Jan. 1983). See: www.vatican.va.

UR: Second Vatican Council. Decree on Ecumenism Unitatis Redintegratio. See: www.vatican.va.

UUS: John Paul II. 1995. Encyclican letter Ut unum sint. In: AAS 87(1995) 921–982. See: www.vatican.va.

Alberigo, Giuseppe, Jean-Pierre Jossua, and Joseph A. Komonchak (ed.). The Reception of Vatican II. Washington DC: The Catholic University of America Press.

Bakker, Freek (ed.). 2004. Rethinking Ecumenism: Strategies for the 21st Century. IIMO Research Publication 63. Zoetermeer: Meinema.

Benedict XVI. 2005. Address of his Holiness Benedict XVI to the Roman Curia offering them Christmas Greetings, December 22, 2005. In: AAS 98(2006), 40–55. English translation: see www.vatican.va.

Bordeyne, Philippe, and Laurent Villemin (eds). 2006. Vatican II et la théologie: Perspectives pour le XXIè siècle. Paris: Cerf.

Communicationes: Pontificia Commissio Codici Iuris Canonici Authentice Interpretando. In: Communicationes 1969ff.

Gaillardetz, Richard R. 2006. The Church in the Making: Lumen gentium, Christus Dominus, Orientalium Ecclesiarum. Mahwah, N.J: Paulist.

Gruppe von Farfa. 2011. Gemeinschaft der Kirchen und Petrusamt: Lutherisch-katholische Annäherungen. Frankfurt am Main: Lembeck.

John XXIII. 1959. Papal Allocution 'Questa Festiva'. In: AAS 51(1959), 65–69. English translation in: The Pope Speaks 4(1959), 398–401.

John Paul II. 1983B. Codex Iuris Canonici. In: AAS 75(1983), Pars II. English translation: Code of Canon Law. Latin-English Edition (Washington DC: CLSA, 1998.

Kasper, Walter. 1989. Theology and Church: New York: Crossroad.

Kasper, Walter. 1989A. The Continuing Challenge of the Second Vatican Council: The Hermeneutics of the Conciliar Statements. In: Kasper 1989, 166–176.

Komonchak, Joseph A. 2011. Benedict XVI and the Interpretation of Vatican II. In: Lacey and Oakley 2011, 93–110.

Lacey, Michael J., and Francis Oakley (eds). The Crises of Authority in Catholic Modernity. Oxford: University Press.

Paul VI. 1973. Allocution to the Pontifical University Gregoriana on December 14, 1973. In: AAS 66(1974), 10. English translation: Canon Law and the Church's Pastoral Mission. In: Canon Law Digest (= CLD) 8(1978),100–101.

Paul VI. 1977. Allocution to the Roman Rota on February 4, 1977. In: AAS 69(1977), 153. English translation: The New Code and the Better Protection of Justice. In: CLD 8(1978),111.

Pottmeyer, Herman-Josef. 1987. A New Phase in the Reception of Vatican II: Twenty Years of Interpretation of the Council. In: Alberigo et al. 1987, 37–38.

Puglisi, James F. (ed.). 2010. How Can the Petrine Ministry Be a Service to the Unity of the Universal Church? Grand Rapids Mi: Eerdmans.

Routhier, Gilles. 2006A. El concilio Vaticano II come estilo. Iglesia Viva 227 (2006-3), 23-44.

Routhier, Gilles. 2006B. L'Assemblée extraordinaire de 1985 du synode des évêques: moment charnière de relecture de Vatican II dans l'Église catholique. In: Bordeyne and Villemin 2006, 61-90.

Routhier, Gilles, and Guy Jobin (eds). 2010. L'Autorité et les autorités: L'herméneutique théologique de Vatican II. Paris: Cerf.

Routhier, Gilles. 2011. Carrying within ourselves the Legacy of Vatican II. Lecture given on March 3, 2011 at the Faculty of Theology at the Catholic University in Louvain (unpublished).

Rush, Ormond. 2004. Still Interpreting Vatican II: Some Hermeneutical Principles. Mahwah: N.J. Paulist Press, 27-30, 42 and 49.

Wijlens, Myriam. 2004. 'Peter and Paul Seminar': A Follow up by Theologians and Canon Lawyers to the Groupe des Dombes' Publication For the Conversion of the Churches. In: Bakker 2004, 229-241; Reprint in The Jurist 64(2004) 6-20.

# LIST OF AUTHORS

Dr. Rein Brouwer is senior lecturer in Practical and Empirical Theology at the Protestant Theological University in the Netherlands (location Amsterdam).

Prof Pieter Coertzen is an emeritus professor of Ecclesiology (Church Law and Church History), and chairperson of the Unit for the Study of Law and Religion in the Beyers Naudé Center for Public Theology, at the University of Stellenbosch, South Africa.

Dr. Harm G. Dane is a study secretary for the relation between church and society of the Protestant Church in the Netherlands.

Prof. Henry DeMoor is professor of Church Polity emeritus at Calvin Theological Seminary in Grand Rapids, Michigan, USA.

Prof. Norman Doe is professor of Law and Director of the Centre for Law and Religion at Cardiff Law School, United Kingdom.

Prof. Allan J. Janssen is an affiliate professor of Theological Studies at New Brunswick Theological Seminary, New Brunswick, New Jersey, USA.

Prof. Leo J. Koffeman is professor of Church Law and Ecumenism at the Protestant Theological University in the Netherlands (location Amsterdam).

Prof. Volker Küster, is professor of Missiology and Comparative Religion at the Johannes Gutenberg University, Mainz, Germany.

Prof. C.J.P. (Nelus) Niemandt is head of the Department of Science of Religion and Missiology at the University of Pretoria, South Africa.

Dr. Mary-Anne Plaatjies van Huffel is senior lecturer in Ecclesiology (Church Polity) at the University of Stellenbosch, South Africa.

Dr. Lazarus H. Purwanto (1951) is a part-time lecturer for Church Polity at the Sekolah Tinggi Teologi Jakarta (the Jakarta Theological Seminary), Indonesia.

Dr. Joseph D. Small is an adjunct faculty at the University of Dubuque Theological Seminary, USA.

Prof. Johannes Smit is extraordinary senior lecturer of Church Polity at the North-West University (Potchefstroomcampus), South Africa.

Prof. Fred A. van Lieburg is professor of the History of Dutch Protestantism at the VU University in Amsterdam, the Netherlands.

Prof. Myriam Wijlens is professor of Canon Law at the faculty of Catholic Theology of the University of Erfurt, Germany.